Toy Stories

Toy Stories
The Toy as Hero in Literature, Comics and Film

Edited by TANYA JONES

McFarland & Company, Inc., Publishers
Jefferson, North Carolina

ALSO OF INTEREST

*The Gothic Fairy Tale in Young Adult Literature:
Essays on Stories from Grimm to Gaiman,*
by Joseph Abbruscato and Tanya Jones (2014)

LIBRARY OF CONGRESS CATALOGUING-IN-PUBLICATION DATA

Names: Jones, Tanya, 1983– editor.
Title: Toy stories : the toy as hero in literature, comics and film / edited by Tanya Jones.
Description: Jefferson, North Carolina : McFarland & Company, Inc., Publishers, 2017 | Includes bibliographical references and index.
Identifiers: LCCN 2017010150 | ISBN 9781476665177 (softcover : acid free paper) ∞
Subjects: LCSH: Toys in mass media. | Courage in mass media.
Classification: LCC P96.T69 T69 2017 | DDC 809/.933564—dc23
LC record available at https://lccn.loc.gov/2017010150

BRITISH LIBRARY CATALOGUING DATA ARE AVAILABLE

ISBN (print) 978-1-4766-6517-7
ISBN (ebook) 978-1-4766-2911-7

© 2017 Tanya Jones. All rights reserved

No part of this book may be reproduced or transmitted in any form or by any means, electronic or mechanical, including photocopying or recording, or by any information storage and retrieval system, without permission in writing from the publisher.

Front cover image © 2017 Choreograph/iStock

Printed in the United States of America

*McFarland & Company, Inc., Publishers
Box 611, Jefferson, North Carolina 28640
www.mcfarlandpub.com*

For Doug. Thank you for all the love and support masquerading as thinly veiled criticism.

For Mom and Dad. Thank you for always saying, "You should…" Even when I don't.

For Mrs. Aten. Thank you for inspiring me as a teacher, a writer and as a person.

Table of Contents

Bears, Bogeymen and Bedtime Heroes: Something Like an Introduction
    TANYA JONES   1

The Stuff of Legend: The Graphic Novel's Re-Imagination of Children's Literature
    REBECCA GORMAN O'NEILL   13

"The Steadfast Tin Soldier" as Romantic Hero and Tragic Lover
    KIRSTEN MØLLEGAARD   27

The Problem of Possession: Objects and Maturation in *The Indian in the Cupboard*
    RACHEL L. CARAZO   45

They Don't Make 'Em Like That Anymore: *Dolls* vs. Modernity
    CRAIG IAN MANN   62

"You are not a live thing. You're a dummy": The Rights and Hierarchy of the Hero-Creations of Oz
    DINA SCHIFF MASSACHI   78

Falterity: The Toy as Otherwise Than Hero
    NATHAN TEBOKKEL   94

"You made the journey, the Long Journey!" Performances of Race, Nation and Toyhood in *Paddle-to-the-Sea*
    THADDEUS ANDRACKI   114

"Even if you can't see something, it doesn't mean it isn't there": Toys as Heroic Agents of Creativity and Cultural Criticism in *Small Soldiers*
    MICHAEL BRODSKI   130

The Lonely Doll Series: Fantasy and Fear MARY BRONSTEIN	143
"Real isn't how you are made": Heroism and the Power of a Child's Love KRISTINE LARSEN	157
Goodbye, Get Lost, Come Back! Parting Ways with Special Toys VALERIE H. PENNANEN	169
About the Contributors	183
Index	185

Bears, Bogeymen and Bedtime Heroes
Something Like an Introduction

TANYA JONES

> "Toy" is a word that feels pleasant in thoughts and memories. But "toy" is also a limited word. Under the right circumstances a toy can become so very much more than something to be played with or amused by.
> It can become miraculous.
> —*Ollie's Odyssey*, William Joyce

At the time of writing, my daughter is two. Like most children, she has a favorite toy. For her, it is a small elephant head attached to a tiny gray blanket with the word "loved" stitched on a tag. It was only natural for me to name him Lovey as I used him to move her from a feeding to her crib during her early months. Now, even in her "big-girl-bed," Lovey maintains the coveted position of favorite. He is the toy that accompanies us on every trip and every errand. We know where he is at all times, even if he is not involved in her active play. And, despite his lack of any suggestive anatomy—having only a square for a body—he even has a gender.

I had encouraged the connection between Lovey and my daughter by using him as her transitional object in her early months, but I was curious to know why Lovey was so treasured since I was in the middle of editing this very collection. So I asked: why was Lovey her favorite? Why did she believe that Lovey was so special? Her answer, at two years of age, surprised me.

"Because he loves me."

He loves *me*. Not because she loved him. But because, even at two, she recognized the power behind the notion that she was loved and cared for. Her favorite toy was granted the privilege of loving her. I thought of all the times Lovey had been sought out when she was angry or upset or frightened. How Lovey was a necessity whenever her anxiety was high. Not just when she felt sick, or was teething, or overtired. But also when she was being reprimanded, because someone has to champion her when Mommy and Daddy are the villains.

In 1953, Donald Winnicott, an English pediatrician and psychoanalyst, introduced the world to his theory regarding, what he called, transitional objects. The transitional object, he believed, is an item used by a child—like a teddy bear or a blanket—as a soother and "becomes vitally important to the [child] for use at the time of going to sleep, and is a defense against anxiety" (Winnicott 5). Parents recognize this object for their own child/children and "get to know its value and carry it around even when travelling. The mother lets it get dirty and even smelly, knowing that by washing it she introduces a break in continuity to the [child's] experience, a break that may destroy the meaning and value of the object to the [child]" (5).

These toys (or items) become more than what they seem. Children that form an attachment to such objects tend to view them more as friends and less like inanimate pieces of cloth or plastic. The child shows not only favoritism to the transitional object, but also begins to trust it. As an outlet for inner dialogue, the toy functions as a companion. But it is a companion that is limited to what the child has already perceived in his or her own world because the toy can only "know" what the child knows. Thus, the transitional object becomes an extension of the child and, traditionally, the mother:

> They attribute their own feelings and worries to them. "The kitty is crying because it's waiting for mommy to come and mommy is late," a little girl kept saying, stroking her favourite toy. The child seems to, transfers him/herself to the toy, which becomes his/her *alter ego*. At the same time the toy is not a mirror and the child is not immediately reflected in it.
>
> It is the child's *alter ego* because any imaginative toy always has **its own** image. A conversation with a toy is thus a conversation of one ego with another one embodied in a material object [Smirnova 7, emphasis in original].

By offering the child her first "not-me" possession, the transitional object is both externalized and internalized. The object is real, tangible, and separate from the child (external), but the child perceives the object as an extension of the self and of the mother (internal). The item exists in a limbo of both real and not real, able to soothe and comfort the anxious or stressed child by both existing and being imbued with the power the child has provided it with.

The transitional object, for all intents and purposes, is a hero to his or her child. So it is little wonder that so many writers, filmmakers, and artists have chosen to use such a familiar hero to tell their stories.

And, truly, we are all familiar with the toy hero in one form or another.

Countless among us have visited the Hundred Acre Woods with Christopher Robin for a smackerel of honey with Pooh, have marveled at the depth of love *The Velveteen Rabbit* had for his little boy, and both celebrated and mourned with Andy's anthropomorphized toys through the *Toy Story* series. And which of us can't remember our own special toy growing up?

These well-loved and well-known characters have served as transitional objects for children all over the world. Winnie-the-Pooh is a classic example. Not only did the original Pooh bear and his menagerie of friends serve as transitional objects for author A.A. Milne's only son, Christopher Robin, but even their stories served to provide Christopher Robin with a way to deal with the very stressful act of simply growing up:

> The stories themselves serve as transitional objects. Milne wrote his son into the stories and Christopher Robin's reflections and questions are sprinkled into the books, thus providing Christopher Robin a narrative serving to contain emotional states and sort life experiences for psychological processing and integration of meaning. As child therapists understand, children play anxiety or other emotional states on characters for purposes of modulation, whether those characters are in stories, or as toys such as dolls, puppets, or figures of superheroes [Sullivan 47].

Throughout the course of Milne's stories and poems detailing Christopher Robin's adventures with Pooh, Piglet, Tigger and the rest, we get a glimpse into Christopher's anxieties about growing up, both as they *play out* within his own character and as they are *acted out* by his stuffed friends, who, as transitional objects, are both *him* and *not-him*. Milne was even fond of noting this himself, actively highlighting particular emotions or activities with capital letters in his writing, such as when Pooh and Piglet emerge from the mist after having become lost: "'Oh, there you are,' said Christopher Robin carelessly, trying to pretend that he hadn't been Anxious" (Milne 266).

Christopher Robin, a child, is seen here as anxious over his beloved playthings' whereabouts. Pooh and Piglet, having become lost in the mist, return home to their child unscathed. However, while lost, the toys—Piglet more-so than Pooh—are frightened, nervous, and "anxious" themselves, wondering how they will find their way back home to their friends again. Milne's story of his son's special toys becoming lost and his inclusion of his own son's feeling about the idea of them being lost is almost a romantic psychoanalysis of a common fear in childhood: that of becoming lost or abandoned. As Michael Howarth points out in his book, *Under the Bed, Creeping: Psychoanalyzing the Gothic in Children's Literature*, the fear of being abandoned/lost "arises from an instinctual need to rely on caregivers for food, clothes, shelter, and protection" (Howarth 225). Hearing the story from the perspective of his transitional objects, Christopher Robin is granted the opportunity to play out the fear of becoming separated from his own loved ones and by being placed in the story himself, he is able to be both the caregiver and nervous child, anxiously awaiting the return of his "family."

Milne was obviously aware of his son's fondness of Pooh, but it is also likely that he recognized his son's dependence upon his favorite bear as is illustrated in one of his poems:

> There's always Pooh and Me.
> "What would I do?" I said to Pooh,
> "If it wasn't for you," and Pooh said: "True" [Milne 54].

Here, Pooh is a different sort of hero. While it may be Christopher Robin that actively scares away the dragons, it is by engaging in play with Pooh and having Pooh to protect that gives him the courage to overcome his fears— even his fanciful ones. The "dragons" are as much make-believe as Pooh is himself, but the act of being brave in the face of danger is quite real to the child at play. Christopher Robin is "not afraid," but holds Pooh's paw as he chases the dragons away and then wonders what he would do if Pooh were not around. While it is easy enough to read the passage and smile at the image of a little boy defending his small toy from danger, it is just as likely that Christopher's claim that he is "not afraid" is only because Pooh is there with him. As his transitional object, Pooh is limited to what Christopher Robin perceives and is written that way by Milne with great effect. Thus, when Pooh says, "I wasn't afraid…. I'm never afraid with you," he is Christopher Robin speaking through Pooh, admitting that being brave is easier when someone you love and that loves you in return is supporting you through your trials. As a toy manipulated by Christopher Robin (and Milne), Pooh is both brave and in need of protection:

> When manipulated by human beings—adults or children—toys embody all the temptations and responsibilities of power. As characters with whom humans identify, they also suggest the relatively powerless relationship of human beings to known or unseen forces: their dreaded vulnerability [Kuznets 2].

Pooh is, of course, not the first—or even the last—bear or bedtime companion to provide his child with a sense of comfort in a world of which they are still trying to make sense. And, in some instances, that world is a much scarier place than the Hundred Acre Woods. Though it is hard to pinpoint exactly when the toy became protector, we see evidence of hero toys guarding their children from boogeys and monsters in countless pieces of literature, film, comics, and even music.

In 1930, Rex Lowton and Ray Benson wrote the novelty fox trot "Hush! Hush! Hush! Here Comes the Bogeyman" that was later recorded by Henry Hall and Val Rosing. The song—featured in both films and video games— advises children of what to do should the Bogeyman ever appear. In the original art advertising the piece, a little girl is shown sending her teddy bear—his paw raised aggressively—toward a ghostly figure. This inclusion of toys is also mirrored in several of the lyrics. There, unlike with Pooh, we see examples of toys acting as heroes against a specific childhood fear: monsters at bedtime. The lead soldiers and the teddy bear are meant to act as heroic protectors, defending their child in the dark when he or she is most consciously aware of their "dreadful vulnerability" and separated from the primary caregiver.

This image is fairly common. Often, we see depictions of children clutching a toy as an unspeakable horror looms in the background. In some cases, like the aforementioned song suggests, the toy is the child's champion, safeguarding them against the nightmares and boogeys that threaten. Since transitional objects are (1) objects of comfort sought out by the anxious child during times of stress and (2) often toys, it is no wonder so many authors and artists recognize the toy as the hero a child's imagination needs. Especially in the dark.

It is the dark the toy heroes must traverse in *The Stuff of Legend*, a graphic novel series from Mike Raicht, Brian Smith, and Charles Paul Wilson III. When their boy is taken "into the Dark" by the Boogeyman, several of his toys—many of which are nursery classics—follow his trail through the closet and into the Boogeyman's realm to win him back. Led, at least initially, by the Boy's two transitional objects and primary playthings—the toy soldier known as Colonel and Max the teddy bear—the toys become real heroes fighting for both their lives and the life of their Boy.

One of the remarkable things about *The Stuff of Legend* is the way the authors and artist have looked at toy heroes in a new light. Rather than simply being passive objects of comfort for their child, the toys in the Boy's bedroom become active heroes determined to rescue their master. The toys, it seems, live in limbo. As we have already discussed in regards to transitional objects, they are both real and not real; tangible objects that "come to life" when the child imagines them to be so in active play. But *The Stuff of Legend* goes beyond this notion and suggests that toys exist in still another limbo: they are comfort objects and do fulfill their roles as playthings, but when they are alone, they exist as both self-aware toys with their own personalities (regardless of the part the Boy gives them during playtime) and as true-to-life versions of their toy shells when they venture into the Dark. Thus, when Max the teddy bear and the miniature toy soldier enter the Dark, they are transformed into a raging grizzly bear and a fully grown man.

All of the toys seem to have two forms and it is interesting to note that the authors never specify which form is, in fact, the *true* form.[1] This is likely because both are, in a sense, real. During play, a child does not necessarily see the toy for what it is and, instead, sees it for its potential. This is illustrated in *The Stuff of Legend* as the Boy's transitional objects (the Colonel and Max) and his other toys provide both comfort and the opportunity for him to, quite literally, play out his own anxieties.

For example, when the Boy plays war with the Colonel in his room, he sees a substitute for his father, an Allied soldier fighting in Europe during World War II. Though he holds the toy soldier in his hands as he plays at fighting Nazis on the beaches of Normandy, his toy hero in those moments may as well be his father, fighting on those same beaches across the sea. There is a very real possibility that his father will die in the war, so he treasures his toy soldier that wears the same uniform as his father. With it, he fights imaginary Nazis (toy knights, cowboys, and Confederate and Union soldiers) on beaches he has constructed out of blankets and sheets (Raicht *Dark*). The Colonel is, of course, victorious because to play otherwise is to believe his father may not return. During play, the Boy perceives a miniature version of his own father's potential, so when the toys enter the Boogeyman's realm—a world seemingly built from both imagination and the abandoned and forgotten toys of childhood—it is only fitting that the Colonel's appearance changes so he shares both the same potential and the same face as the Boy's father.

While the Colonel plays a more active role as a transitional object, allowing the Boy to work through his emotions with play, Max the teddy bear is no less important. Recognized by all the toys as the Boy's "favorite," Max keeps a coveted place on the Boy's bed, is the recipient of the Boy's affection, and is the only remaining stuffed animal in the Boy's possession (all others have been lost to the Dark or handed off to the younger brother). Though the Boy uses the Colonel as the hero during active play, it is Max that the Boy looks to for comfort and safety.[2] This is most evident in *Book 1: The Dark*. As the Boy is being dragged into the closet by the Boogeyman, we see a series of several panels in which the Boy reaches desperately for Max. It is not the Colonel, his other toys, or even his "real" puppy that the Boy looks to as savior, but Max, his favorite teddy bear, as he lays crumpled on the floor by the bed (Raicht *Dark*). Later, in *Book 2: The Jungle*, Max explains his role as the Boy's favorite: "I was always his best friend. Always by his side at night to keep him company. To keep him safe" (Raicht *Jungle*).

As a transitional object for the Boy, Max understands that he has two roles to fulfill: companion/comfort object and protector. He fulfills the first role; he is a companion to his child and the Boy speaks to him and about him as such. The Boy reads to Max and sleeps with him at night and, though he is not always involved in the active play, he is never out of reach. In this position, Max is more of a friend than a toy. Toys are played *with*; friends provide companionship. His role, therefore, is to be both involved and separate. Being the favored transitional object, Max is special and both the Boy and the other toys recognize and respect his position.

It is his secondary role as protector that causes Max so much grief throughout the series. Max believes his duty is to keep the Boy safe and since transitional objects are meant to provide a feeling of safety, this is understandable. However, Max not only failed to keep his child safe, he betrayed him as well. It is Max that opens the closet door to the Boogeyman to rid himself of his new rival (the Boy's new puppy) and solidify his position as favorite. The Boy, unaware of this betrayal and still believing his toys to be inanimate objects—though he later learns differently—frantically tries to reach Max during his abduction because he *is* the "best friend" and the one that he trusts and loves. This is a curious position from a psychoanalytic standpoint. In the eyes of the Boy, Max has both failed and not failed. Logically, the Boy does not expect Max to protect him from any real danger. Max is a transitional object, a toy, but not one that possesses any real authority (or so the Boy thinks). However, because of Max's position as favorite transitional object, the Boy, in his panic, reaches for him as if he truly will become his savior. During play, the Boy sees Max's potential as best friend and so turns him into such while still recognizing that he is a toy. But during that moment of extreme stress when he is being dragged backwards into his closet, the Boy sees Max as a potential hero. He reaches for Max because, in that instant, Max is real to him.

Of course, the toys in *The Stuff of Legend* are not the only toys whose allegiance to their child means they will be tested. In spring 2016, William Joyce introduced the world to Billy and Ollie in *Ollie's Odyssey*. Ollie, a stuffed animal somewhere between a teddy bear and a rabbit, was crafted by Billy's mother using pieces from her own favorite childhood toy. And while an infant Billy forms an instant bond with Ollie, it is Billy's mother that gives Ollie a purpose:

> [W]hen it came time for bed, Billy always got a good-night slobber from his parents. Then Mom would tuck Billy in at night, she'd say "Keep him safe, Ollie" before she left the bedroom and turned off the light.
> Ollie took this request very seriously. "Safe." Ollie liked the way it sounded. He liked what it meant. He liked the way it made him feel. It was like "soft and warm" but better.
> So keeping Billy safe was Ollie's favorite thing to do. He'd put his head on Billy's chest and listen to his heart.
> *I am Mr. Safe*, he'd say to himself. *I am the Keeper of Safeness. The Grand High Safemaster of Planet Billy* [Joyce 18].

Ollie, recognizing the power behind words such as "belonged," "safe," and "favorite," is determined to be everything that Billy requires in a favorite.

As Billy's favorite, Ollie has spent his and Billy's life learning and adapting to fulfill Billy's needs at the time. When Billy was an infant, this meant being his crib companion. When Billy was a little older, he was a teething tool. A little older still, and he is Billy's constant friend and confidant. Winnicott addresses this issue with transitional objects and, what he called, "good-enough mothers." According to Winnicott, a "good-enough mother (not necessarily the infant's own mother) is one who makes active adaptation to the infant's needs … that gradually lessons, according to the infant's growing ability to account for failure of adaptation and to tolerate the results of frustration" (14). As a transitional object, Ollie functions as Billy requires even when his parents (specifically his mother) fail because it is Billy in the position of power. Ollie "belongs" to Billie and has been tasked with the job of keeping Billy "safe" and that is what he will do.

When Billy is kidnapped by Zozo—a bitter and malevolent clown doll—and his henchmen of Creeps, Ollie realizes he is needed and he answers the call to action: "The Code of the Toys was unshakeable, even for the tiniest of playthings. The code was simple: that a toy would always help whenever possible. Help make their child's day full of adventures, full of joy, full of comfort" (199). But this "A-venture" is not a game invented by Billy, but one where Ollie will have to become a real hero. And while the prospect of returning to Zozo's lair frightens Ollie, the chance to be the hero is exciting for him: "Billy was the hero when they pretended.… But this time, Ollie was the hero person, and it wasn't pretending, it was *real*. And this kind of REAL felt even stronger than pretending, and maybe even better" (Joyce 214). Like Pooh, Ollie has always been the companion, the one that inspires Billy's bravery by being someone in need of protecting. This is a standard purpose for transitional objects. However, with Billy captured, Ollie must take up the mantle of hero of their story and be brave for Billy's sake, much like his counterparts in *The Stuff of Legend*. He succeeds, freeing his child and accompanying him on his way home, thereby living up to the potential his child has fantasized him to have.

Yet, this "A-venture" comes at a price. By searching for Ollie, Billy knowingly broke several understood "laws" (sneaking out at night, crossing streets alone, etc.). He also sacrificed himself to the Creeps in an attempt to save Ollie from re-capture. In doing so, Billy has been exposed to several harsh realities and has had to make very adult decisions alone. When he is rescued and their adventure is over, he seems different to Ollie and Ollie realizes that his Billy also has potential: the potential to grow up. And while Ollie has been the hero of the real adventure, he instinctively lets Billy take the lead and carry him home. Ollie has also been changed by their trials; he feels regret and, for the first time, worries about his future with Billy. The journey has made them both "different *inside*. And in ways they couldn't quite grasp" (Joyce 287).

The journey has both brought Billy and Ollie closer together and begun their separation. Billy has taken his first real steps into the world alone without parent or substitute parent (Ollie). Ollie has become a true hero, but must face the possibility of future abandonment. Their first real adventure is over, but in the aftermath Billy realizes he will grow up and that means he can begin to see Ollie for what he is: a toy. Ollie sees the same reality. As the book closes, we find Ollie in a limbo befitting his status as transitional object: "Ollie sat there on the threshold. Not inside or out, but in between" (Joyce 293). Here, we see him as both what he is and as a symbolic representation of his role: he is neither real nor imaginary, but both; he is neither just-Ollie nor just-Billy, but both. It is this remarkable duality that allows him to be a hero for his child.

As discussed earlier, toys as transitional objects are very much the heroes of the stories that are imagined for them, but also for the reality they inhabit. Christopher Robin needed Pooh to deal with the struggles of growing up. The Boy needs Max to comfort him and the Colonel to show him true bravery. Billy needs Ollie to keep him "safe." Children everywhere rely on their toys for these same reasons. As Joyce says, the toy "can become miraculous" and, given the opportunity, can become a hero (3).

It is with this very idea in mind that this collection came about. The essays herein all take miraculous and iconic (and not-so-iconic) toys of childhood and detail what makes them so heroic. Why is it so mesmerizing to consider the possibility that our childhood transitional objects inhabit a world we know nothing about? What is it about the toy we find so fascinating that we have breathed life into it in so many different mediums? In her book, *When Toys Come Alive: Narratives of Animation, Metamorphosis, and Development*, Lois Kuznets suggests that our interest in the secret world of toys is due to the way toys play out human stories. Toy stories are full of existential questions about what it means to be "real," hint at the secret world behind closed doors, illustrate how we are both powerful and vulnerable, and ask us to confront the concept of creation and, in a sense, divinity (2). In this collection, you will see academics from around the world examining these issues and more. Each author has brought a unique perspective to the toy as hero.

Rebecca Gorman O'Neill traces the history of "Toy Fantasy" tropes as they have appeared in Children's Literature. In *"The Stuff of Legend*: The Graphic Novel's Re-Imagination of Toy Fantasy," O'Neill begins her discussion focusing on early toy narratives and their passive playmate heroes and shows an evolution of not only the toy heroes themselves, but of the laws that govern them. She argues that it is *The Stuff of Legend* that has finally "re-imagined" these laws and tropes by subverting or enhancing them.

Kirsten Møllegaard follows with her essay on "The Steadfast Tin Soldier" where she discusses the trope of the romantic hero as tragic lover and Andersen's attempt to criticize societal norms of the Biedermeier period in Central Europe. As she delves into the fairy tale turned tragic romance in "'The Steadfast Tin Soldier' as Romantic Hero and Tragic Lover," she examines the tiny tin hero's complex makeup as he self-sabotages his chances to be with his love due to his rigid adherence to conforming to social rules.

In "The Problem of Possession: Objects and Maturation in *The Indian in the Cupboard*," Rachel L. Carazo argues the idea of problematic possession as it is made evident in stories where toys come alive. Her argument that society values objects as something to be possessed rather than for what we can learn from interaction with them (especially in regards to children at play) is one that asks the reader to examine the self in relation to the material world.

The idea of the preoccupation with modern materialism is also a cornerstone of "They Don't Make 'Em Like That Anymore: *Dolls* vs. Modernity" by Craig Ian Mann. Using the 1987 horror film *Dolls* as the vehicle for his theory, Mann takes a very different approach to the toy as hero trope. The murderous dolls and toys in the film, he claims, *are* heroes determined to shield the modern youth from the horrors of the adult world that sees them only as consumers and destroyers. Mann studies *Dolls* as an anti-consumerist parable and its well-loved toys as the heroes willing to get their hands dirty to help stop the spread of capitalist corruption.

In "'You are not a live thing. You're a dummy': The Rights and Hierarchy of the Hero-Creations of Oz," Dina Schiff Massachi journeys into the land of Oz and details the social struggles of the anthropomorphic heroes of Baum's creation. While those hero-creations are just as heroic as their "living," breathing counterparts, the author claims that those citizens that are made have little opportunity to rise above servitude regardless of their societal contributions.

A journey of self-discovery is a focus of Nathan TeBokkel's essay. In "Falterity: The Toy as Otherwise Than Hero," TeBokkel examines perceived faults and the oscillation between the struggle with alterity and the acceptance of identity using a dialectic he calls falterity. The joint allegiance to both other and self is a struggle with which all readers will likely be intimately familiar and many will find a kinship with Buzz Lightyear or Wreck-It Ralph as TeBokkel explains the manifestation and eventual acceptance of falterity.

Denial of equality is also a topic of Thaddeus Andracki's essay on the 1942 picture book *Paddle-to-the-Sea*. "'You made the journey, the Long Journey!' Performances of Race, Nation and Toyhood in *Paddle-to-the-Sea*" scrutinizes performances of race and nation. Drawing upon native studies, possession, and posthumanist ideas, Andracki suggests that the stereotypical portrayal of the book's toy hero almost argues for white settler colonialism and illustrates a trend regarding what kinds of toys become real in ways denied to the colonized.

In "'Even if you can't see something, it doesn't mean it isn't there': Toys as Heroic Agents of Creativity and Cultural Criticism in *Small Soldiers*," Michael Brodski offers insight into the notion that toys demonstrate the repression of youth in a culture dominated by adults determined to both hoard power and safeguard social norms. By studying the structure versus agency debate as it is related to a child's place in society, in the film, and in reality—including strained relationships between children and their parents—Brodski champions the importance of creativity and self-expression in childhood.

A child's perception of reality and their place in the world is also considered in Mary Bronstein's essay titled *"The Lonely Doll* Series: Fantasy and Fear." Using *The Lonely Doll* series by photographer Dare Wright, Bronstein analyzes themes of loneliness, love, fear, and belonging as they pertain to child development studies and feminist theory. Bronstein includes close studies of some of the dramatic photographs found in the series that depict Edith, Wright's childhood doll and companion, to enhance her discussion.

In "'Real isn't how you are made': Heroism and the Power of a Child's Love," Kristine Larsen uses *The Velveteen Rabbit* as a springboard into her discussion of love as the catalyst necessary to become a hero. Her essay considers the toy heroes from Tolkien's *Roverandom* and the 2007 film *The Last Mimzy*, detailing how their heroic acts are ultimately inspired by the love of the children they have come to love in return.

We close, fittingly, with Valerie H. Pennanen's essay "Goodbye, Get Lost, Come Back! Parting Ways with Special Toys." Her essay chronicles several literary "goodbyes" between children and their best friends: their most valued toys/transitional objects. Pennanen analyzes these goodbyes and the children who so treasured their friend as they struggle with where growing up leaves them in relation to their beloved playthings.

This collection—with its diverse interpretations of toy heroism—aims to be a valuable resource for a variety of academic studies. It is the hope of both this editor and the authors that the scholarship within is a starting point for further research into the complicated world of toys.

Notes

1. In the Colonel's war journal, the Colonel writes about his fascination that he and his companions became "Real" when they entered the Dark (Raicht *Dark*). This could lead us to believe that their toy form is their true form. However, in the Dark, the toys seem to have natural abilities that had nothing to do with their regular play with the Boy and more to do with whom they believed themselves to be. The Princess, always the damsel in distress during play, is a stoic, proficient warrior, meant to lead her people to victory. The Jester, a Jack-in-the-Box on the Boy's bedroom shelf, becomes a duel wielding assassin with a gentleman's mannerisms. Without the Boy dictating their moves through play, they are at liberty to be themselves. Thus, the Dark may be where they are at their most "Real."

2. If the Colonel is a substitute for the father, it is not a far leap to imagine Max as a substitute for the mother. Traditionally, according to Winnicott, transitional objects are the first "not-me" possessions discovered through an infant's relationship with his/her mother. Since Max fulfills the Boy's need for comfort and safety, he is the more common transitional object that stands in for the mother.

Works Cited

Howarth, Michael. *Under the Bed, Creeping: Psychoanalyzing the Gothic in Children's Literature.* Jefferson, NC: McFarland, 2014. Digital.

Joyce, William. *Ollie's Odyssey.* New York: Atheneum/Caitlyn Dlouhy Books, 2016. Print.

Kuznets, Lois Rostow. *When Toys Come Alive: Narratives of Animation, Metamorphosis, and Development.* New Haven: Yale University Press, 1994. Print.

Milne, A.A. *The World of Pooh: The Complete Winnie-the-Pooh and The House at Pooh Corner.* London: Dutton Children's Books, 2010. Print.

Raicht, Mike, and Brian Smith. Illus. Charles Paul Wilson III. *The Stuff of Legend—Book 1: The Dark.* San Diego: Th3rd World Studios, 2010. Print.

_____. *The Stuff of Legend—Book 2: The Jungle.* San Diego: Th3rd World Studios, 2011. Print.

_____. *The Stuff of Legend—Book 3: A Jester's Tale.* San Diego: Th3rd World Studios, 2012. Print.

_____. *The Stuff of Legend—Book 4: The Toy Collector.* San Diego: Th3rd World Studios, 2013. Print.

Smirnova, E.O. "Psychological and Educational Evaluation of Toys in Moscow Center of Play and Toys." *Psychological Science and Education* 2 (2011): 5–10.

Sullivan, Laura. "Calvin and Hobbes to the Rescue: The Therapeutic Uses of Comic Strip and Cartoons." *Popular Culture in Counseling, Psychotherapy, and Play-Based Interventions.* Ed. Lawrence C. Rubin. New York: Springer, 2008. pp. 54–56. Print.

Winnicott, D.W. *Playing and Reality.* London: Routledge, 2005. Print.

The Stuff of Legend
The Graphic Novel's Re-Imagination of Children's Literature

REBECCA GORMAN O'NEILL

The Boogeyman is real, and he has come out of the Dark and taken the Boy. The toys, who love and are loyal to the child, follow him into the Dark to save him. As this point, a reader might easily fall back on common tropes of the subset of Children's Literature referred to as "Toy Fantasy" (Russell) and guess what happens next. *The Stuff of Legend*, story by Mike Raicht and Brian Smith, with graphite illustrations by Charles Paul Wilson, III, designed and colored by Jon Conkling and Michael DeVito, takes the reader's comforting toy tropes and explodes them, leaving its readers in a truly postmodern narrative. *The Stuff of Legend* works on the toy-literature knowledge of its older audience, delivering something refreshingly, and sometimes shockingly, new.

Toy tropes were first established in early toy narrative, invariably children's books, and by the 21st century had solidified for audiences through picture books, comic strips, and films. These tropes work on several basic, natural childhood fantasies. First, toys, as objects that are designed to look like little people and animals, have the capacity to think and act like little people and animals. Second, the child, who loves his or her toys, is loved by the toys in return; toys aspire to please or serve their child, and so the child is the center, leader, or god of this miniature world. The child, usually not a primary focus or decision maker in his or her own life, is all of these very satisfying things in the world of his or her toys. With toys, the child becomes the adult.

In earlier toy literature, toys are largely passive. In *Hitty: Her First Hundred Years* by Rachel Field (1846) and Johnny Gruelle's *The Raggedy Ann Stories* (1918), the dolls are sentient but only sometimes animate. When Hitty picks up a quill to write her memoirs, she describes how she was lost, dropped, shipwrecked, and turned into a pincushion. Her sturdy build of mountain-ash wood allows her survival through these adventures and finally into a peaceful antique shop (Kuznets, "Taking Over" 24–33). Raggedy Ann is more active in her adventures but is also dependent on her build as a rag doll for survival as she is dropped in paint, washed, boiled, wrung, tied to the end of a kite, dropped in a river, and attacked by birds. These dolls live through battering, loss, and passively experienced adventures, accepting battering as "the price not only of love but of life" (Booth). Other, notably male, toys, including Williams' *The Velveteen Rabbit* (1922) and Collodi's *Pinocchio* (1880) aspire to be real, finding their toys-ness not the gateway to adventures, as Hitty and Raggedy Ann do, but as a constraint to a full and fulfilling life. The Velveteen Rabbit is mocked and troubled by real rabbits. He is cast aside after comforting his child through scarlet fever, and he is in danger of being incinerated when he is repaid, finally, for his loyalty by the Nursery Magic Fairy, who makes him real so he can run and play and live in "Rabbit-land." Pinocchio becomes sentient as he is being carved. After many misguided adventures, most of which no human boy could have endured, including starvation, imprisonment, and burning, Pinocchio finally matures, giving all his money to "the Fairy with Azure Hair," going to bed on time, and working hard. After proving his worthiness, he is magically turned into a real boy. In Pinocchio and the Velveteen Rabbit's cases, their wishes to be real are a parallel to the child's wish to be grown-up. Realness allows the toys freedom from the whims and control of others, it allows the fulfillment of being able to move and choose their own fates, and it gives vague, yet certain, paths to happiness. How exactly realness is attained—external love, proof of one's goodness, and subsequent magical intervention—is a satisfying parallel of a child's perception of how *to* grow up.

A.A. Milne's *Winnie-the-Pooh* (1926), E.T.A. Hoffman (Hoffmann)'s *The Nutcracker and the Mouse King* (1816), and Lynn Reid Banks' *The Indian in the Cupboard* (1980) pull on a different aspect of Toy Fantasy; toys are a conduit to a special, secret world. In this world, the child is a central and powerful figure, able to change and often improve the lives of the anthropomorphized toys. The books empower children by portraying them as having power over something—the lives and actions of their toys (Nikolajeva 47–55). In *Winnie-the-Pooh* and *The House at Pooh Corner*, especially, Christopher Robin appears as the only sane and reasonable person, a proxy parent, in the lives of the "large dysfunctional family" that are his toys—"a hyperactive tiger, a manic-depressive donkey, a paranoid pig, a dyslexic owl, and a feeble-minded bear" (Russell). Christopher Robin is often placed as the mentor and savior: "Here comes Christopher Robin—*he'll* know what to do" (Milne, *House* 26). The heroism and control of Christopher Robin, who is drawn, when he is drawn, as physically larger, indeed, adult-sized in comparison with his toys, as well as the wholesome idyll of the Hundred Acre Wood, have made the Pooh books a perennial favorite among children for decades.

The Pooh books' Hundred Acre Wood is a prime example of a frequent attribute of Toy Fantasy narrative, which theorist Maria Nikolajeva calls the "Secondary World Fantasy." The world in which toys move and transform, whether it be the Hundred-Acre Wood, the Christmas Eve battleground of E.T. A. Hoffmann's *The Nutcracker and the Mouse King*, or the cupboard of *The Indian in the Cupboard*, is a mythic world. In this mythic world, the rational rules regarding time and space are cast effortlessly aside. In Children's Literature, an entire adventure may be had, and years may even pass, without the "real world" even noticing, an expression of the scope of the imagination of a child. *The Lion, the Witch, and the Wardrobe*, for example, allows the children of the story to battle, conquer, grow up, and then return to the moment they left the real world, as children again. The same malleability of time occurs in Lewis Carroll's *Alice's Adventures in Wonderland* and *Through the Looking Glass*, in which Alice apparently has all of her adventures in Wonderland while only taking brief naps in the real world. While not considered Toy Fantasy, Lewis and Carroll's works fit in the closely related field of anthropomorphic animal literature, and work within Secondary World paradigms (Nikolajeva 126–128).

Through the 20th century, Toy Fantasy developed in newer media, in picture books like Don Freeman's *Corduroy* (1968), Peter Collington's *The Midnight Circus*, and James Stevenson's *The Night After Christmas* (1981); illustrated books such as Russell Hoban's *The Mouse and His Child* (1967) and Rumer Godden's *The Story of Holly and Ivy* (1958); and finally into film and television. Disney adapted *Pinocchio* (1940) and *Winnie-the-Pooh* (1966–2011) to animated film, and Columbia pictures built a live-action adaptation of *The Indian in the Cupboard* (1995). CBS's television specials such as *Rudolf the Red-Nosed Reindeer and the Island of Misfit Toys* (1964) brought Toy Fantasy to an even wider audience.

Audiences were thus fluent in toy tropes by the time of the release of Pixar's *Toy Story* films (1995, 1999, 2010). First and foremost, toys exist to serve the child. They are usually a family or group, with individual identities and skills, who share a common goal: be the child's playthings and love the child as much as the child loves them. As with any group, there may be friction in the ranks, but it is usually minor, and resolved in the course of the story. In the commentary track of the DVD of the first *Toy Story* movie, the writers explain how the group of toys act as if they are actually at work. They have meetings and tasks, which Woody, as leader, runs and assigns. The child's favorite toy is invariably the leader of the group of other toys, or, as in *Winnie-the-Pooh*, the central figure of the narrative. The common child's fantasy of toys being alive (especially when no one's looking) is fully engaged here. When the child is not playing with the toys, the toys have a life of their own, whether the child is aware of this life, as in *Winnie-the-Pooh*, or is not, as in *Toy Story*. Generally, when the toys are alone, they feign to be or are forced to be inanimate. Usually this in presented in the form of vague rules (as in *Toy Story*) or laws (as in *The Stuff of Legend*) which the toys may not, or dare not, break, except in the most extreme circumstances.

Bill Watterson's comic strip *Calvin and Hobbes* (1985–1995) is unusual in that it straddles this line. Hobbes is a full tiger to Calvin, but appears as a toy tiger to everyone else. *Calvin and Hobbes* similarly blurs the boundary between the real world and Nikolajeva's Secondary World, as the reader is at once shown Calvin and Hobbes in a spaceship, battling dinosaurs, or fending off monsters, as well as his real-world cardboard box, school desk, or unappetizing dinner.

Threats to the toy's comfort, happiness, or wellbeing similarly fall into established tropes. These threats mirror an average child's anxieties. Major threats include the loss, either of the child, as in the *Velveteen Rabbit*, or the loss or misplacement of the toys themselves, as in *Toy Story*. The outside or unfamiliar world is also a threat, firmly established in all the *Toy Story* films, whether it be moving to a new house (*Toy Story*), being sold in a yard sale (*Toy Story 2*) or being accidentally relocated to an insane day care (*Toy Story 3*). Furthermore, parents who don't understand the value of the toy to the child, or the child outgrowing his or her toys (*Toy Story 3*), are a persistent threat, mirroring growing-up anxieties of losing the magic, wonder, and freedom of childhood. Other children who don't see the value of the toys, especially girls, such as Susie Derkins in *Calvin and Hobbes* or Sid's sister in *Toy Story*—both of whom demasculinize a male toy by forcing it into the inevitable tea-party—threaten the well-being of a toy, mimicking loss of or change to a child's known identity. Tangible threats to a toy's physical safety often takes the form of the uncontrolled dog, whether it be the new Christmas puppy or Sid's vicious mongrel, as these may damage the toy, either by innocent roughhousing or by intentional targeting.

The ultimate threat to a toy is being replaced. Buzz threatens to replace Woody in *Toy Story*, and the Velveteen Rabbit, as well-loved as he is, is tossed "in the bin" and forgotten by the child, who gets a new toy rabbit and a trip to the sea-side. *The House at Pooh Corner* includes this replacement anxiety, as the toys first busy themselves to find out what Christopher Robin does with his days (he's been learning to read) and then throw him a farewell party, as he is apparently going off to boarding school. Milne's assurance to the reader, "wherever they go, and whatever happens to them on the way, in that enchanted place on the top of the Forest a little boy and his Bear will always be playing" (Milne, *House* 56), may read a little hollow. If the boy is off to school, this "boy always playing" is now only a memory, as real as Pooh's adventures were.

The Stuff of Legend takes these tropes of toy "rules" and threats to the toy, and other more subtle staples of Toy Fantasy narrative, and explodes them, using the reader's expectations of what toys can do and how toys can act, and either going beyond or subverting these expectations. This graphic novel spans, as of this writing, 15 "parts" or issues, collected in to four volumes: "The Dark," "The Jungle," "A Jester's Tale," and "The Toy Collector." Two more volumes are projected, with "A Call to Arms" being released in 2017.

"The Boy," referred to as such throughout the story, lives in Brooklyn in 1944. His father is fighting in Europe, and he, his younger brother Johnny, and his female relatives have been left behind. Through a series of flashbacks, the reader comes to understand that Max, the Teddy Bear, is the favorite toy, though the Colonel, a toy soldier, has recently become favored as well. The toy soldier mimics the boy's sense of the War, where his father is and what his father faces, as the Colonel fights his way to the tops of hills to rescue the Indian Princess.

Toy soldiers and male miniature toys have a unique status in Toy Fantasy, going back as far as Hans Christian Andersen's "The Steadfast Tin Soldier" (1838) to Pauline Clarke's *Return of the Twelves* (1962) to Banks' *The Indian in the Cupboard*; their very smallness is at odds with their vibrant roles as combatants. In the *Toy Story* movies, the tiny plastic solders are extremely serious. "Just … just go on without me!" cries the Minesweeper Soldier, to great comic effect (*Toy Story*). A child holding a toy soldier does not immediately imagine war and carnage, but tends to project on this toy his or her "hopes, fears, joys, bad dreams…. Above all, the holder imagines its feelings of powerlessness" (Kuznets, "Taking Over" 79). In *The Stuff of Legend*'s Boy's case, his soldier, the Colonel, is a substitute for his father who is away at war. Toys often, in Toy Fantasy, fill the role of "missing friends, siblings, or even parents" (Nikolajeva 51) to the lonely child. The Boy's loneliness is eased not only by his toy-play, but also by a new puppy. This puppy, Scout, causes his toys the inevitable discomfort and distress with its rough play and tendency to chew on them, and, more powerfully, with the boy's fondness of it. Keeping with another common trope, the toys may be animate when alone with the animal, while they are inanimate to any child.

One night, from the dark of the closet, the tentacles of the Boogeyman reach through and take the Boy into the Dark. How the Boogeyman was able to reach into the Boy's room is, at first, a mystery. The toys, inanimate and helpless when the boy is awake, quickly mobilize, with the Colonel as organizer, guide, and heart of the expedition. The Colonel will lead the expedition into the Dark. Max the bear and the Indian Princess, two other favorites of the Boy, quickly agree to join the expedition. Quackers, the toy duck, and Jester, the slightly insane Jack-in-the-Box, eagerly join the group, the latter out of a fondness for the princess. The Colonel asks Percy the Piggy Bank to go as well, as his intellect will be vital to the "mission." Percy resists, but is finally persuaded to go by Harmony the ballerina-top—but only if she goes, too. The other toys stay behind as they are favored by the Boy's younger brother, and so owe their allegiance to him. Scout, the boy's puppy, comes along.

In this move, *The Stuff of Legend* starts to distinguish itself from Children's Toy Fantasy to Toy Fantasy geared toward older readers. In leaving "home" (the Boy's Room) for a cause (the Boy), *The Stuff of Legend* becomes a quest narrative. In Rumer Godden's *The Dolls' House* and Russell Hoban's *The Mouse and His Child*, home is the goal, and the establishment of a safe home is the result of the perseverance and the goodness of the protagonists. In the *Toy Story* films, getting back home or, ultimately, to a new and fitting home (*Toy Story 3*), is the reward of trials the toys go through. A movement away from home, as in *The Stuff of Legend*, indicates a more mature readership. Christopher Claussen, in his article "Home and Away in Children's Fiction," states, "When home is a privileged place—when home is where we ought, on the whole, to stay—we are probably dealing with a story for children. When home is the chief place we must escape, either to grow up … or to maintain innocence, then we are involved in a story for adolescents or adults" (as cited in Kuznets, "Taking Over" 149). The toys of *The Stuff of Legend* leave their home with a goal, and they have no way to be content at home any longer without that goal. The leaving-home narrative pushes to a more mature readership, but is still flavored with a child's faith that the goal can be attained, the quest successfully ended, and the home easily returned to. This is, as the story unfolds, far from the case. Once in the Secondary World of the Dark, the toys find that there is no clear way to the Boy, and no clear way to return home. Only the Boogeyman has ever "gone back" from the Dark, and with or without the boy, the toys find themselves essentially and profoundly changed simply by having crossed the threshold of the closet.

After the little people and animals troop into the closet with Harmony's childlike, simple words to Percy, "You are not alone, you have to have faith that together we will prevail," a turn of the page reveals a break from one of the most basic tropes of toy literature. When toys become animated in most narratives, they generally keep most attributes of their toy selves: size, temperament, and/or appearance. Hobbes is more tigerish in Calvin's imagination, but he's about the same size; Pooh and friends are slightly more "real" versions of their cuddly selves, their seams and stitching erased. Woody and company are physically identical to their inanimate selves—the toy soldiers must even manage walking on their static plastic bases. So what happens in *The Stuff of Legend* to a toy in the Dark is jarring. All the toys become full-life-sized versions of their toy selves—Max is a grizzly bear, the Princess a knife-wielding warrior, and the Jester brandishes hatchets and has the unnerving ability to set things on fire. The tiny toy Colonel becomes a full-sized soldier with weapons in hand—a soldier whose face is identical to that of the boy's father. The puppy, Scout, remains the relative size of a puppy, and is now dwarfed by the very toys he once chewed on. The toys show no surprise or wonder at the change, but step into their new bodies and forms and directly into the Battle at Brooklyn Creek; the now-real toys fight the Boogeyman's army. This army, the reader soon learns, is made up of other toys that have been discarded into this or other closets, lost, broken, or forgotten. The Boogeyman has earned his army's loyalty by fixing them and giving them purpose, and they fight for him relentlessly, with the unnerving mantra, "his will is the way."

Many children's Toy Fantasy stories work on perceived danger which soon is diffused as non-threatening. Sid, in *Toy Story,* threatens to blow up Buzz Lightyear with a firework, but there are enough allies and opportunities to diffuse the threat, handily—indeed, this is one of the times when the toys break their rule of inanimateness: Woody and his friends come "alive" to frighten Sid into stopping his torture. Calvin and Hobbes face dinosaurs, aliens, and gooey monsters which soon resolve into less threatening reality when Calvin's imagination is interrupted. *The Stuff of Legend* wastes no time in making clear that these toys are in true, mortal danger, and that they are physically capable of facing it. The Boogeyman's forces are a range of male toy types: cowboys with pistols, Vikings with axes, knights with pikes, who fight to kill and are killed in turn, their bodies piled along the battlefield. The Boy's toys are strong warriors, for the most part, though Harmony is too tender-hearted for battle, and Percy too cowardly.

Each of the toys in the Secondary World, as with most toy narratives, are imbued with the attributes of both their physical forms—Max has the teeth and claws like a bear; Quackers can fly like a duck—and also the attributes the Boy has given them—the Colonel is brave; Harmony is sweet. Unlike other toy narratives, however, the attributes are not distributed equally. Where Pooh and his animal friends are all equally animal-like, and the *Toy Story* toys are all equally toy-like, the level of "real-ness" that the toys have in the Dark, according to illustrator Charles Paul Wilson, III, is proportionate to the amount to life, time, and thought the Boy has given them. Harmony, not much played with, looks mechanical. The favorite Colonel looks fully real. A toy train and the men who run it admit that they were thrown in the closet before being taken out of the box, and so they look barely human (Wilson). The puppy, naturally, remains a puppy.

Furthermore, the more time they spend in the Dark, the more these toys grow and develop into their own personalities. Usually toys in the Secondary World of the Toy Fantasy exist on a constant, as in *Pooh* and in *Calvin and Hobbes*. Their unchanging nature is predictable and comfortable. When a toy does grow or change, it is sudden, drastic, and magical, as in *The Velveteen Rabbit* or in *Pinocchio*. *The Stuff of Legend*'s toys, by contrast, work on a slowly developing learning curve, and their priorities and values change as the story goes on. The Jester, for example, at first wacky and whimsical, is violent and deadly by the end of the third book.

His focus on the Boy is gradually replaced by his love of the Princess, and it is for her, and not the Boy, that he fights, and quests, even to the point of hunting and killing other toys (Book 3). Percy the pig, who is intelligent but skittish to begin with since spending his life as a piggybank leads to a terror of being dropped and broken, becomes not only a coward, but a conniving betrayer. The Boogeyman shows Percy that here, in the Dark, Percy cannot be dropped and broken, and reminds Percy of the Boy's plans to smash him one day. This earns the Boogeyman Percy's loyalty over his duty to the Boy, ultimately leading to Percy's betrayal of his friends. Harmony, the ballerina-top, becomes more assertive and strong in defense of and because of her "family," by which she means the other toys, and not the Boy. Because of their developing personalities, the longer they are in the Dark, the more real these toys become—with no contact whatsoever with their Boy, and with no overt discussion of "realness." To be a real boy, to be a real rabbit, is never an aspiration for *The Stuff of Legend*'s toys, as it is with *Pinocchio* and *The Velveteen Rabbit*. In the Dark, it would seem, realness is compulsory. In the Boy's world, inanimateness is a limiting, but not necessarily unfavorable, condition. Indeed, Harmony remembers the stillness of the Boy's world wistfully, in the face of the violent and dangerous Dark, and the many violent toys that call it home.

When, in either the Primary or the Secondary World of toy narratives, the Child's toys meet "other" toys, that is, toys not belonging to the child, these other toys are usually friendly, even if they are first perceived as threatening, as with Sid's mutant toys in *Toy Story*. In *Toy Story 2*, Stinky Pete tears Woody's arm, but it doesn't seem to hurt. In *Toy Story 3*, the day care toys are organized and do form a true nemesis force; but while they have the power to entrap the hero toys, they make no overt moves to physically harm them.

In *The Stuff of Legend*, the other toys are not only a direct and violent threat, but different kinds of toys pose different threats. The residents of Hopscotch, a town designed around a maniacal and unfair board game, live their lives by bizarre and capricious rules, forced on them by a megalomaniacal Mayor—also a minion of the Boogeyman. In Book 2, "The Jungle," the realness of the toys moves a significant step further. The animal toys have lived in the Jungle for so long that they refuse to call themselves toys, not because a Blue Fairy or enough love has made them "real," but because the Boogeyman has instilled in them a hatred of all things human. To belong to a human and be its plaything has become disgusting to the animals of the Jungle. Human toys are hunted for sport by the animals, who care nothing for their common origin. The most terrifying "other" toy, a destroyer of Boogeyman-allies and good-Toy forces alike, are the mindless Golems: clay men and dinosaurs bent on simple destruction. Deeper into the Dark, the Boy's toys meet a community of Dolls, complicit with the Boogeyman in exchange for his protection, as well as Storybook characters who are at war with one another, one side hoarding the Night Light, as the Wolf and the Little Pigs play out their endless struggle. The most capricious and dangerous toy, however, is the one that shares a common origin with the Boy's toy Jester. The Laughing Ghost is the Jester's "brother." Both, in the real world, were Jack-in-the-Boxes given to the Boy and his little brother, Johnny. The Boy played with and loved his Jack-in-the-Box, but Johnny immediately broke and discarded his. Now, in the Dark, the Laughing Ghost has become a vicious killer, loyal to no one. This stratification and differentiation of toy types allows a level of complexity of narrative: who is friend? Who is foe? Who is willing to switch sides, and who is secretly loyal to the Boogeyman? This is a level of complexity absent from earlier, children's Toy Fantasy, and is made possible in *The Stuff of Legend* by, compared to children's books or films, the extended length of the narrative. Indeed, when the simple map of the Dark needs extending, the map literally changes, as the imagination of the creators, and the Boogeyman, require it to.

The primary agent of this narrative complexity is, however, a clear, named, and shown foe—an element absent from most Toy Fantasy. Vague outside threats may shake a toy community from time to time—a new toy, a new puppy, a blustery day. Even *Toy Story*'s Sid, the crazed toy-destroyer next door, can, with the right gaze, be seen as more of a misguided mad scientist. But the Boogeyman is real, is insidious, and is, apparently, everywhere. The Boogeyman can easily be a metaphor working with the time and setting of the story; an America in 1944 was a mass of fears of vague yet palpable threats: the Boogeyman is Hitler; he is the German spy next door; he is the possibility that the letter the Boy received from his father is the last one. Indeed, he could be a metaphor for the present-day preoccupations of *The Stuff of Legend*'s contemporary readers.

And there is comfort in a metaphoric Boogeyman, because a metaphor is removed from real-ness. But the Boogeyman in *The Stuff of Legend* is named and shown, and he relentlessly and tirelessly pursues the Boy's heroes. He is omnipresent in his ability to manifest from the shadows. Most significantly, he is a threat to the real Boy in the real world, dragging him from his bed, as much as he is a threat to the toys in the Dark. The excuses that the reader instinctively makes, that the Boogeyman somehow not really a threat, that the boy is actually safe somewhere, that this is his dream, or that maybe the Boogeyman is a manifestation of the Boy's dark side/fears/social conditioning—all of these attempts at self-comfort are taken from the reader when the reader sees the Boy in the Dark, alone and frightened. As the Boy's toys seek him, the Boy tries to find his own way home, oblivious to his toys' efforts, and harried by the Boogeyman and his forces. The Boy is, in fact, the most innocent and naïve character in the story. The Boy, still steeped in childlike innocence, travels through the Dark, happily following a vague path, forgiving all those who wrong him. He frequently faces actual danger, which he treats as an adventure, rushing toward the Boogeyman's soldiers to fight them, and even spending most of his time in the Dark with another lost boy, a boy whom he instantly befriends, and who turns out to be the Boogeyman in disguise. The Boy's greatest foe is next to him nearly every time we see him, but the Boy is blind to this darkness. No child's Toy Fantasy has so crossed the line from fantasy world to real world to the extent of truly endangering the toys' child. In traditional Toy Fantasy, the child is the savior, the god, and the hope and focus of his toys. In *The Stuff of Legend*, seeing the Boy in the Dark pushes the reader into unfamiliar territory. Shown this bemused and powerless Boy, the reader is forced to ask: What if his toys did find him? The Boy is, if anything, less capable of navigating the Dark or vanquishing the Boogeyman than his toys are.

Absent the child as leader, traditional Toy Fantasy casts the favorite toy as hero or leader. Here, again, *The Stuff of Legend* not only subverts this trope, but tears it to pieces. The Colonel leads his little group into the Dark and through battle with the simple and clear goal of finding the Boy. The Colonel is the Boy's father-proxy, brave and loyal. But the Colonel, soon after entering the Dark, comes face-to-face with the Boogeyman himself. The reader has seen the Colonel in flashbacks, as the Boy plays with him, get to the top of the hill and defeat the foe. But, as the Boogeyman says, the Dark has different rules than the Boy's world, and the Colonel has not learned them yet. Getting to the top of the hill, for example, is sometimes "only the beginning of the fight" (Book 1, Part 1). The Boogeyman approaches the Colonel, unfazed by the Colonel's bullets. He expresses how the Boy has failed to prepare the hero for this battle, and then he tears the Colonel in two. And so, before the first issue of *The Stuff of Legend* ends, the leader is destroyed. The other toys decide to soldier on with Max the Teddy Bear taking the lead, but the death of the Colonel decisively shows the reader that this is a world in which no toy is safe, and to which the surviving toys must adapt.

In most Toy Fantasy, toys are more or less immortal. Hitty the doll recounts her first hundred years; Woody and Jessie are old enough to be collector's items, but they never age. Christopher Robin's toys live on in the Hundred Acre Wood forever. By the fourth book of *The Stuff of Legend*, "The Toy Collector," the reader has learned that anything that can happen in the real world can happen to the toys. They may die, like the Colonel; lose hope, like Quackers and Harmony; become sick, like the Princess who suffers a wound that becomes infected; and be scarred or broken, like Percy who is maimed by the Boogeyman and the Jester who is maimed by his twin. The final comfort the reader may cling to, that a broken toy may be mended, is torn away in "The Toy Collector." There is a Toy Collector in The Dark, who gathers the fragments of the many toys that have been killed in battles, and there is a Toy Maker, who can reassemble the toys. The toys, however, have no life, except that which the Boogeyman gives them. The Boogeyman can restore toys to life with a whistle, but upon their return to life, the toys are twisted, dark, evil, and completely loyal to the Boogeyman, ready for him to send them into battle—for him to play with them—again.

With the death of the Colonel comes the natural confusion of whether the toys should go on or go back. After some debate, and not yet realizing that no one knows how to get back, they move on, but under the shadow of yet another broken toy trope. Toy Fantasy will have sometimes have minor or perceived betrayals. Hobbes takes endless joy in tricking and pouncing on Calvin when Calvin least expects it. In the first *Toy Story* movie, Woody is rejected by the other toys when they think, wrongly, that Woody has done away with Buzz out of jealousy. Pooh and Piglet steal Eeyore's house—an honest mistake. But *The Stuff of Legend* works on a deep betrayal, centering perhaps the most powerful trope in Toy Fantasy.

Almost every Toy Fantasy includes some level of replacement anxiety. This comes in many forms: the child may be moving on to more mature times, as in *Toy Story 3* and *The House at Pooh Corner*. The toy may be defective in some way, as in *Corduroy* or *The Velveteen Rabbit*. Even Hobbes has to go in the washing machine from time to time. But the most common incarnation of this replacement anxiety is a favored toy being replaced by a newer toy, losing the favor of the child, who is, for the toy, the center of existence. Buzz Lightyear threatens Woody. Jessie the Cowgirl is left behind in favor of teen-girl concerns. The Island of Misfit Toys is populated by toys which each have a correlating, better version: the Charlie-in-the-Box, the Cowboy who rides an ostrich, the train with square wheels. S.D. Schindler's picture book *The Curious Island of Abandoned Toys* (2007) makes it clear that inhabitants, politely, do not ask how other toys ended up there. To be abandoned is not only a source of pain, but a source of shame. The toy has somehow failed its owner. If, as the King of the Island of Misfit Toys says, "a toy is never truly happy until it is loved by a child," then it follows that a toy is in true despair if it does not have a child's love. The universality of this trope speaks to its strength, as most children, as some point, feel this replacement anxiety themselves. "Toy" is to "child" as "child" is to "parent." A child may not feel good enough in the eyes of their parent, or may be threatened by the arrival of a younger sibling, or may be fearful of the loss of a parent to separation or death—the latter being the very anxiety the Boy of *The Stuff of Legend* must feel with a father away at war.

This replacement anxiety is the chief motivating factor in Percy's betrayal, as Percy has heard the Boy looking forward to destroying his piggy bank to get the money inside. But the strongest replacement anxiety comes with the toy that is the favorite—Max. While the Boy tends to actively play with the Colonel more now his father is a soldier, Max is secure in the status of being best-loved, as expressed by his place on the boy's bed at night. But the toy that is best loved has the most to lose in the loss of that love. Max, the reader learns, had replaced the boy's first favorite toy, Monty the cymbal-monkey. Monty was greeted in the Dark by the Boogeyman, who then was showing a kind face, comforting the displaced Monty and other discarded toys. The Boogeyman also tempted and won the allegiance of the Knight, another favorite who suffered the terrifying toy-fate of being lost; the pride of being best loved also comes with a fear of being left behind. Monty and the Knight are both instrumental in building the Boogeyman's empire in the Dark.

Max is most threatened by the Boy's new puppy, Scout, "the toy that could play back" (Book 2, Part 4). When Scout takes Max's place on the Boy's bed, and Max is left on the floor, the Boogeyman starts to whisper to the despairing Max. The Boogeyman successfully tempts Max into opening the closet door just enough. Max thinks the puppy will be taken, but it is the Boy the Boogeyman wants. The replacement anxiety over the puppy drives Max to rash and destructive action and, subsequently, the loss of the Boy, which he spends the balance of the books trying to correct. His single-minded focus on the quest, the reader learns, is not fueled by bravery so much as guilt. Max-the-hero's unmasking as Max-the-villain shatters the quest, leaving yet another trope subverted.

In *The Stuff of Legend*, it is not so much the toy that has been replaced in the eyes of the child, but the child and the quest for the child that is replaced in the eyes of the toys. The ultimate trope is ultimately subverted. With the knowledge of Max's betrayal, and inflamed by Percy, the group of toys falls apart. Their single-minded focus on the Boy has fallen apart as well. Max has won the place of King of the Animals, and the only one to stay by his side is, ironically, Scout the puppy. Max, the favorite toy, is left alone and broken, still wishing to search for the Boy, but convinced he cannot succeed without his friends. The loss of those friends hurts him more deeply than the loss of his Boy. Max wanders the Dark with Scout and Monty the Monkey, looking for anyone with wisdom on how to proceed. The Princess returns to the Indians and is reunited with her tribe. The Jester's love for the Princess is eventually all that drives him, but when he kills one of her kinsmen, she spurns him. The Jester is set at odds with his twin, the Laughing Ghost, and ends up battered and nearly broken, cared for by Rebecca, the leader of the Dolls. Harmony and Quackers abandon the quest for the Boy, having "endured enough," and wander the Dark, looking for a way home and mourning the loss of their "family." Their return to the quest for the Boy is more to mend the bond with Max than find the Boy. Percy, the least willing member of the group, is ironically the one to find the Boy, and then only by a coincidental crossing of paths. The Boogeyman is quick to reclaim Percy from the Boy, and as the fourth book closes, the fractured narratives continue, with characters lost, dead, bewildered, and trapped in the Dark.

The establishment of toy tropes in the Toy Fantasy subgenre of children's literature reflects the needs and interests of the children for whom that literature is made. Children's own fears, fantasies, and worldviews are played out by their toys when their toys come to life in their stories. *The Stuff of Legend* quite skillfully takes the tropes with which its grown readers are already intimately familiar and subverts or expands on them, leading the reader to a fresh, surprising world, both familiar and unpredictable.

WORKS CITED

Booth, Allyson. "Battered Dolls." In *Images of the Child*. Ed. Harry Eiss. Bowling Green, OH: Bowling Green State University Press, 1994. Print.
Carroll, Lewis. *The Annotated Alice: The Definitive Edition*. Illus. John Tenniel. Ed. Martin Gardner. New York: W.W. Norton, 2000.
Collington, Peter. *The Midnight Circus*. New York: Alfred A. Knopf, 1992. Print.
Collodi, Carlo. *The Adventures of Pinocchio*. 1883. Trans. Carol Della Chiesa. *PublicLiterature.org*. Web. April 16, 2011.
Freeman, Don. *Corduroy*. New York: Viking Press, 1968. Print.
Godden, Rumer. *The Story of Holly and Ivy*. Illus. Barbara Cooney. Reprint ed. New York: Puffin, 2010. Print.
Gruelle, Johnny. *Raggedy Ann Stories*. New York: Little Simon, 1918. *Project Gutenberg*. Web. March 30, 2011.
Hoban, Russell. *The Mouse and His Child*. 1967. Illus. David Small. New York: Scholastic, 2001. Print.
Kuznets, Lois R. "Taking Over the Doll House: Domestic Desire and Nostalgia in Toy Narratives." *Girls, Boys, Books, Toys*. Ed. Beverly Lyon Clark and Margaret R. Higonnet. Baltimore: Johns Hopkins University Press, 1999. 142–153. Print.
Lewis, C. S. *The Lion, the Witch, and the Wardrobe*. Reprint ed. New York: HarperCollins, 2008.
Milne, A.A. *The House at Pooh Corner*. Illus. Ernest H. Shephard. New York: Dell, 1981. Print.
_____. *Winnie-the-Pooh*. Illus. Ernest H. Shephard. New York: Dell, 1988. Print.
Nikolajeva, Maria. *From Mythic to Linear: Time in Children's Literature*. Lanham, MD: Scarecrow Press, 2000. Print.
Raicht, Mike, and Brian Smith. Illus. Charles Paul Wilson III. *The Stuff of Legend*. Th3rd World Studios. Volume I: The Dark, Book 1. 2009.
_____. *The Stuff of Legend*. Th3rd World Studios. Volume I: The Dark, Book 2. 2009. Print.

———. *The Stuff of Legend*. Th3rd World Studios. Volume II: The Jungle, Part 1. 2010. Print.
———. *The Stuff of Legend*. Th3rd World Studios. Volume II: The Jungle, Part 2. 2010. Print.
———. *The Stuff of Legend*. Th3rd World Studios. Volume II: The Jungle, Part 3. 2010. Print.
———. *The Stuff of Legend*. Th3rd World Studios. Volume II: The Jungle, Part 4. 2011. Print.
———. *The Stuff of Legend—Book 3: A Jester's Tale*. Th3rd World Studios. 2012. Print.
———. *The Stuff of Legend—Book 4: The Toy Collector*. Th3rd World Studios. 2013. Print.
Rudolf, the Red-Nosed Reindeer. Dir. Kizo Nagashima and Larry Roemer. 1964. Sony re-release, 2002. DVD.
Russell, David. "Toy Fantasy." *Literature for Children: A Short Introduction*. 8th ed. Boston: Pearson/Allyn & Bacon, 2014, 198. Print.
Schindler, S.D. *The Curious Adventures of the Abandoned Toys*. New York: Henry Holt, 2007. Print.
Stevenson, James. *The Night After Christmas*. New York: Greenwillow Books, 1981. Print.
Th3rd World Studios. "The Stuff of Legend." 2016. Web. March 27, 2016.
Toy Story. Dir. John Lasseter. Disney/Pixar, 1995. DVD.
Toy Story 2. Dir. Ash Brannon and John Lasseter. Disney/Pixar, 1999. DVD.
Toy Story 3. Dir. Lee Unkrich. Disney/Pixar, 2010. DVD.
Watterson, Bill. *The Indispensable Calvin and Hobbes*. Kansas City: Andrews and McMeel, 1992. Print.
Williams (Bianco), Margery. *The Velveteen Rabbit—or—How Toys Become Real*. Illus. William Nicholson. New York: Doubleday, 1922. *The Digital Library Project*. Web. March 22, 2016.
Wilson, Charles Paul. "Stuff of Legend Paper at the Pop Culture Convention in San Antonio—A Quick Question?" Message to the author. March 15, 2011. E-mail.

"The Steadfast Tin Soldier" as Romantic Hero and Tragic Lover

KIRSTEN MØLLEGAARD

Illustration by Vilhelm Pedersen, 1850

It is a convention to call a story's main character, or protagonist, its "hero" (Abrams 224). But not all story heroes are heroic in the sense of being brave, strong, and willing to sacrifice themselves for the common good. "The Steadfast Tin Soldier"[1] by Danish poet and author Hans Christian Andersen (1805–1875) features a toy protagonist, who, despite his stoic fortitude and military decorum, at heart is as soft as the material[2] from which he is made.

The tin soldier has none of the folksy, swashbuckling humor of another uniformed Andersen hero, the strapping soldier of "The Tinderbox,"[3] who kills the witch and wins the princess. Instead, "The Steadfast Tin Soldier" features a romantic hero who struggles against the pietism, middle-class conventions, and smug conformity of the Biedermeier[4] period, which dominated Scandinavian culture from about 1815 to 1848 in the wake of the Napoleonic wars and transitioned into the Romantic era. The historical subtext of war, sieges, and death informs the ambiguous ways in which Andersen uses subtle humor to question social values about heroism, masculinity, and domestic bliss. A close reading of "The Steadfast Tin Soldier" in conjunction with some of Andersen's other object-centered fairy tales, notably "The Sweethearts, or The Top and the Ball" (1844) and "The Shepherdess and the Chimneysweep" (1845), reveals a complex perspective on Andersen's treatment of the romantic hero as tragic lover.

Andersen and the Biedermeier Period

The Biedermeier period, known in Denmark rather grandiosely as *guldalderen* (the Golden Age), was "characterized by restraint, conventionality and utilitarianism" (Wullschlager 53). It developed in response to the fateful politics that had plunged Denmark, then an absolute monarchy, into economic and political turmoil, and produced a strong apolitical climate with an emphasis on Denmark as a small, industrious, and peaceful nation.[5] On the surface, the Danish Golden Age appears to be a time of harmony, quiet comfort, and idyllic nationalism. In reality, Denmark entered the 1800s through a series of chaotic events that thwarted the country's ambitions to become a major European power and reduced it to a small, impoverished nation. In 1795, a fire that started in the naval shipyards destroyed over 900 houses in the capital of Copenhagen. During the following decade, sieges, warfare, and fires took their toll on the nation's capital. Denmark, priding itself on its naval strength, was on the losing side in the Napoleonic wars (1803–1815). In 1801, the British navy, under the command of Admiral Horatio Nelson, destroyed most of the Danish navy. The British returned in 1807 and bombarded Copenhagen, leveling the medieval part of the inner city. The British also demolished Copenhagen's military defenses and took away the remainder of the navy. National bankruptcy in 1813 was followed by the loss of sovereignty over Norway to Sweden in 1814. While social and political reforms were in the works across Europe at the time, there were huge gaps between social classes. The poor had little opportunity for social advancement coupled with the fact that the majority of Danes lived in rural areas. In major towns and cities, the bourgeoisie, solidifying their assets and investments, developed a pronounced home culture, turning the eye away from the havoc of the outer world onto the small pleasures of home. Margaret Doyle explains, "[T]he bourgeois home was at the center of Biedermeier culture, and Gemütlichkeit, or coziness, was the principle behind its interior decoration" (89). Andersen, who had grown up in great poverty in Odense, the largest city on the island of Funen, was ironic and suspicious of bourgeois coziness, and he used the contrast between the perceived security of the home and the perceived dangers and disillusionment of the outside world with great critical effect in his fairy tales. He recognized that Biedermeier culture was philistine, yet world-weary. "The basic attitude was resignation and humor with a tendency towards the melancholic and idyllic. The aim to strike a harmonic balance between the material world and the ideal often produced a sense of disruption" ("Biedermeier" n.p.).[6] Home was seen as a refuge from the storms of politics and war, and the humorous banalities and cozy routines of everyday life were celebrated in visual and literary art as bulwarks against the world of politics, that external "playground of evil forces" ("Biedermeier" n.p.). In "The Steadfast Tin Soldier" and other object-centered stories, Andersen adeptly unsettles the illusion of domestic idyll by placing an agent of evil, often a troll, in a strategic position that will set in motion the protagonist's journey from the sanctity of home into the turbulent world outside.

The architecture and material culture of the Biedermeier period not only included comfortable, well-lit houses and spacious apartments for the middle and upper classes, with practical furniture and room for social gatherings, it was also the burgeoning era of new developments in children's culture. "The child assumed a role of unprecedented importance in Biedermeier society" (Doyle 89), and consequently so did the material culture centering on childhood. The market for toys grew with bourgeois prosperity, and the possession of toys implicitly taught children mercantile principles about trade and ownership. Andersen biographer Erik Haugaard observes, "[W]e live in an age of toys; and toys are pleasant to own" (2). Handmade toys fashioned by craftsmen or at home gradually became replaced by mass-produced toys. As a reflection of the wars in Central and Northern Europe, tin soldiers,[7] painted in the bright colors of the Napoleonic armies, became popular among boys of all ages and stations in life.[8] War toys have existed since antiquity, but tin soldiers were not mass-produced until the 1800s (Tatar 224, note 1). They were sold in boxed sets and marketed specifically for boys, thus contributing overtly to the pronounced gendering of toys that is evident in Andersen's tales of animated objects. The steadfast tin soldier is always a "he," never an "it." His masculinity is accentuated by his metallic form, uniform, arms, and steadfastness in neat binary opposition to the way the object of his romantic desires, the fragile paper ballerina, is portrayed as the essence of femininity in her flimsy dress, bright spangle, and elegant pirouette.

During the Biedermeier period, war toys allowed children to process the death and destruction of warfare within the cozy security of home. The imaginary world created through play transposed the reality of bloodshed to the safety zone of the nursery, where the toys in Andersen's stories form their own social hierarchies, and humans' role merely is to play with the toys. Interestingly, in Denmark, tin soldiers' uniformity and lack of individual expression gave rise to colloquial sayings about the human condition, which reflect the intersection between rational, common-sense Biedermeier values and idealistic Romantic sentiments. Among the examples of such colloquial sayings listed in the historical *Ordbog over det danske Sprog* (*Dictionary of the Danish Language*) we find the expression *dusinmennesker* (literally, "dozen people"), meaning people who are commonplace, unremarkable, and lack individuality. The existentialist philosopher Søren Kierkegaard, a contemporary of Andersen's, derisively compared such commonplace, unremarkable people to "tin soldiers in a box" (*Ordbog*).

It is evident from Andersen's diaries, letters, and literary works that he detested the commonplace and in particular the Biedermeier period's valorization of fitting in, not calling attention to oneself, and meek acceptance of one's station in life.[9] In one of his autobiographies,[10] *The Fairy Tale of My Life* (1871), he describes himself again and again as "fortune's child" (408). His meteoric literary career was indeed remarkable.[11] Reared in the slums of Odense, he ended up becoming Denmark's national poet. But there were formidable obstacles along the way. While he harvested recognition and accolades abroad, he felt that Danish critics punished him for being ambitious and different. One person told him, "For God's sake don't believe you are a poet because you can make verses!" (Andersen, *The Fairy Tale of My Life* 57). Kierkegaard's review of his novel *Only a Fiddler* (1837) devastated Andersen: "I learned from it that I was no poet, but a poetical figure that had escaped from my group, in which my place would be taken by some future poet" (*The Fairy Tale of My Life* 137). Diana Crone Frank and Jeffrey Frank correctly maintain that "it is an understatement to say that Andersen frequently felt misunderstood, even abused, by Danish critics" (11). Thus, the stigma of low-class birth, petty jealousies, and the lack of recognition among peers, which Andersen experienced in the closely confined literary circles in Denmark, might be seen as a source of inspiration for the torments suffered by the steadfast tin soldier.

Romantic Dreamer and Ambiguous Hero

"The Steadfast Tin Soldier" was one of Andersen's first stories to endow toys with human emotions and aspirations and situate them in a strict social hierarchy. It was also one of his first fairy tales not based on a folktale.[12] The idea of the toys coming to life and playing among themselves was not new. Andersen had read E. T. A. Hoffmann's dream-fantasy *The Nutcracker and the Mouse King* (1816), and he had seen animated toys in children's ballets and puppet performances on his travels in Europe (Kofoed 245). In fact, he had already experimented with bringing inanimate objects to life in "Little Ida's Flowers," which was published in his first fairy-tale collection in 1835.[13] However, "The Steadfast Tin Soldier," published in his third fairy-tale collection in 1838, marks a new beginning in his authorship because in this story the hero is a toy living, loving, and dying among other toys in a complete social and material world that in many ways parallels, but is largely independent of, human society, though located in a shared domestic setting. The toys' relative isolation from the human world is underscored by the fact that none of the characters are given names, neither amongst themselves nor by their owners, the children.[14] Rather, toys and humans live in parallel social universes that intersect in the nursery, but the strong emotional bond between child and toy that characterizes many other animated object stories is absent here. "The Steadfast Tin Soldier" is, literally, a toy story in which human characters remain on the margin.

"Little Ida's Flowers" uses a child's point of view to bridge the magical realm of animated objects and the dreary, common-sense world of grown-ups. By showing how magical the child's world is, Andersen lampoons the story's dry, old professor who keeps telling Little Ida that she is silly for believing that dolls and flowers come alive at night to dance and make merry. Little Ida is the precocious, innocent child protagonist, who acts as intermediary between the fantasy world of dancing flowers and talking dolls and the tedious rationality of the grown-up world. In contrast, in "The Steadfast Tin Soldier" humans are fleeting nameless characters,[15] who skirt the periphery of the toys' social arena, thus opening up the narrative to the titular toy as the story's romantic hero.

Our hero is one of twenty-five tin soldiers "born of the same old tin spoon" (Hersholt n.p.),[16] which a little boy receives for his birthday. The soldiers are all alike except for the one who was made last. He has only one leg because the tin ran out. The tin soldiers are placed on a table in the crowded nursery, and the tin soldier immediately falls in love with a paper ballerina in a gauze dress adorned with a single spangle. He believes that since she is balancing on one leg and he can't see her other leg, she must be one-legged like himself and hence suitable to be his wife. His only worry is that she may be above his station in life because she lives in a grand cardboard castle and he shares a box with the other tin soldiers. At night, when the children sleep, the toys play amongst themselves, doing somersaults and moving about. The tin soldier, however, is merely gazing at the ballerina. At the stroke of midnight, a troll hiding in a snuffbox pops up and tells the tin soldier to stop staring at the ballerina. The tin soldier ignores the warning and keeps looking at the dancer. The next morning, he is placed on the windowsill and is suddenly—perhaps by the troll, perhaps by the wind—blown out into the street below. A maid helps the little boy search for him, but they can't find him. As the rain comes pouring down, two street boys spot him and place him in the gutter in a boat made from old newspaper. Throughout the dangerous, high-speed journey down the culvert where a nasty sewer rat demands to see his passport, the tin soldier remains stoic and silent. He is washed out into the canal and swallowed by a fish, which is caught, bought, and brought up into the very same home from where he came. There is great wonder when he is taken from the belly of the fish and once again placed on the table within view of the pretty ballerina. They gaze at one another, but remain silent. Suddenly, one of the little boys grabs the soldier and throws him into the fireplace. As he is melting, a draft from an open door blows the paper ballerina into the fire where she immediately is reduced to ashes. When the maid cleans out the oven the next day, she finds the soldier's remains "in the shape of a little tin heart. But of the pretty dancer nothing was left except her spangle, and it was burned as black as coal" (Hersholt n.p.).

The tin soldier is certainly the hero of the story. But is he heroic? His heroism is ambiguous, in part because his missing leg marks him as a victim of a cruel, whimsical fate. Just because he happened to be the last soldier to be born from the old tin spoon, he is not fully developed. However, the narrator assures us that he "stood as steady on the one leg as any of the other soldiers on their two" (Tatar 226). This assurance justifies the lack of impairment the soldier actually suffers because of his missing leg and shifts the narrative attention from his outside deformity to his inner character as a dreamy romantic pining for a flimsy paper princess. The story explores the duality between inner and outer worlds, which much Romantic literature focuses on, by keeping the tin soldier's outer appearance as rigid and unflinching as that of a real toy soldier, while taking the reader into the toy's innermost thoughts to reveal his anxieties and desires. The duality between stoic outer appearance and inner *Weltschmerz* ("world-pain," an important concept for the Romantics) is also a central theme in Andersen's other animated object and animal tales (e.g., "The Ugly Duckling," "The Fir Tree," "The Old Tombstone," and "The Silent Book"). In the fairy tale "The Old House," for example, a little boy gives an old man a tin soldier to keep him company. The tin soldier is homesick for the bustling nursery and cries out, "I simply can't stand it any longer!" because the sad loneliness, or *Weltschmerz*, prevailing in the old man's house is too much for him to bear (Hersholt n.p.).

A second ambiguous aspect of the tin soldier's heroism is his lack of action. Chance and accidents, rather than strategic planning, define his topsy-turvy journey through the world outside. Due to circumstances beyond his own control (the wind or the troll), he is whisked into a series of events that tests his valor, but at the same time subverts the pietistic values and codes of military honor he has internalized. Joan Haahr remarks, "[T]he narrative questions the very decorum it praises" (497). The soldier's rigid steadfastness and unflinching military demeanor make him appear to be brave and constant[17] on the outside, but he is quite the opposite inside. His inner thoughts are marred by insecurities, fears, and worries. He clearly lacks the qualities that would make him a valiant warrior. This lack is symbolized by his missing leg. The impairment makes him remarkable, as the narrator emphasizes, because out of all the twenty-five tin soldiers in the box, he is the only one who is different. His missing leg is not so severe a defect that he is discarded from the collection of tin soldiers. On the contrary, although he is the runt, the weaker one born last with a deformity, he is the only one who is special. All the other tin soldiers look alike and are therefore, within the logic of the story, neither interesting nor remarkable. Only the steadfast tin soldier stands out as remarkable. In Andersen's story universe (as it was in his real life), difference is a sign of romantic splendor blemished by suffering and victimization. Another famous romantic Andersen hero, the titular character of "The Ugly Duckling" (1843), is also unique because he, like the tin soldier, "didn't turn out right" and is consequently "picked on by everyone" (Tatar 104, 105). The ugly duckling is harassed and tortured in the duck yard, kicked by the maid, ridiculed by the wild drakes, and lectured to by the pompous chicken. The tin soldier is yelled at by the troll, abused by the street boys, threatened by the sewer rat, swallowed by a fish, and thrown into the fire by a little boy. Both characters are singled out by misfortune (or fortune as the case eventually turns out to be for the duckling) because they stand out as different, one for being ugly, the other for being one-legged.

The Missing Leg

Several scholars discuss the tin soldier's missing leg in the context of disability studies. David T. Mitchell and Sharon L. Snyder argue that "The Steadfast Tin Soldier" gains narrative momentum precisely because "the outward flaw 'attracts' the storyteller's—and by extension the reader's—attention" (54). The tin soldier's "disability establishes the uniqueness" of his character, but Mitchell and Snyder note that it is otherwise not used to compromise his endeavors in any way (55). Vivian Yenika-Agbaw goes deeper into the underlying reasons for the tin soldier's romantic pining for the paper ballerina. She argues,

This attempt to link up with someone who shares his physical disability serves as a motivating factor that enables him to survive the abuse he suffers at the hands of the humans. He chooses to blame his mishaps not on the humans but on the black goblin who had taunted him earlier, thereby introducing a racial dimension to the tale, and blackness as another symbol of otherness. In so doing, he refuses to acknowledge the superiority of the boys; instead, he holds steadfast to his love of the dancer in hope of having her reciprocate [96].

It is possible, as Yenika-Agbaw suggests in her reference to blackness as a symbol of otherness, that contemporary readers may see the black troll in the snuffbox as giving the tale a racial dimension, but Scandinavian folktales and legends abound with dark, hairy trolls and goblins. For example, in Norse mythology, blackness is associated with chthonic, earthy powers like the giant Narfe, whose daughter Nat (Night) is "black and dusky" (Bæksted 43). In the Danish folktale *For Tre Skilling* ("For Three Shillings"), a soldier plays cards with three black creatures that emerge from the chimney and take the form of devils (*Danske Sagn og Æventyr* 53–60). Similarly, the black troll in "The Steadfast Tin Soldier" emerges from a place of black material: the snuffbox. If blackness is seen as a racial dimension, or a symbol of the other, it is hard to explain why the paper ballerina's entire existence is reduced to the spangle burnt "black as coal," or why Andersen describes the heroic chimneysweep from "The Shepherdess and the Chimney-Sweep" as "saa sort som et kul" (*Eventyr og Historier*, Vol. I, 115), meaning "as black as coal" (Hersholt n.p.). Moreover, "as black as coal" is a colloquial idiom echoed in the snippet of a traditional children's singing game, "Bro, bro, brille," which the tin soldier recalls as the paper boat starts to disintegrate and he thinks he is about to drown. Translators take great liberties with the translation of this song line and its child-speak vocabulary, "Fare, Fare, Krigsmand! Døden skal Du lide!" (*Eventyr og Historier*, Vol. I, 207),[18] which literally means, "danger, danger, war-man! You shall suffer death." "Bro, bro, brille" is a so-called arch game, where two children, who represent the sun and the moon, face one another and join hands up high, thus forming with their arms a high arch or bridge through which the other children pass single file, while they sing the song. The game is related to "London Bridge Is Falling Down."[19] The lyrics of "Bro, bro, brille" describe an emperor's castle thus: "så hvidt som et kridt, så sort som et kul" ("as white as chalk, as black as coal"), and when the verse ends with the lines "den, som kommer allersidst, skal i den sorte gryde" ("the very last one shall get into the black cauldron"), the moon and sun lower their arms and "catch" someone, who will then "die" and have to choose to join either the sun's or the moon's side. When all the children have "died," the game ends with a tug-of-war between the moon's and the sun's sides. To the tin soldier, the references to danger embedded in "Bro, bro, brille" are very literal, and the blackness evoked (the powerful emperor's castle and the black cauldron) signifies the death he believes he is heading toward. Sure enough, he is shortly swallowed by a fish and thus buried alive in its dark womblike tomb: "My! how dark it was inside that fish! It was even darker than under the gutter-plank and it was so cramped" (Hersholt n.p.). In consideration of these contexts for Andersen's metaphorical uses of blackness, the black troll in the snuffbox can be seen as part of the evil, deadly, uncontrollable forces that snatch away soldiers' and children's lives in war and games, respectively.

In the specific context of Andersen's fairy-tale universe, trolls are the harbingers of misfortune and, mirroring Andersen's Christian beliefs, are seen as akin to devils and demons (Johansen 548–550). "The Snow Queen" famously opens with a description of the devil, who creates the magical mirror that splinters and sends millions of fragments out into the world to distort people's perception of good and evil. The troll in the snuffbox that pops up at the stroke midnight—"the witching hour" as Tatar points out (228, note 10)—obviously scares the tin soldier to the point that he, as Yenika-Agbaw argues, believes that the troll is behind the haphazard misfortunes that befall him: falling out the window and getting thrown into the fire by the little boy. None of these unfortunate events are associated with his one-legged-ness. In other words, while the tin soldier's impairment can be read as a symbolic reference to the very real dangers of maiming, death, and war of the 1800s,[20] within the narrative logic of the story itself, the tin soldier is never inconvenienced by his missing leg. In fact, it makes his character all the more heroic that his handicap does not prevent him from aspiring to marry the lovely ballerina and that he is able to return to the nursery in one piece after his dangerous journey. From the limited narrative perspective of the tin soldier, his one-legged-ness is advantageous in allowing him to rationalize that he and the ballerina are well suited for one another, since she—or so he believes—is also one-legged. This perspective both valorizes and satirizes the Biedermeier norm of marrying within one's social class and contradicts the folktale tradition of the hapless, but street smart folk hero who marries up, as when the opportunistic soldier of "The Tinderbox" or the impossible titular character of "Clod Hans" end up marrying princesses.

The narrator of "The Steadfast Tin Soldier," however, clearly identifies the tin soldier's impairment as that which makes him interesting and marks him as the story's main character. Andersen introduces him thus: "det er just ham, som bliver mærkværdig" (*Eventyr og Historier*, Vol. I, 204). The adjective *mærkværdig* means "remarkable" or "striking," but can also mean "strange," "odd," or "peculiar." Jean Hersholt translates this passage very close to the original as "he'll be the remarkable one" (n.p.). Maria Tatar and Julie K. Allen change the verb tense from future to past tense and select a more awe-inspiring adjective: "he's the one who turned out to be astonishing" (226). Interestingly, Robert MacLean quotes a translation that takes even greater liberties with the original text: "he's this story's hero" (280). These three examples of translations show some of the difficulties not only in pinpointing the meaning of the text in translation, but also the meaning of the tin soldier's character. Is it the missing leg that makes him remarkable, or is it his romantic sentiments and tragic fate?

Lacking a leg is not an obstacle for the tin soldier's romantic ambitions, but leaving the small world of the nursery is. Once he falls out the window, there is no way of knowing if he'll ever get back home. Through the ages, the sanctuary of home shines a bright beacon in children's literature about animated toys. Separation from home is conceived as one of the most dreadful things that can happen to a toy (and by extension, to a child). Andersen's toy heroes typically face formidable challenges when they get lost or leave the safe, though typically oppressive, world of home and go out into the world. Nevertheless, for the tin soldier to go AWOL does represent an unexpected occasion to earn valor and prove his manliness.

The voice of the tyrannical troll represents the patriarchal authority that rules the nursery. The troll's words are both the law and the verdict: don't look at the ballerina, or else. The troll's voice is as harsh and authoritarian as that of headmaster Simon Meisling, who practically tortured Andersen when he was at school in Slagelse and punished him for hoping to become a poet.[21] The troll's commanding tone is evident in Andersen's original text, where the exclamation marks underscore the tone: "'Tinsoldat!' sagde Trolden, 'vil Du holde dine Øine hos Dig selv!'" (*Eventyr og Historier*, Vol. I, 205). Tatar translates this harsh bark of an order almost verbatim: "'Tin soldier,' the troll shouted. 'Keep your eyes to yourself!'" (228). Surprisingly, Hersholt makes the troll sound quite polite: "'Tin soldier,' he said. 'Will you please keep your eyes to yourself?'" (n.p.). The tone is important here, because the tin soldier's defiance of the troll's order is what causes the ill wind to sweep him out the window the following day, just as the troll predicted. "The bogey said, 'Just you wait till tomorrow'" (Hersholt n.p.). Thus, while the nursery may seem like a feminized space in the Biedermeier home, mainly frequented by children, teen-aged maids, and occasionally the mother, it operates under the patriarchal hegemony of the malevolent troll who does all he can to keep apart the two lovers. The tin soldier is not allowed to look at the ballerina, and he understands why. Even before the troll starts shouting at him, he has reasoned that she is too "grand" (Hersholt n.p.) or "noble" (Tatar 226) for him. The tin soldier's inner monologue articulates time and again how he has internalized the oppressive social norms and values that prevent him from following his heart.

In spite of that, the tin soldier hopes to overcome social stigma and marry the paper ballerina. That is why his accidental journey in the world outside, as unplanned and tumultuous as it is, has the benefit of empowering his suit because it gives him an opportunity to earn valor. Just like a real soldier must brave the dangers of the battlefield in order to prove himself, so must the tin soldier leave the cozy safety zone of the nursery to show that he is brave and steadfast. There is hope that upon his return, he will have proved himself worthy of the ballerina and thus be able to override the troll's authority.

At the same time, "The Steadfast Tin Soldier" makes it clear that the world outside the safety of home is full of danger, adventure, unsettling unfamiliarity; *das Unheimliche*, literally the "un-homely" (in Freudian terms, "the uncanny"). As much as the tin soldier resents the troll's harsh rules in the nursery, he is overwhelmed by the chaos reigning in the world outside where he is literally swept along by currents and events. Anxiously he yearns for the safety of home and the pretty ballerina: "'Where can I be going?' the soldier wondered. 'This must be that black bogey's revenge. Ah! if only I had the little lady with me, it could be twice as dark here for all that I would care'" (Hersholt n.p.). Perhaps none of Andersen's fairy tales captures the dual yearning for home (Danish: *hjemve*) and for the world outside (Danish: *udve*)[22] better than "The Shepherdess and the Chimneysweep" (1845), which features two porcelain figures living in an old wooden cabinet. The tin soldier has many characteristics in common with the fearful, handwringing shepherdess, who elopes with the chimneysweep to avoid an arranged marriage to the devilish carved male figure jutting out of a wooden cabinet. An "old Chinaman" figurine, who claims to be her grandfather, has nodded his approval for the hideous figure to marry the shepherdess (Hersholt n.p.). The shepherdess begs the chimneysweep to take her away. After a dark and dangerous journey through the stove and stovepipe into the chimney, the two lovers finally reach the top of the chimney:

> Overhead was the starry sky, and spread before them were all the housetops in the town. They looked out on the big wide world. The poor shepherdess had never thought it would be like that. She flung her little head against the chimney-sweep, and sobbed so many tears that the gilt washed off her sash. "This is too much," she said. "I can't bear it. The wide world is too big. Oh! If I only were back on my table under the mirror. I'll never be happy until I stand there again, just as before. I followed you faithfully out into the world, and if you love me the least bit you'll take me right home" [Hersholt n.p.].

Like the shepherdess, the tin soldier is stunned by the magnitude of the outside world. But there are also important differences between the two characters' experiences. The shepherdess is overwhelmed by the endlessness of a starry night whose beauty she cannot appreciate. It only triggers acute homesickness in her. She and the chimneysweep reenter their home by returning to the maternal womb through the same birth canal—the chimney—that they used to get out. "'Here we are,' said the chimney-sweep. 'Back where we started from. We could have saved ourselves a lot of trouble'" (Hersholt n.p.). The chimneysweep's laconic remark underscores the futility of their journey and their failure to embrace the wide world. The tin soldier's journey, in contrast, is much more dramatic and mythic in nature considering his life cycle: he is formed in fire from a spoon, falls through the air into the street, is swept along by water, entombed in the belly of the fish, reintroduced into human society, and then again transformed by fire into a heart.

Death, Silence and the Hero's Journey

The tin soldier completes the cycle of the hero's journey, with the ordeals and tests of valor famously outlined by Joseph Campbell in *The Hero with a Thousand Faces* (1949). But he is not a triumphant hero. He is different. He is sensitive. He is silent. He dies. Those are exactly the characteristics that Andersen employs to bring to life the romantic hero turned tragic lover. The tin soldier goes through three births: when he is born from the tin spoon, when the little boy (on his birthday, naturally) tears off the lid on the box and shouts, "tin soldiers!" (Tatar 224), and when the he is taken from the belly of the fish. Yet, he ends up dying not as a result of a mighty battle, but rather as the victim of the irrational whims of a little boy (or, perhaps the malevolent influence of the troll). Throughout this journey, he is remarkably passive and never says a word, not even to the ballerina. He does nothing to save himself when he has the opportunity, but simply goes with the flow of wind and water wherever chance takes him.

We may ask, why does he not try to save himself when he is on the perilous journey? Why is he so quiet? When the maid and the little boy search for him after he has fallen out the window, he chooses to remain quiet for fear of losing his dignity as a man in uniform. Hersholt's translation reads, "If the soldier had called, 'Here I am!' they would surely have found him, but he thought it contemptible to raise an uproar while he was wearing his uniform" (n.p.). The term "raise an uproar" is a rather free translation of Andersen's term "at skrige høit" (*Eventyr og Historier*, Vol. I, 206), which means to "cry out" or "scream loudly." Maria Tatar and Julie K. Allen translate the same passage, "he felt it was beneath his dignity to shout while in uniform" (229). His reluctance to shout or scream suggests that he finds it incompatible with his soldierly demeanor to use such an effeminate mode of calling attention to himself. More to the point, he is afraid of looking like a fool.

He obviously looks ridiculous when, after he falls out the window, he is standing on his head between the cobblestones with his single leg sticking up for the world to see. His journey would have ended before it began if he had called for help. It is tempting to conclude that although he is terrified of never being found, he is even more terrified of being laughed at. Similarly, when the two street boys whoop and yell as he rushes down the gutter in the paper boat—again a ridiculous situation far beneath his dignity—he "remained steadfast, without changing his expression and looking straight ahead of him, standing tall with his rifle on his shoulder" (Tatar 229). Of course, the irony is that since he really is a tin soldier he can't change his expression even if he wanted to. He is literally cast in a mold, meaning a social gender role, from which he cannot escape. However, although his very essence at heart is romantic, he has internalized that rigorous masculine gender role's values and obligations to the point that he accepts that he must give the ultimate sacrifice for his honor, namely the death awaiting him in the fireplace into which the whimsical little boy tosses him.

Nameless little boys are also agents of their toys' death and disappearance in other Andersen tales, for example "The Old House" (1847) and "The Sweethearts, or The Top and the Ball" (1844). As previously mentioned, in "The Old House" a little boy visits a lonely old neighbor and decides to give him one of his tin soldiers to keep him company. This tin soldier can speak, but only to the boy. He complains of how boring and miserable it is to live in the old man's house:

> I can't bear it!" wailed the tin soldier. "I've been shedding tin tears—it's too sad here! I'd rather go to the wars, and lose arms and legs; at least that would be a change! I just can't stand it!" [...] "You were given away as a present," said the little boy firmly. "And you must stay here! Can't you understand that?" [Hersholt n.p.].

The complaining tin soldier eventually flings himself onto the floor, falls through a crack, and is not found again until many years later when the little boy, now a grown man with a wife, finds him in the dirt after the old house has been demolished. The reemergence of the tin soldier out of the dirt is not unlike the rebirth of the steadfast tin soldier from the belly of the fish. But in the years that he has been lost and forgotten, the boy has become a man and the distance between him and the toy is unbridgeable. Getting lost and forgotten is often synonymous with death for the toy.

Andersen's story "The Sweethearts, or The Top and the Ball" combines the theme of death by disappearance with aging, another death sentence for an active toy. The top (a male toy) and the ball (female) live in the same drawer full of toys. The freshly painted red and yellow wooden top woos the leather ball, declaring that "we are just made for each other. You bounce and I dance" (Hersholt n.p.).[23] The ball begs to differ. She thinks the top is below her social rank because she is made from leather and he from wood. She is taken out to play and bounces so high up that she disappears. The top thinks that she has eloped with a swallow she said she liked. As the years go by, the top mends his broken heart. He is getting worn and old, but then he is gilded and is as good as new again. He spins and leaps. "But suddenly he jumped too high, and disappeared" (Hersholt n.p.). He falls into the rubbish bin and cannot be found. He realizes that his gilding will soon fade and he'll look like the "riffraff" of discarded things surrounding him (Hersholt n.p.). One of those dirty, old, broken things in the dustbin is the ball. Now that he is gilded, she does not recognize him as her old suitor. She exclaims, "[T]hank goodness. At last I have an equal to talk to!" (Hersholt n.p.). Uninvited, she tells him that she never married the swallow, but landed in the roof gutter. The golden top is disgusted with her appearance and remains silent. Then the maid discovers him and he returns triumphantly—like the tin soldier rescued from the belly of the fish—to the sanctity of home, where he is "admired by everybody. But the ball was never heard of again" (Hersholt n.p.). Where the top returns in golden glory, the discarded old ball is left to rot in the rubbish bin.

Chance, (mis)fortune, social snobbery, and cruel everyday banalities determine the hero's journey in Andersen's story world. Death and silence often await the returning toy hero. For the steadfast tin soldier, it could be argued that even in his absurdly tragic death he defies the odds. He and the ballerina are united in death and thus in eternity, with his entire being transformed into a tin heart, while she, made only of a light and flimsy material, is reduced to just a blackened sequin. The soldier's inner romantic essence becomes a lovely objet d'art, a curio, and a memento of a tragic, but romantic destiny.

Conclusion

Critics predominantly decipher Andersen's fairy tales in search of biographical clues to his unsuccessful real-life romances. Andersen's letters and diaries seem to support such an interpretative angle. Jackie Wullschlager introduces her Andersen biography with a telling quote taken from a letter Andersen wrote in 1834: "every character is taken from life; *every one of them*; not one of them is invented. I know and have known them all" (original emphasis, quoted in Wullschlager 3). (In)famous for his narcissism, he states, "the history of my life will be the best commentary to all my works" (*The Fairy Tale of My Life* 274). From this perspective, we might see the steadfast tin soldier as a personification of Andersen who yearned to be loved, and the flimsy paper ballerina as an incarnation of the graceful Lucile Grahn, who danced in August Bournonville's ballet "*La Sylphide*, which opened in Copenhagen in 1836" (Wullschlager 176). Bournonville had revived and modernized Filippo Taglioni's original romantic ballet. Bournonville and Grahn danced the principal roles, but Grahn became unhappy with her relationship to Bournonville and left Denmark for good the very same year in order to dance at the famous Paris Opera Ballet. The reference to the *La Sylphide* ballet and burning, destructive, love is evident in Andersen's fairy tale: "hun fløi ligesom en Sylphide lige ind i Kakkelovnen til Tinsoldaten, blussede op i Lue og var borte" (*Eventyr og Historier*, Vol. I, 209), which Hersholt translates, "She flew like a sylph, straight into the fire with the soldier, blazed up in a flash, and was gone" (n.p.). Andersen had had a romantic crush on Grahn, the incarnation of the elegant sylph, who appeared to dance on air. Her career at the Royal Danish Ballet was a bright flash, and then she was gone. Like many of Andersen's other crushes, she inspired him to hope and yearn, but he never did find a life partner.

While acknowledging the valid interest in the minutiae of Andersen's personal life and his deserved iconic status as the inventor of the literary fairy tale, this essay has focused on the tin soldier as a *Sinnbild*, or symbolic allegory, of the Biedermeier period's attempt to conform and domesticate the unruly, sensitive spirit of the romantic hero. The tin soldier is indeed the story's hero in the sense that he is the focalizing character whose perspective and inner feelings we follow. Moreover, our discussion of his character in conjunction with other Andersen fairy-tale heroes points to the presence of a complex subtext of resistance within the tale itself to the rhetoric of military stoicism and uniformity. As Ann Schmiesing has demonstrated in a recent study of disability in the Grimms' collected stories, the historical background of the Napoleonic wars informed the 19th century perception of the destructive powers of war on the human body. Enormous numbers of disabled veterans, many of them amputees, returned from the wars, where "the use of packed columns on the field led to an increase in casualties and also a spike in the number of amputees" (56). The tin soldier's missing leg alerts us to consider the implication of warfare on the human body. For although the one-legged tin soldier, to use a contemporary expression, is "born that way" and is accepting of his deformity, his uniqueness is that the missing leg marks him as different from the other tin soldiers. He is a unique individual entrapped in a strict social world where he is allowed neither voice nor gaze, and where he has internalized the very values that oppress him.

Andersen criticizes Biedermeier values such as sentimental piety and domestic security by situating the one-legged tin soldier in a social world of totalitarian rule, social injustice, and ultimate death. Andersen's irony forms an important basis for this criticism: the tin soldier has internalized the very values, which work against his ultimate goal of being united with the ballerina in marriage. By conforming to proprietary ideals about valor and soldier's honor, he remains a passive figure, unable to break rules and take action against the forces that conspire to destroy him. The tragic death of the two lovers can be seen as both the triumph of the Romantic spirit and its destruction as the two lovers go down in flames.

Notes

1. "The Steadfast Tin Soldier" ("Den standhaftige tinsoldat") was published in Andersen's third collection of fairy tales, *Eventyr, fortalte for Børn* (*Tales, Told for Children*) in 1838.
2. Tin was used in alloys such as pewter to manufacture household items. The fact that the tin soldiers in Andersen's story are mass made from a recycled old spoon underlines their base social class, lack of individuality, and low military rank.
3. "The Tinderbox" ("Fyrtøjet") was published in 1835 in Andersen's first collection of fairy tales.
4. The term Biedermeier derives from an everyman, conventional middle-class character in the satirical poems by Ludwig Eichrodt and Adolf Kussmaul, which made fun of the period's introspective complacency and emphasis on domestic idyll. The German prefix *Bieder* means "honest but ordinary" (Daverio 395).
5. National hymns of that era practically wallow in pietistic humility. See for example Andersen's contemporary, N. F. S. Grundtvig's "Langt højere bjerge så vide på jord" ("Far, Greater Mountains in the Wide World") (1820), which contains two lines often quoted in Danish political rhetoric of that time: *vi er ikke skabte til højhed og blæst / ved jorden at blive det tjener os bedst* ("we are not made for grandeur and storm / it serves us best to stay close to the ground").
6. Unless otherwise noted, all translations are by the author.
7. Tin soldiers were also made from materials other than tin, such as wood, stone, silver, lead, and other metals. In the story, the tin soldiers are cast at home in a mold. Factory-made tin soldiers, prized by collectors, became common in the mid to late 1800s.
8. "Crown Prince Ludwig was especially taken with Andersen's stories. He became so absorbed in 'The Steadfast Tin Soldier' and the main character's amputated relationship to life that he subsequently became greatly distressed when he found three of his best toy soldiers missing their heads. 'Three brave tin soldiers are dead! I wonder what Andersen will say when he hears about it'" (Jens Andersen 438).
9. See Wullschlager, Jens Andersen, and Bredsdorff.
10. Andersen wrote four autobiographies in total. See Møllegaard: "The Fairy-Tale Paradigm: Contemporary Legend on Hans Christian Andersen's Parentage," note 2 (43).
11. Andersen's rags-to-riches life story is in fact so remarkable that some scholars believe that it is too good to be true. Some researchers argue that he was not at all the son of a washerwoman and a shoemaker, but the secret lovechild of a prince and a noble lady. See Møllegaard: "The Fairy-Tale Paradigm: Contemporary Legend on Hans Christian Andersen's Parentage."
12. Although Andersen is usually credited with inventing the literary fairy tale, he drew on folktale material in many of his stories.
13. In one of his autobiographies, Andersen writes that "Little Ida's Flowers" was his own invention "although it bore a tolerably near affinity to a story of Hoffman's [sic]" (*The Fairy Tale of My Life* 204).
14. It is a notable feature that Andersen does not name animated objects, not even when they are protagonists.
15. Lois Rostow Kuznets argues that "distance between animated man-made objects and human subjects ... tends to prevail in Andersen's tales" (81).
16. Only six of Andersen's 156 fairy tales begin with the formula *der var engang* ("once upon a time"). "The Steadfast Tin Soldier" is one of them. Jean Hersholt, whose translations of Andersen's works will be used as the primary reference in this essay, chooses to shorten the phrase to "there were once twenty-five tin soldiers" (n.p.), which verbatim parallels the wording of the Danish text: *Der var engang fem og tyve Tinsoldater* (Andersen 203). Hersholt's translations are endorsed by The Hans Christian Andersen Center website.
17. Some translations render the Danish adjective *standhaftig* as "constant" or "brave" (Owens; MacLean).
18. Hersholt translates these two lines as "Farewell, farewell, O warrior brave/ Nobody can from Death thee save" (n.p.). Tatar's translation goes further, "Flee the waters, warrior brave / Here below is thy shadowy grave" (230).

19. "London Bridge" is listed as number 502 in the Roud Folk Song Register. See also Milbank 366.
20. Even if the Napoleonic wars are usually not directly mentioned in 19th century fairy tales, "these wars would in any case have profoundly shaped the readers' understanding" of the tales (Schmiesing 57).
21. Meisling forbade Andersen to write poetry and stories. "'You are a stupid boy, who'll never be any good,' Meisling told him. 'When you start to stand on your own two feet you can write a lot of nonsense, but no one will read what you write, and it will be sold as pulp.... Don't start crying, you overgrown boy!'" (Wullschlager 62).
22. Andersen was familiar with both notions. He loved to travel, but was always nostalgic for home, even though he found his literary endeavors stifled in Denmark. Jens Andersen summarizes, "Andersen's numerous trips and encounters with other people provided the author with essential spaces in his occasionally quite painful life" (492).
23. The top's rhetoric parallels the tin soldier's. They both look for similarities between themselves and the female objects of their desire in order to justify their romantic quests. The top finds the bouncing ball comparable to his spinning, while the tin soldier perceives the ballerina's one-legged-ness as reason enough to desire her.

Works Cited

Abrams, M. H. *A Glossary of Literary Terms*. 7th ed. New York: Harcourt, 1999. Print.
Andersen, Hans Christian. *Eventyr og Historier*. Vol. I & II. Hans Brix, ed. København: Gyldendalske Boghandel Nordisk Forlag, 1952. Print.
_____. *The Fairy Tale of My Life. An Autobiography*. London: Cooper Square Press, 2000. Print.
Andersen, Jens. *Hans Christian Andersen: A New Life*. Trans. Tiina Nunnally. New York: Overlook Duckworth, 2005. Print.
"Biedermeier." *Minilex*. Gyldendal: Copenhagen. No Date. Web. February 12, 2016.
Bredsdorff, Elias. *Hans Christian Andersen: The Story of This Life and Work 1805–75*. New York: Charles Scribner's Sons, 1975. Print.
Bæksted, Anders. *Guder og Helte i Norden*. Copenhagen: Politikens Forlag, 1978. Print.
Danske Sagn og Æventyr. Axel Olrik, ed. København: Gyldendal, 1967. Print.
Daverio, John. *Robert Schumann: Herald of a "New Poetic Age."* New York: Oxford University Press, 1997. E-book.
Doyle, Margaret. "Biedermeier." *Encyclopedia of the Romantic Era 1760–1850*. Vol. 1. Christopher John Murray, ed. London: Taylor & Francis, 2004. 88–89. E-book.
Frank, Diana Crone, and Jeffrey Frank. "The Real H. C. Andersen." *The Stories of Hans Christian Andersen*. Durham: Duke University Press, 2005. Print.
Haahr, Joan G. "The Steadfast Tin Soldier." *The Oxford Companion to Fairy Tales*. Jack Zipes, ed. Oxford: Oxford University Press, 2000. Print.
Haugaard, Erik. *Portrait of a Poet: Hans Christian Andersen and His Fairytales*. Washington, D.C.: Library of Congress, 1973. Print.
Hersholt, Jean. Trans. "The Old House." *The Hans Christian Andersen Centre*. August 11, 2015. Web. October 24, 2015.
_____. "The Shepherdess and the Chimney-Sweep." *The Hans Christian Andersen Centre*. August 11, 2015. Web. October 24, 2015.
_____. "The Steadfast Tin Soldier." *The Hans Christian Andersen Centre*. August 11, 2015. Web. October 24, 2015.
_____. "The Sweethearts, or The Top and the Ball." *The Hans Christian Andersen Centre*. August 11, 2015. Web. October 24, 2015.
Johansen, Ib. "The Demons of the Text." *Hans Christian Andersen: A Poet in Time*. Johan de Mylius, Aage Jørgensen, and Viggo Hjørnager Pedersen, eds. Odense: Odense University Press, 1999. 541–554. Print.
Kofoed, Niels. "Hans Christian Andersen and the European Literary Tradition." *Hans Christian Andersen: Writer and Citizen of the World*. Sven Hakon Rossel, ed. Amsterdam: Rodopi, 1996. 209–257. Print.

Kuznets, Lois Rostow. *When Toys Come Alive: Narratives of Animation, Metamorphosis, and Development*. New Haven: Yale University Press, 1994. Print.

MacLean, Robert. "Hans Christian Andersen's 'The Steadfast Tin Soldier': Variations upon Silence and Love." *Ritsumekan Bungaku* 589 (2004): 25–42. No Date. Web. October 23, 2015.

Milbank, Anna-Marie. "London Bridge." *Encyclopedia of Play in Today's Society*. Vol. 1. Rodney P. Carlisle, ed. London: Sage, 2009. E-book.

Mitchell, David T., and Sharon L. Snyder. *Narrative Prosthesis: Disability and the Dependencies of Discourse*. Ann Arbor: University of Michigan Press, 2000. Print.

Møllegaard, Kirsten. "The Fairy-Tale Paradigm: Contemporary Legend on Hans Christian Andersen's Parentage." *Contemporary Legend* 8 (2005): 28–47. Print.

Ordbog over the danske Sprog [Dictionary of the Danish Language]. No Date. Web. October 28, 2015.

Owens, Lily, ed. *The Complete Collection of Hans Christian Andersen*. New York: Gramercy Books, 1996. 13–15. Print.

Schmiesing, Ann. *Disability, Deformity, and Disease in the Grimms' Fairy Tales*. Detroit: Wayne State University Press, 2015. Print.

Tatar, Maria. *The Annotated Hans Christian Andersen*. Trans. Maria Tatar and Julie K. Allen. New York: W. W. Norton, 2008. Print.

Wullschlager, Jackie. *Hans Christian Andersen: The Life of a Storyteller*. Chicago: University of Chicago Press, 2000. Print.

Yenika-Agbaw, Vivian. "Reading Disability in Children's Literature: Hans Christian Andersen's Tales." *Journal of Literary & Cultural Disability Studies* 5.1 (2011): 91–108. Print.

The Problem of Possession
Objects and Maturation
in The Indian in the Cupboard

Rachel L. Carazo

> "In a culture such as ours that is starved of meaning, people often find meaning in life through the things they own."
> —Hade 161–162

Play is a central component of childhood, especially play with objects that children can physically touch and imaginatively control. In fact, play is so integral to the notion of childhood, as opposed to adult working life, that the toy industry has even commodified play and marketed it to families (Brown 454). Thus, the possession of objects/toys has become the mainstay of childhood play. Yet what happens when toys become alive and challenge norms of possession, through which the development of life skills and imaginative faculties occurs (Ogata 129)? In Lynne Reid Banks's famous work, *The Indian in the Cupboard*, the problem of possession, which appears during Omri's interactions with Little Bear, situates Little Bear, the living toy, as the hero of the novel and creates a medium through which to inspect the unresolved issues inherent in childhood play.

Problematic possession is also a very complicated issue, and it intersects with concerns of materialism, consumerism, and the objectification of animate/inanimate things (Nava 165). The main aspects of the problematic possession of the toy/object include power, age and maturation, and inheritance and gender. Yet Omri, who inhabits a society infused with problematic possession, cannot overcome these biases on his own. He needs a hero who can problematize the process and present a counter-narrative, which involves the secondhand/gifted object, self-worth and self-possession of power, self-criticism and the development of tolerance, and becoming transformative.

Little Bear is this hero, and even though problematic possession is not completely resolved at the conclusion of the novel (Banks 196), Omri has taken the first steps to understanding the true power of objects/toys in society and how he can allow them to exist on their own (Bennet vii).

Heroic Dynamism: The Strengths and Weaknesses of Little Bear

> "Plastic, the quintessential postwar material, had been adapted for the production of toys even before the [Second World] war."—Ogata 137

Plastic is stagnant. It has no feelings. It is bought, controlled, inherited, and destroyed on a whim. Therefore, a plastic toy seems like a lifeless, unimportant object. However, Little Bear possesses none of these static qualities. Even though his plastic form is possessed by Omri and Patrick, he is never truly owned. This reality makes Little Bear a dynamic protagonist and an unquestionable hero whose personal strengths and weaknesses allow Omri to recognize the dual nature of the possession of objects/toys and that, although it is a complex problem, it is a problem quickly re-conceptualized and reevaluated.

First, Omri does not purchase Little Bear. The plastic Indian is a birthday gift from his friend Patrick and is therefore a secondhand toy (Banks 1). In addition, Omri's brother Gillon does not actually purchase the cupboard. Instead, Gillon finds it in the alley next to the house, where neighbors discard unwanted objects (Banks 2). The special key for the cupboard, which Omri receives from his mother, is also secondhand (Banks 3). It once belonged to his grandmother and has become a family heirloom. Consequently, an overview of the main objects/toys in the novel reveals that the most important *things* to the plotline cannot actually be purchased; they must be given secondhand or inherited. Thus, before Little Bear even comes to life, he, the key, and the cupboard defy the norms of materialism and consumerism, in which objects are valued for being new and improved. Instead, these very objects already provide a philosophical position from which objects can both become "a form of subjection to it and a form of resistance" to human material culture (Nava 165).

The living Little Bear also opposes these notions of materialism and objectification. When he first interacts with Omri, Little Bear is already educated. He has experienced the complexities of life, losing a wife and taking thirty scalps during a war (Banks 34). He also shares his culture with Omri and explains that he is Iroquois, not Algonquin (Banks 31). Little Bear has life skills; he builds longhouses, hunts, and tends horses. Even his tolerant taming of Crazy-horse demonstrates his dynamism:

> Then, quite calmly, Little Bear reached up and laid his hand on the horse's neck. That was all. He did not hold the reins. The horse could have jumped away, but he didn't. He raised his nose a little, so that he and the Indian seemed to be breathing into each other's nostrils [Banks 39].

Little Bear therefore has multiple skills and experiences because he is more than just plastic. He is a toy that exerts a living force on the people who try to possess him (Bennett vii).

If Little Bear, the toy/man, must be inherited, then he will be inherited with all of these dynamic qualities, not just the inanimate, plastic ones. The difference in possession is that Omri cannot buy Little Bear firsthand or improve him materially since Little Bear has years of personal experiences and since Little Bear only transforms *himself* when he is alive, interacting with other people. Omri notices these qualities during his attempt at possession, causing him to question events in his own life and believe that "[h]e had an experiment to do" with Little Bear (Banks 29). Omri therefore matures because a plastic toy (Little Bear) exerts its own force (Bennett vii) and reminds his supposed owner that no toy, especially a secondhand one, can be easily *purchased* and subsequently controlled.

Second, Little Bear maintains an incontestable sense of self-worth and the self-*possession* of his own power. Little Bear exhibits pride in his Iroquois/Native American heritage and he judges Omri by these cultural standards. For example, since wives in Little Bear's culture cook, Little Bear believes that Omri has a wife who has been cooking for them. When Omri corrects this assumption, Little Bear then quickly asks: "Omri not got wife? Who grow corn, grind, cook, make clothes?" (Banks 36). Little Bear also adheres to his culture when he requests a horse, a longhouse, and animals to hunt (Banks 37). In response, Omri often negotiates with Little Bear, and this disputation determines the outcome of events. When Little Bear wants to fight Boone, Omri tells him: "All right, you kill him. But then I won't bring you a wife" (Banks 103). Omri often wins these debates. However, when Little Bear encounters resistance, he uses other tactics. When he first meets Omri,

> after a few moments he decided it was more dignified to stop struggling. Instead, he folded his tiny arms across his chest once again, put his head back, and stared with proud defiance at Omri's face, which was now level with his own [Banks 24–25].

Even when he is overruled, Little Bear exhibits his dignity and his heroic faith in himself despite his size and strange circumstances. Consequently, even before he claims the headdress from the dead chief, Little Bear always assumes that his self-possession and culture are primary values with which Omri must cooperate (Banks 66).

Little Bear's power, despite Omri's supposed ownership of him, overturns the idea that "when characters are playing Indian, [...] it reifies the sociocultural differences being assumed by these representations" (Meek 118). Little Bear cannot *play* an Indian since he really is one; Omri then quickly reexamines his biases about Native American lifestyles, speech, and personalities. The power difference between the two cultures therefore remains dynamic and interdependent since Little Bear and Omri continually reevaluate their perspectives about each other, creating the dichotomy of subjection and resistance that Mica Nava attributes to consumerism and materialism (165). For Little Bear, his self-worth and self-possession, not his Native American culture, are critical points of contention in the novel since he still proudly displays and matures with his culture intact.

Little Bear's promotion to chief also reflects the force of objects in Omri's life (Bennett vii). To gain status, Little Bear gains an object: a headdress (Banks 66). At the beginning of the novel, Omri believes that having a skateboard will increase his popularity and self-worth (Banks 2). However, like Little Bear's authority, Omri's view of objects as reflections of his own importance becomes problematized (Banks 66). Being a leader is a demanding task, as is caring for a small, plastic toy/man (Banks 77). Little Bear's difficult tenure as chief directly reflects the toy/object's power over materialistic, human culture (Bennett vii), and as Little Bear's power grows, so too does Omri's multi-faceted understanding of consumerism and materialism (Nava 165). Omri demonstrates this relationship when he states, "He says he's a chief now. It's made him even more bossy and—and *difficult* than before" (Banks 77). Thus, the costlier and more authoritative the object becomes for its supposed possessor, the more difficult ownership really becomes.

Little Bear, a living toy, is also heroic because he problematizes the power of the object and demonstrates how all objects are essentially alive (Bennett vii), subsequently belonging to humans and resisting their proclaimed power over them (Nava 165). Little Bear is therefore a heroic living *object* since he exhibits his own self-worth to Omri and uses this influence to teach Omri why toys are dynamic forces instead of immutable, plastic objects.

Third, Little Bear remains a dynamic hero due to his self-critical nature, which allows him to evaluate his actions and tolerantly regard others. These self-reflective qualities are normally absent in inanimate objects. Little Bear, though, has life as a man and as an object/toy. His self-reflection also creates a similar philosophical space for Omri, who begins to question, if not erase, his reliance on objects and reevaluate the intolerance that this materialistic belief fosters toward other people and objects.

Little Bear's own reflective spirit appears during his interactions with Boone: a cowboy and a socially accepted opponent. Yet these social norms, which are already debatable due to problematic possession, cannot endure.

Little Bear and Boone agree and disagree often, culminating in Little Bear's awkward shooting of Boone with an arrow (Banks 164). However, Little Bear realizes his mistake and jumps on his headdress, resisting the power and authority that this object supposedly gives to him (Banks 168). He then risks his life to find the key, which has been lost beneath the floorboards, and saves the life of another toy/object (Banks 178). This heroic moment, when "Little Bear, a tiny, vulnerable figure, strode off through the dust into the darkness under the floor," epitomizes Little Bear's struggle and how he overcomes it, by admitting his mistakes and by trying to reconcile his actions with what he has learned about materialism (Banks 175).

Little Bear's tolerance directly results from this self-reflection, and Omri learns from him. During one scene, Little Bear refuses to eat with Boone. Later, though, "Little Bear, after hesitating, was first to shoot his arm out and dip the bread into the egg," making peace (Banks 110). Little Bear also cares for Boone after Omri summons Tommy, a First World War medic/toy, from the cupboard to heal his wounds (Banks 50).

Another self-critical assessment that Little Bear makes symbolizes problematic possession and alerts Omri to the same issue. Little Bear asks, "How be brave, how be chief with no other Indians?" (Banks 160). Consequently, Little Bear cannot be himself or lead without other Native Americans or other toys. In effect, Omri cannot understand problematic possession without other people or objects/toys. Little Bear is more heroic with Boone, Tommy, Bright Stars, Omri and Patrick around since each must face the power of the object and an audience that uses these objects to evaluate them. Little Bear also helps Omri apply his knowledge of problematic possession to his family and society. Omri then reacts to material expectations from his parents, Gillon, Adiel, and Patrick.

Most importantly, when Omri returns Little Bear to plastic, this self-reflective spirit does not vanish. Omri becomes a blood-brother with Little Bear, and Little Bear with Boone, suggesting that the connection between the toy/object and humanity remains valuable (Banks 195). Little Bear is therefore dynamic because he makes Omri aware of problematic possession, and like Little Bear, Omri develops a better sense of tolerance for other people and objects that he did not express before his *possession* of Little Bear. His blood and self-reflective spirit will therefore remain in Omri, ensuring that the toy Indian will still affect Omri despite his *material* composition.

Fourth, Little Bear is transformative and thus able to influence the lives of others as well as his own. This ability directly opposes Michael Dorris's claim, which Michelle Pagni Stewart shares, that Little Bear, a Native American under a child's supervision, remains powerless. Dorris maintains that "Native American characters are often not allowed to change, contrary to the growth of characters in most children's literature" (181). However, Little Bear *does* change. Little Bear's initial treatment of Omri and Boone progresses to acceptance and cultural relativism.

The first major transformative aspect includes Little Bear's acts that change others, especially Omri. Omri learns to adapt to and understand Little Bear's personal demands even if he does not immediately enact them. For example, Omri refuses to offer a certain type of food or bring a bear to life (Banks 78). Yet Little Bear always receives proper care and equipment from Omri. Most importantly, when Omri confronts Little Bear's assertion of power, he does not deny Little Bear respect or the ability to self-actualize (Stewart 181). Instead, Omri relates:

> yet when he saw how the Indian, who was altogether in his power, faced him boldly and hid his fear, he lost all desire to handle him—he felt it was cruel, and insulting to the Indian, who was no longer his plaything but a person who had to be respected [Banks 25].

Therefore, Omri, and even the novel itself, allow Native Americans their own power and humanity. The fact that Little Bear begins as a plastic toy does not confirm this bias since Little Bear is a heroic object/man *with* a story and *within* a story (Ulrich 6).

The second major aspect involves Little Bear's own transformations. He decides to go to school with Omri, and the experience changes everyone (Banks 102). As a result, Little Bear spends positive time with Boone and gains a wife afterward (Banks 187). Omri learns that Patrick, although his friend, represents a social threat toward Little Bear and Boone. Omri accuses Patrick: "You *use* them. They're people. You can't use people" (Banks 141). Omri also learns about trust and friendship, especially when Patrick, after his major mistake, still appears at Yapp's and helps acquit him of stealing toys (Banks 151). Even Little Bear and Boone aid Omri during this tense situation, since they "played along beautifully. There they lay, side by side, stiff and stark, as like lifeless plastic figures as could possibly be" (Banks 151–152). Little Bear uses his influence as a toy/man to transform situations into positive ones for his friends.

The last image, when Little Bear, Boone, and Omri become blood brothers, solidifies this transformation (Banks 195). Little Bear, who is sometimes plastic and always a Native American, Iroquois man, has the power to transform his life and the lives of others. By the end of the novel, Little Bear is still a toy but much more human since he can now use his strengths and weaknesses to affect everyone. Little Bear also returns to his plastic state with something that he had once lost: love; he loves Bright Stars and esteems Omri, Patrick, and Boone. He therefore maintains his transformative power and will continue forward with it to his next adventure.

Lastly, Little Bear's interactions become a counter-narrative to Omri's own culturally-assumed linearity of time and maturation (Roemer 16). The flow of time in Native American literature tends to be disjointed or interrupted by other historical voices (Porter 39). This literary experience also exhibits Native American culture, specifically and in general, as a counterbalance to other cultures (Murray 70). Thus, Little Bear's presence in Omri's world disrupts the modernized, linear flow of time as well as historical time (Roemer 16). Little Bear, Boone, and Tommy Atkins are all from different centuries, and their entrances and exits from Omri's life indicate that time, and thus objectification and possession, are not simply linear.

In addition, Little Bear's personal maturation does not occur chronologically (Roemer 16). Little Bear is already an adult when he arrives; he had a wife and a tribe (Banks 34). When Little Bear returns to his plastic state, he also returns to these affiliations. Yet his critical period of heroic maturation occurs in the middle of his life, between his toy/object states, which interrupts Omri's time expectations and demonstrates Little Bear's own dynamic force. In fact, the modern-day heroism of Little Bear counters Barbara A. Meek's notion that certain "linguistic images perpetuate the historical placement of Native Americans as characters who exist only in a national past and not in a modern present" (121). Little Bear, a hero in his own time, is also a modern hero, ensuring that Native Americans and their traditions are still visible in the twentieth and twenty-first centuries.

Little Bear's counter-narrative also alters the way that Omri views himself and his society. Omri tended to be more self-centered, but Little Bear offers Omri a vision of polyvocality common to Native American tradition that broadens Omri's worldview (Roemer 18). Even Tommy Atkins and Boone share their perspectives about life, affecting Omri's change:

> Might as well, I suppose. Not that there's much to look forward to except mud and rats and German shells coming over.... Still, got to win the war, haven't we? Can't desert, even into a dream, not for long, that is—duty calls and all that, eh? [Banks 52].
>
> I seen him bring a pal o' mine back from the dead, near enough, by puttin' a hot coal in his belly button. He never operates till a man's dead drunk, *and* he don't charge extry for the likker neither! [Banks 190].

These counter-narratives, which oppose the modern view that Omri experiences, allow Omri to evaluate his family's and friends' actions differently (Banks 43). They also demonstrate how Little Bear's dynamism inspires a series of events that are guided by different voices and cultures, times with meaning for their narrators and descriptions that follow the Native American tradition of assigning meaning to place and storytelling (Roemer 18).

Another counter-narrative involves naming, which, when performed in English by a Native American, can also be interpreted as a method of self-actualization (Coulombe 19). According to Joy Porter's evaluation of Native American history, many Native traditions and perspectives were destroyed simply by renaming them. She explains: "He [Columbus] went on to progressively rename and recontextualize the islands he encountered so as to mark non–Indian possession of them, and to rename all the indigenous peoples of the Americas with one single collective descriptor" (44). Consequently, many Native American places and peoples were renamed to fit European standards. However, Little Bear gives his own name to Omri, and this name continuously counters the "Indian" title of the work, which seems to loom over the narrative. There may be an Indian in the cupboard, but this Indian is Little Bear, and Omri will not forget. The real man, not just his ethnicity or toy/object state, therefore remains the hero. In fact, Little Bear provides names for his horse, Crazy-horse (Banks 39), and his wife, Bright Stars (189), maintaining his personality and the heroic power to counter the longtime domination of other cultural forces (Porter 44).

Porter's argument that "they judged Indians to be culturally static and somehow *outside of* history" also faces resistance in the novel (45). For Omri, Little Bear is a historical figure, but he also affects many of Omri's present activities. Boone and Tommy follow this same process, and this mixture of historical forces directly challenges the historicity of the future. Even when Little Bear, Boone, Bright Stars, and Tommy return to their "own times," the possibility and *probability* that they will return in the future is always evident, keeping Little Bear's counter-narrative alive.

Maturation follows a similar path. Little Bear, an adult from the past, learns to live in and to respect the present. Omri, a maturing, modern boy, learns to value the past. These elements then combine in the future, during which time their identity and maturity will evolve. Therefore, Joy Porter's assessment of Native American literature, as a narrative and, in this instance, a counter-narrative, remains crucial. She writes: "The great transformative power of Indian literature from any era derives in part from its ability to invoke a past with direct implications for the present" (Porter 39). Little Bear, a dynamic hero *and* toy accomplishes just this; he invokes his past identity, power, and maturity and uses them to transform the present, influencing Omri and others along the way.

Problematic Possession: Power, Maturation and Gender in Human Society

> "He wanted to keep him. But he knew, now, that that was impossible. Whichever way he thought about it, the end was the same—disaster of some kind. Whatever magic had

> brought this strange adventure about must be put to use again, to send the little people back to their own place and time."
> —Banks 186

Once Little Bear's heroic dynamism is evident, Omri's own heroic development and encounter with problematic possession follows. Omri is indeed a hero. However, his affiliation with a materialistic society reveals that what he gains in knowledge he still cannot completely actualize. Thus, possession of the toy/object remains problematic at the conclusion of the novel. Nevertheless, the process of reviewing problematic possession, which includes issues of power, age and maturation, and gender and inheritance, suggests that understanding this possession is the first heroic step to contradicting it.

Omri's major problem is that the Indian is a *toy*, and this realization has several implications. First, Omri believes that as a plastic toy, the Indian is fairly worthless, retaining the mid-eighteenth century definition of being "a trifle or petty commodity" (Ogata 130). Omri also knows that Patrick paid a few cents for the Indian at Yapp's, supporting this assumption of its trifling worth (Banks 1). In addition, the modernity of the toy affects Omri's perspective. The Indian, a supposed historical figure, is meant to be owned, displayed, and traded with the belief that the process is harmless to those involved (Brown 454).

Consequently, Omri begins his tenure as the owner of the Indian as any possessor would. He does not treat the Indian like a living man, and he therefore undervalues it. Instead, it is a used toy "that [Patrick] himself had finished with" (Banks 1). Yet when the Indian later becomes Little Bear, a hero, the value that Omri places on this object/toy clearly does not match its actual relevance. In fact, toys/objects are highly influential and simultaneously worthless for Omri (and his society); Omri undervalues everyday objects that actually exert great influence on him (Bennett vii), and he, like others, misses the ubiquity of objects to every human experience (Ogata 131).

For Omri, the problem of the object occurs due to his suspension of this reality once Little Bear becomes "alive." Thus, as Bill Brown relates about Stephen Crane's work, toys in novels are problematic since the toys "[come] to life not as toys but as subjects released from the condition of being a toy, [and they] appear (when out of sight) to be recovering from the seriality of modern life" (456). The implications of this idea are important. First, it is easy for Omri and readers to assume that once Little Bear is alive that his "toyness" is essentially erased. Second, as Brown suggests, being a toy/object is not ideal; being alive is better. However, as has already been discussed, the two sides of Little Bear, the heroic toy *and* man, are equally necessary to highlight problematic possession. Third, when Omri only esteems

Little Bear, the man, he assumes that modern plastic toys are boring and powerless.

In effect, the toy Indian is just as alive and powerful as Little Bear. Toys/objects exert a force over Omri and his society since even their static, inanimate forms are highly desirable (Bennet vii). Omri exemplifies this dependency on their influence when the narrator describes his birthday: "After school, there was a family tea, and all the excitement of his presents… . He got his dearest wish—a skateboard complete with kickboard and kryptonic wheels" (Banks 2). Consequently, when Omri receives the secondhand Indian, about which he has not fantasized, he mistakenly believes that his adventure has ended. Yet, as Brown explains, "fantasized adventures are inspired—crucially—not by books but by things" (457). As a result, Omri learns that toys/objects constantly guide his actions and influence his perceptions of the world. Little Bear's changing states cannot alter this reality. Nevertheless, the living, heroic Little Bear is the best agent through which Omri learns about problematic possession, when things that seem lifeless control human decisions and feelings (Bennett vii).

Inherently related to the problematic object is problematic power. Since Omri views objects, especially the plastic Indian, as static and cheap, he places himself in control of them. Omri also believes that he should control what kinds of toys/objects he owns. For example, the narrator explains: "The trouble was, though, that Omri was getting a little fed up with small plastic figures, of which he had loads" (Banks 1). This material exhaustion demonstrates how Omri and his society view objects and choose to manipulate aspects of their ownership (Giddings and Halverson 70). It also supports Brown's proprietary stage in childhood development, a stage that possibly replaces the mirror stage and teaches children how to possess toys/objects (460).

Omri's reaction to receiving the cupboard, which is not a repetitive plastic figure, reflects this psychological development (Brown 460).

> You might suppose Omri would get another disappointment about this because the cupboard was fairly plain and, except for a shelf, completely empty, but oddly enough he was very pleased with it. He loved cupboards of any sort because of the fun of keeping things in them. He was not a very tidy boy in general, but he did like arranging things in cupboards and drawers and then opening them later and finding them just as he'd left them [Banks 3].

Omri's happiness is therefore directly linked to objects/toys and how much power he can exert over them. With the cupboard, Omri controls what objects he keeps inside, where he can locate them, and where they remain until he moves them. Consequently, power and its development over objects/toys become inherent in childhood play (Rustin and Rustin 26). Children also learn this power from social and historical forces, suggesting that Omri's sense of control is deeply indebted to his social interactions (Ogata 131). Omri thus realizes the simultaneous *fun of keeping things* and *fun of keeping things in them* (cupboards) (Banks 3).

Omri's power remains problematic since it does not immediately diminish when the Indian becomes alive. In fact, Omri's desire to control Little Bear and the resistance that he faces allow for Omri's and Little Bear's heroic maturation. Omri's power also depends on his sense of touch. As soon as Little Bear appears, Omri wants to hold him: "His next thought was that he must somehow get the Indian in his hand. He didn't want to frighten him any further, but he *had* to touch him. He simply had to. He reached his hand slowly into the cupboard" (Banks 7). Clearly, Omri will not negotiate this desire with Little Bear. Omri wants to hold and control him, and he does so, much to Little Bear's frustration.

Nevertheless, Little Bear immediately exerts his own human and object power, making him heroic and countering Omri's socially assumed power over toys/objects (Bennet vii).

> Omri was quite taken aback by all this. While giving Little Bear every respect as a person, he was not about to be turned into his slave. He began to wonder if giving him those weapons, let alone letting him make himself into a chief, was such a good idea [Banks 66].

Omri therefore remains ambivalent about Little Bear's own assertions of identity and control. Omri respects Little Bear for his courage and perseverance. Yet Omri prefers to maintain his control over this small toy/man, even daring to compare Little Bear's autonomy to slavery. However, Omri often relents and accepts Little Bear's wishes, such as his becoming chief and wanting a wife. At last, Omri realizes: "You couldn't just—set them up and make them do what you wanted them to. They'd do what *they* wanted to" (Banks 77). This understanding makes power problematic and dependent on the inherent power of the object/toy (Bennet vii).

Omri's acceptance of Little Bear's power reflects Brown's comment that "[f]arfetched as it may seem to imagine an object revealing the history of its own production" it is possible, especially in this instance (456). When Little Bear shares his history with Omri, he reveals the production process of his personality and existence; his maturation and dynamic heroism are also produced when Banks tells the story of Omri and Little Bear, highlighting the production of problematic possession and how it can be understood through their interactions.

Pauline Turner Strong's summary of the novel also supports this negotiation of power between a human and a toy/object. She writes:

> the moral of the tale is clear: although Omri at first cherishes his power over Little Bear, calling him "my Indian," he comes to respect Little Bear as an autonomous human being with (as Omri tells Patrick) his own life, times, country, language, and desires [409].

Omri is therefore a hero, and the fact that problematic possession still lingers at the end of the novel cannot undermine his understanding and reactions to the power of the object/toy (Bennet vii). These notions of power and the object also depend on society's view of childhood, when certain conditions, such as age and maturation, are supposed to directly affect the enactment of possession.

Maturation and its assumed association with age are important aspects of problematic possession. This connection is why scholars such as Perry Nodelman delineate childhood as a period when adults see specific qualities in children, who are in the process of reaching this maturation point (226). Maturation is also meant to demonstrate how humans interact and control objects/toys with the assumption that possessive impulses should decrease with age. However, Omri *and* his parents have problematic interactions with objects, and while Omri becomes more enlightened, adults' attachment to things suggest that the inverse relationship is a false one.

At first, Omri is immature because he wants to own Little Bear. However, "Omri realizes very soon that his Indian is a responsibility, not merely a plaything," highlighting the inevitability that Omri will return the toys to plastic and mature into a man (Rustin and Rustin 106). Patrick's personal struggles with possession also serve as a counterpoint to Omri's supposed maturation, where Omri believes that he has overcome such babyish behavior and left behind his childhood games (Banks 118). Thus, according to Rustin and Rustin, "[w]hile this isn't for him yet, he and his friend Patrick are now ready to give up those kinds of play with little toys in which some of their feelings of caring and being cared for could find expression" (117). However, as has been discussed, Little Bear's heroic dynamism and personal search for identity allow Omri (and readers) to question this simple progression from a possessive childhood to an object-free adulthood (Stewart 19).

Clearly, problematic possession does not decrease with age. Omri's mother has safeguarded the key since her youth (Banks 4). Omri's father angers over his missing seed tray, and Omri must replace it to make him happy again (Banks 67). Gillon frets over his missing shorts, which are *his* and which he accuses Omri of taking (Banks 117). Therefore, the need to possess and control objects does not disappear with increased age.

In addition, children seem to be much better judges of this problematic behavior. Omri not only evaluates and learns from his own actions toward objects/toys, but he also supposes that "[t]he trouble was that although grown-ups usually knew what to do, *what* they did was very seldom what children wanted to be done" (Banks 35). Omri therefore understands that adults struggle as much with objects/toys/possession as he does. Mr. Johnson becomes ill when he sees Little Bear and "gave him a shake of his own that rocked him back and forth on his feet like one of those weighted dolls that won't fall down. Then, abruptly, he let him go and strode back to his desk" (Banks 135). He is ill because he misunderstands the object/toy and its actual power over him (Bennet vii).

Omri then considers his mother's tears, which have emotional and material causes; he supposes that "[w]hen his mother cried, as she did sometimes when things got too much, she only asked to be left alone till she felt better. Maybe all grown-ups were like that" (Banks 97). These issues suggest that children like Omri can best evaluate problematic possession before physical maturation and before embedded social norms fail to confront and enlighten those who are supposedly no longer affected by objects/toys.

As a result, when Omri expresses how he "had heard about people going gray-haired almost overnight if they had too much worry. He felt it might easily happen to him," he is reiterating socially accepted norms about aging and maturity (Banks 142). Childhood play, which has been constructed by the same social processes, also fails to recognize how dynamic heroism can awaken mature thoughts in children better than it can in adults (Ogata 130). Thus, the change of the plastic Indian into Little Bear disrupts these assumptions and allows Omri to exemplify how maturity and the possessive age are not the same as maturity and physical age. Understanding this difference is critical, and the attitudinal divide toward objects/toys between Omri and Patrick is a major component of demonstrating the (un)acknowledged power of the object in the novel (Bennet vii).

Therefore, since physical age cannot really determine maturity, especially with objects, problematic possession still exists at the end of the novel, supporting Brown's comment, "Thus *always* the child (puerile) but *already* grown up (modern)" (452). Adults can remain children in the social sense, and their treatment of objects/toys highlights this disparity. Omri, although still a child, has real insights about himself and others that the transformative qualities of Little Bear, the toy/man, continue to make possible.

Inheritance remains an integral part of problematic possession, which can be passed down to each generation just like objects/toys. Thus, even though living in the present seems central to the novel, concepts of the past and how the future will inherit them are critical themes (Rustin and Rustin 108). Objects and toys are clearly kept over time, and how they affect Omri directly influences his actions.

The key is the main symbol of inheritance for Omri since it came from his mother and his grandmother:

> Most of the keys were much too big, but there were half a dozen that were about the right size. All but one of these were very ordinary. The unordinary one was the most interesting key in the whole collection, small with a complicated lock part and fancy top. A narrow strip of red satin ribbon was looped through one of its curly openings. Omri saved that key to the last [Banks 3].

This key enables the magic in the cupboard, and its affiliation with the cupboard also relates directly to inheritance since "[a] cupboard was a little castle, an edifice for preserving and displaying family wealth" (Ulrich 112). Therefore, in the novel, inheritance functions with problematic possession since Omri and his society value and find magic in items that must be passed down and kept even by adults.

Inheritance is therefore more than just the sharing of one object with children and grandchildren. It suggests, contrary to Bill Brown's assessment of childhood before and after war, that there can be no "literary return to boyhood" that actually escapes crises (451). Omri can return Little Bear and Boone to plastic and leave them in his cupboard, but he can still pass these objects down to his children or keep them for another time. This assumed donation of objects/toys becomes a normalized part of family life, and as Laurel Thatcher Ulrich relates, "history teaches us that material objects were not only markers of wealth but devices for building relationships and lineages over time" (111). Omri enacts the same possession of a toy that his grandmother did with the key or that his brother did with the cupboard when he *inherited* it from another family. Omri inherits objects and he will also bequeath them, even if this event is not yet enacted in the story.

Gender also makes possession and inheritance problematic. Omri relies on female possessors rather than the male line of inheritance. As Ulrich relates, larger property tended to descend from men, while "movables formed the core of a female inheritance" (111). Thus, even though Omri himself is a boy, the legacy of the cupboard, the key, and their magic come from his female relatives. In addition, problematic possession that includes inheritance and gender also reflects a female counter-narrative against the novel's male heroes. Omri's grandmother, according to Omri's mother, "was most terribly poor when she died, poor old sweetie, and kept crying because she had nothing to leave me, so in the end I said I'd rather have this little key than all the jewels in the world" (Banks 4). Omri's grandmother therefore accepts the process of sharing movables with her children and cries when she has little to offer. This psychological pain demonstrates the enduring power of the object/toy and the social force that objects exert on everyone (Bennet vii). Omri's mother then continues the process; she chooses an object and gives it meaning, thus appeasing her grandmother and ensuring that her own children will follow these efforts.

Consequently, through these actions, and contrary to Brown's idea of "restricting the child/adult opposition to one gender," the power of the female to distribute and maintain objects becomes a counter-narrative to the masculine nature of inheritance, which seems to follow male protagonists in the novel (452). In fact, these men—Omri, Little Bear, Boone, Patrick, Gillon, and Adiel—have inherited their life skills from their female ancestors—the keepers of the keys and cupboards. Thus, female power, especially female material power, remains central to the novel despite their seeming relegation to the backstory. In addition, Rustin and Rustin believe that "[t]he key that [Omri's] mother will wear round her neck, which was to remind her of her grandmother, is now also to keep her youngest son in her mind, as he grows away from his infancy and the time of his closest touch with her" (117–118). Even though Little Bear's dynamic heroism has problematized Omri's childhood experience, the notion that the key still remains a generational link solidifies Omri's connection to the feminine experience of childhood, maturation, toys/objects, and inheritance.

Lastly, this female counter-narrative reveals the inherent divide that exists between types of objects/toys and gender (Brown 467). According to Omri's society, boys should concentrate on physical actions and objects/toys that represent these actions, such as trucks, sport, and warfare; girls, on the other hand, should focus on caring, dolls, and toys/objects that will enhance their caretaking skills (Rustin and Rustin 117). The plastic Indian, which seems to be a masculine toy, still has a connection to feminine dolls, which have been defined as "[a]ll small scale figures of human beings," of which Little Bear is indeed (Giddings and Halverson 70). Omri, who follows the line of female inheritance in his family, seems to have connections to both genders since he wants to control and manipulate objects (Giddings and Halverson 70) while he also takes care of them (Banks 46). Rustin and Rustin support this mixing of social norms and gender divisions when they write, "The story is able to explore, through a boy's relationship with toys which are conventionally masculine, the more feminine aspects of his character" (104–105). Subsequently, Omri, as another dynamic hero, symbolizes the competing aspects of inheritance and gender; he creates a counter-narrative to social mores about childhood and play with toys/objects as he experiences the world with Little Bear, the hero/toy that inspires the entire process and reveals the problems of possession.

(In)Conclusion: The Enduring Problem of Possession

> "There they were, the two plastic groups—forms, outlines, shells of the real, real creatures they had been.... The figures were there, but the people, the personalities, were gone."
> —Banks 196

Little Bear's heroic dynamism allows Omri to recognize and evaluate the problematic aspects of possession. However, despite Omri's personal enlightenment, these aspects remain problematic at the end of the novel. The process of inheritance guarantees that people will still view objects/toys in the manner that Omri has attempted to discard. As Amy F. Ogata emphasizes, "Faith in objects to teach lessons is a continuing motivator of today's toy market," and Little Bear, a toy, has reenacted this process (156). Nevertheless, Omri still learns how to understand and live with problematic possession, maturation, and the continued force of objects in his life (Bennet vii).

However, just because problematic possession still exists without a neat resolution does not mean that Omri or Little Bear has failed. Little Bear and Omri *are* heroes, suggesting that the process of learning from objects can and should overpower the human desire to possess them. With this outcome in mind, it is clear that society cannot destroy all objects. Instead, society must use toys/objects as dynamic heroes that can at least illuminate problematic possession and allow for a better evaluation of the self in the material world. The true victory is to allow objects/toys to continue to exist as they really are. Even if Omri never brings them back to life again, problematic possession is always an issue. Yet when children like Omri need help assessing these problems, the plastic Indian is still there, waiting. And as Omri succinctly relates, "Just to know you *could*. That was enough" (Banks 197).

WORKS CITED

Banks, Lynn Reid. *The Indian in the Cupboard*. New York: Avon Books, 1980. Print.
Bennet, Jane. *Vibrant Matter: A Political Ecology of Things*. Durham: Duke University Press, 2010. Print.
Brown, Bill. "American Childhood and Stephen Crane's Toys." *American Literary History* 7.3 (Autumn 1995): 443–476. JSTOR. Web. 15 January 2015.
Coulombe, Joseph L. *Reading Native American Literature*. London: Routledge, 2011. Print.
Giddings, Martha, and Charles F. Halverson. "Young Children's Use of Toys in Home Environments." *Family Relations* 30.1 (January 1981): 69–74. JSTOR. Web. 15 January 2015.
Hade, Daniel D. "Curious George Gets Branded: Reading as Consuming." *Theory into Practice* 40.3 (Summer 2001): 158–165. JSTOR. Web. 15 January 2015.
Meek, Barbara A. "And the Injun Goes 'How!' Representations of American Indian English in White Public Space." *Language in Society* 35.1 (February 2006): 93–128. JSTOR. Web. 15 January 2015.
Murray, David. "Translation and Mediation." *The Cambridge Companion to Native American Literature*. Ed. Joy Porter and Kenneth M. Roemer. Cambridge: Cambridge University Press, 2005. Print.
Nava, Mica. *Changing Cultures: Feminism, Youth, and Consumerism*. London: Sage, 1992. Print.
Nodelman, Perry. *The Hidden Adult: Defining Children's Literature*. Baltimore: Johns Hopkins University Press, 2008. Print.
Ogata, Amy F. "Creative Playthings: Educational Toys and Postwar American Culture." *Winterthur* 39 (Summer/Autumn 2004): 129–156. JSTOR. Web. 15 January 2015.
Porter, Joy. "Historical and Cultural Contexts to Native American Literature." *The Cambridge Companion to Native American Literature*. Ed. Joy Porter and Kenneth M. Roemer. Cambridge: Cambridge University Press, 2005. Print.
Roemer, Kenneth M. "Introduction." *The Cambridge Companion to Native American Literature*. Ed. Joy Porter and Kenneth M. Roemer. Cambridge: Cambridge University Press, 2005. Print.

Rustin, Margaret, and Michael Rustin. *Narratives of Love and Loss: Studies in Modern Children's Fiction*. London: Karnac, 1987. Print.
Stewart, Michelle Pagni. "Judging Authors by the Color of Their Skin? Quality Native American Children's Literature." *MELUS* 27.2 (Summer 2002): 179–196. JSTOR. Web. 15 January 2015.
Strong, Pauline Turner. "Animated Indians: Critique and Contradiction in Commodified Culture." *Cultural Anthropology* 11.3 (August 1996): 405–424. JSTOR. Web. 15 January 2015.
Ulrich, Laurel Thatcher. *The Age of Homespun: Objects and Stories in the Creation of an American Myth*. New York: Vintage, 2001. Print.

They Don't Make 'Em Like That Anymore
Dolls vs. Modernity

CRAIG IAN MANN

The overarching theme of the collection you hold in your hands is of the toy as hero; a childhood friend given life, imagined or otherwise, so that they might protect the children who cherish them—and, of course, those select adults who refuse to let their inner child die—from the horrors of the outside world at any cost. But while the treasured toy is often depicted as a child's ally, it must be said that there is something intrinsically unsettling about toys, dolls and puppets. Inanimate objects that often approximate the appearance of living things, their blank, unblinking eyes and motionless limbs can easily become a source of disquiet rather than comfort in a suitably darkened room. And as much as the idea of a beloved toy suddenly gaining sentience—or enjoying a secret life while we sleep—might seem desirable, fantastical and enchanting, in the horror film that same notion has more often been subverted to become a source of fear, paranoia and dread in the "killer toy" sub-genre.

Directed by Stuart Gordon—more famous as the writer-director of loose H.P. Lovecraft adaptations *Re-Animator* (1985), *From Beyond* (1986), *Castle Freak* (1995) and *Dagon* (2001)—written by Ed Naha of *Troll* (1986) fame and produced by genre powerhouses Brian Yuzna and Charles Band, *Dolls* (1987) is ostensibly one such film. However, *Dolls* is unique amongst its sub-genre in that the antiquated toys that serve as its antagonists are also its heroes. The film discards the popular cultural perception of toys in the 1980s and instead imbues its eponymous dolls with a sense of wonder and nostalgia more common to toys as they were imagined in the late nineteenth and early twentieth centuries; we are encouraged to cheer for the film's murderous dolls because they are lovingly-crafted playthings motivated solely by a desire to protect a seven-year-old child in danger of having her imagination, youth and innocence quashed by a group of adults—including her impatient father and acid-tongued stepmother—representative of urban modernity, mass-market capitalism and the most deplorable aspects of materialistic consumer culture.

Before coming to discuss *Dolls* further, it is important to contextualize the "killer toy" sub-genre, an enduring facet of the horror film which has spanned several decades. Toys, dolls and puppets have served as stock antagonists in the horror film since the release of *The Great Gabbo* in 1929, in which a brilliant ventriloquist begins to speak and act through his dummy as he spirals into insanity. The ventriloquist's dummy has remained a popular horror monster ever since, appearing in such films as *Devil Doll* (1964), *Magic* (1978), *Joey* (or *Making Contact*, 1985), Dead *Silence* (2007), *Triloquist* (2008) and perhaps most effectively in Alberto Cavalcanti's chilling segment for Ealing Studios' portmanteau horror film *Dead of Night* (1945). These tales often draw on the central conceit of *The Great Gabbo* to generate fear by eroding the division between a human ventriloquist and what should be a soulless vessel for their disembodied voice; whether it is the puppet or the puppeteer who is ultimately responsible for committing evil deeds is often left unconfirmed for increased impact.

Elsewhere, four thieves are menaced by voodoo dolls in the Mexican *Muñecos Infernales* (*The Curse of the Doll People*, 1961); hideous toy jesters attack middle class families in *Poltergeist* (1982) and *The Hole* (2009) as part of wider supernatural events; Santa Claus' playthings turn murderous in *Silent Night, Deadly Night 5: The Toy Maker* (1991) and *Krampus* (2015); militaristic action figures attack American suburbia in *Small Soldiers* (1998); a sadistic serial killer speaks through a grotesque puppet named Billy in the *Saw* franchise (2004–2010); a porcelain doll acts as a portent of doom in *Curtains* (1983), while another becomes possessed by a displaced, angry spirit in *The Conjuring* (2011) and its prequel *Annabelle* (2014). The sub-genre is prolific enough to have devolved into self-parody in recent years in films such as *Black Devil Doll* (2007), *The Gingerdead Man* (2005) and its two sequels. Even Pinocchio has had his turn as a lurid horror monster in the sensationally titled *Pinocchio's Revenge* (1996).

While it is clearly still prolific today, it was in the 1980s and 1990s that the "killer toy" film would reach its apex. The latter half of the 1980s saw the release of two films that would launch the sub-genre's most popular and enduring cinematic franchises: *Child's Play* (1988) and *Puppet Master* (1989). Written and produced by Charles Band as the flagship title for his newly-founded production company Full Moon Features, *Puppet Master* quickly gained a cult following and spawned nine sequels over the next three decades, the latest of which—*Puppet Master X: Axis Rising*—was released as recently as 2012. Written by Don Mancini and directed by Tom Holland, *Child's Play* would launch undoubtedly the best-known horror series concerning a monstrous toy: the infamous Chucky, a doll—ironically from the fictional "Good-Guy" toy line—possessed by the spirit of vicious serial killer Charles Lee Ray (Brad Dourif). Immensely popular with horror fans, Chucky would go on to appear in *Child's Play 2* (1990), *Child's Play 3* (1991), *Bride of Chucky* (1998), *Seed of Chucky* (2004) and, most recently, *Curse of Chucky* (2013). With the exception of *Seed*—in which Chucky himself becomes an unwilling father—all of these films see the psychopathic doll menace children and teenagers either in the hope of transferring his displaced soul into their young bodies or for mere sport. And, of course, both *Puppet Master* and *Child's Play* were preceded by *Dolls*.

The unparalleled popularity of both *Child's Play* in particular and the broader concept of the "killer toy" generally in the late 1980s are not difficult to explain. Throughout the twentieth century the production and marketing of toys and their cultural and social meanings had changed dramatically from the close of the nineteenth century. Before the Victorian era, toys were not thought of as children's playthings; as consumer items, they were sold as amusements for adults rather than children (Buckingham 73). This began to change in the nineteenth century but, as Stephen Kline suggests, before 1900 it was still rare for children, aside from the wealthiest, to possess many toys. When children did find or were given items to play with, they were not the mass-produced consumer products we find on the shelves of toy stores today.

In short, the Victorian world of child's play was not a world of manufactured things: sometimes it included found and discarded objects (wheel hoops, sticks, rags) and occasionally folk toys of archetypal form (dolls, balls, carved animals, wheels)—things that parents, relatives and children might carve, sew or otherwise craft.

Before they were factory manufactured, toys belonged in the sphere of folk culture. They were objects produced in one of three ways: by the kids themselves, by parents for their kids, or by local specialized craft producers as gifts or for ceremonies or special occasions. In this context toys had a very special and personal meaning for the child. They were rarely used as just another thing to use to while away idle moments (Kline 144–145).

During the Victorian era, then, for all but the wealthiest toys were either items that were found and transformed into playthings by resourceful children or rare, hand-crafted gifts, usually designed to be given to a specific child and to be cherished for generations. This was a time when toys were singular items: unique and precious to the children and families who owned them.

It was towards the end of the nineteenth century that toys were commoditized. While they were still largely marketed towards adults—in the hope of convincing parents to buy toys for their children—this was the point at which the active marketing of toys began. Though, it must be noted, they were still the source of some sentimentality even as they underwent a transformation into consumer products. As David Buckingham recounts: "The late nineteenth and early twentieth centuries saw the rise of toy marketing, in shop displays, catalogues and advertisements, though this was still mostly targeted at parents. Toys were often invested with parental nostalgia, and a notion of childhood as a time of timeless innocence" (73). This went hand-in-hand with the development of a new, sentimental perception of children and childhood that developed through the late nineteenth century and into the twentieth century, as children were removed from the workplace and the notion that minors should financially support their families began to lose favor. By the 1930s, "the new, sacred child occupied a special and separate world, regulated by affection and education, not work and profit" (Zelizer 209).

As the twentieth century progressed, toys—along with many other facets of American culture—became increasingly disposable and commercialized, especially with the birth of television. TV advertising allowed for marketers to bypass parents and target children directly, effectively creating the concept of the child consumer. As Kline asserts, "Advertisers could now direct their communication specifically at children—to explore new ways to shape children's wants and win their influence within the family circle" (167). Advertisers now had a way of stimulating desire in children for a specific product and creating a communal 'buzz' around the new must-have toy. However, Gary Cross argues that, even with the birth of the child consumer, it was not until the 1970s and 1980s that toys became disposable items to be forgotten and replaced with something new at the whims of advertisers:

> Those adults who were children before the 1970s remember receiving erector sets and dollhouses as rites of passage. These were toys that grandparents had enjoyed as children and seemed to tell the young about what they could expect as adults in their future world of business and the home. These playthings crossed the boundaries of generations, even if they were not really "timeless" [Cross 228–229].

The 1970s brought with it the exponential growth of consumer culture, and soon cherished, hand-me-down playthings were a thing of the past. As the 1970s wore on, even the administration began to take issue with America's rampant materialism; in his televised and controversial "crisis of confidence" (or "malaise") speech of July 15, 1979, Jimmy Carter expressed concern that "too many of us now tend to worship self-indulgence and consumption. Human identity is no longer defined by what one does, but by what one owns" (Hamilton 356). Shortly afterwards, Carter would lose his presidential election race against Republican candidate Ronald Reagan, who, through pro-business rhetoric, financial deregulation and a series of extensive tax cuts for businesses and individuals, would usher in an age of profound materialism; as Michael Schaller asserts, "Not since the Gilded Age of the late nineteenth century or the Roaring Twenties had the acquisition and flaunting of wealth been so publicly celebrated as during the 1980s. Income became the accepted measure of one's value to society" (70).

Reagan's administration urged Americans to earn more and spend more or, in the case of children, to convince their parents to spend more on their behalf. As Kline notes, by 1956 advertisers were spending a combined $25 million a year on marketing aimed at minors; by 1987, the year that witnessed *Dolls'* theatrical release, that amount had risen to an astonishing $750 million (167). And the *types* of toys that were on sale were changing radically. As Cross states, "By the 1980s… the endlessly changing displays of action, fashion, and cuddly figures bore little relation to parents' childhood toys and even less to do with children's actual future" (229). Toy companies found new ways to increase their financial returns, either by basing their toys on pre-existing intellectual property or by turning their toys into the heroes of cartoons, television shows, comic books and films. Geoff King has argued that in the late 1980s and early 1990s, this aggressive marketing to the child consumer became such that films aimed at children would contain sequences explicitly designed to sell merchandise. In particular, King draws attention to a scene in *Jurassic Park* (1993) that takes place in the fictional theme park's gift shop—where we see myriad items that would later be available to buy in reality—and deconstructs *Toy Story 2* (1995) as a children's film designed almost exclusively with the explicit purpose of selling toys (211–212).

By the time *Dolls*, *Child's Play* and *Puppet Master* saw release in the late 1980s, parental attitudes to toys had changed dramatically from the adult perception of children's playthings at the dawn of the twentieth century. Items once sentimentalized as symbolic of childhood innocence were now viewed with suspicion and fear. As Cross states, "[Parents] see the rows of aggressive purple-and-green action figures and conclude that these inhuman creatures teach violence or make children fearful" (229). Buckingham notes that toys have long been venerated for their educational value, but argues—particularly in modern times—that

> [Y]et, on the other hand, they have also increasingly become a focus of fears and anxieties about economic exploitation, declining cultural values and false ideologies. As parents have gradually been written out of the marketing equation, they have frequently come to blame toymakers for the broader problems they face in disciplining children—for promoting violence, gender stereotyping and materialism [73].

It is from this context that the "killer toy" films of the 1980s arise. It is interesting that before the 1980s, the sub-genre was dominated by puppets—

inanimate objects that are traditionally designed to create the *illusion* of life. The fear at the heart of the pre–1980s "killer toy" film, then, is essentially a primal one, of something that artificially appears to think and feel literally coming to life and gaining a malevolent sentience. The 1980s mark a major transition in the sub-genre: where the majority of antagonists were once dummies and puppets, they become dolls and toys. Like *Gremlins* (1984)—in which a father misguidedly purchases a volatile life form for his son as a Christmas present with disastrous results—these post–1980 films are better understood as anti-consumerist parables, with *Dolls* and *Child's Play* standing to this day as the most interesting examples of the sub-genre.

Dolls was produced in 1985 by Charles Band's Empire Pictures, using the company's studio facilities in Rome and shot on the same sets utilised for *From Beyond*, which began its American theatrical run in October 1986. *Dolls* was actually completed first, but due to the extensive post-production work needed to realize the sequences in which the film's toys come to life and attack their deserving but unsuspecting victims, it would not be released in the United States until March 1987 (Gordon and Naha). *Child's Play* entered cinemas soon after in November 1988 and its success quickly overshadowed *Dolls*, a picture that is now a relative obscurity in comparison to the later film. This is unfortunate as, while their narratives are very different, the two films have a great deal in common on a thematic level. They are both anti-consumerist allegories that use toys as metaphors through which to lament various aspects of capitalist modernity: soulless mass-production, rampant materialism and the unfortunate development of the child consumer. It is *how* the two films express this fear of a materialistic society that sets them apart from one another.

Child's Play uses its possessed doll to concentrate on the ills of the toy industry in the 1980s: Chucky is a mass-produced, aggressively marketed commodity with an excessively high price-tag designed to give the product an illusion of exclusivity and create a consumerist furore amongst children. This is why, of course, the film's young protagonist is desperate to receive a Good-Guy doll for his birthday, and why his hardworking single mother—a Chicago urbanite—is forced to buy one from a decidedly unsavory backstreet vendor. *Child's Play 2* goes even further in drawing attention to the fact that Chucky is just one in millions of cheaply-made, identical dolls by setting its climax in the factory where the toys are manufactured. Chucky, then, is very much a product of his time. In fact, many contemporary viewers believed the evil doll to be directly based on Hasbro's "My Buddy" toy line, though writer Don Mancini eventually revealed that he was, in fact, inspired by Coleco's "Cabbage Patch Kids" (Pollard 11). It is not hard to see why Mancini was inspired to imagine a Cabbage Patch Kid as a monster; they were given an air of quality and exclusivity by their exploitative $40 to $50 "adoption fees" and became an unlikely aspirational item (Muir 644). As Sharon M. Scott recounts, this marketing practice only fed the consumerist desires of both children and adults: "Parents behaved like toy store terrorists to get the perfect doll for their child. The shelves assigned for Cabbage Patch Kids were emptied just as soon as they were filled" (52).

And so Chucky—a stand-in for any number of "must-have" toys sold to children through exploitative marketing tactics—is very much the villain of *Child's Play* and its sequels and a metaphor for the unfortunate state of the toy industry in modern capitalist America. In short, as Dominic Lennard suggests, "*Child's Play* uses the doll to dramatize adult frustration toward the consumer child and the financial strain that accompanies him" (134). But while *Child's Play* paints its "Good-Guy" doll as monstrous, *Dolls* depicts its sadly outmoded, uniquely hand-crafted toys as protectors of children. These are heroes of porcelain, wood and tin, deeply steeped in nostalgia and willing to kill in order to shield the young from the horrors of modernity. In short, if Chucky is representative of toys in the 1980s, the ornate and antiquated playthings of *Dolls* represent a throwback to the turn of the century, when toys were still associated with the innocence of childhood: singular items to be cherished and treasured. Ultimately, this is a unique example of the "killer toy" horror film that tries to reinvest in its heroic toys the sense of nostalgia and sentimentalism that was lost with the development of the child as consumer.

Dolls sees a number of people take shelter in an isolated mansion after becoming stranded in the British countryside during a violent storm. An American family—seven-year-old Judy Bower (Carrie Lorraine), her yuppie father David (Ian Patrick Williams) and obnoxious stepmother Rosemary (Carolyn Purdy Gordon)—are the first to arrive, followed swiftly by Isabel (Bunty Baily) and Enid (Cassie Stuart), a pair of hitchhiking British punks travelling with a mild-mannered American named Ralph (Stephen Lee). The mansion is owned by Gabriel Hartwicke (Guy Rolfe), who introduces himself as a retired toymaker, and his wife Hilary (Hilary Mason). Excepting Judy and Ralph, most of the guests are horrified to find the house adorned with all manner of handmade toys, dolls and games. Of course, neither the toys nor the Hartwickes are at all what they seem. A pair of powerful occultists, Gabriel and Hilary's collection of ornate dolls is made up of past houseguests who have been transformed into playthings as punishment for perceived transgressions—presumably because they have embraced the "modern" world. Now, each of their new guests must prove their moral fiber or face death at the hands of their murderous toys.

The film's opening titles, designed by Robert Dawson—who had previously designed the opening titles of *Re-Animator* for Gordon—work hard to render toys as objects to be feared. The credits appear alongside the disembodied heads of various dolls, both male and female, which have been positioned and lit in such a way that their faces are cast in a disquieting shadow, while their eyes seem to stare ominously into the distance. However, it is not long before *Dolls* comes to establish the true purpose of toys in its narrative as heroic protectors of children and those adults who value the innocence of childhood; only those who wholeheartedly embrace the consumerist and capitalist ideals of the 1980s need fear the film's sentient toys.

As the film opens, it swiftly becomes clear that Judy's father and stepmother are two such people: selfish materialists who care little for the young child in their care. Our first glimpse of the couple tells us everything we need to know about them: dressed in expensive and impractical attire befitting of a high-class country club and travelling in a spotless Jaguar, David and Rosemary are the picture of 1980s yuppie culture. Rosemary's first on-screen action immediately underlines the callous nature hinted at by her clothing—she purposely attempts to run down Isabel and Enid, who we first see hitchhiking on the side of the road. Shortly afterwards, the family encounter a vicious localized storm and are forced to abandon their car. Importantly, throughout this entire opening sequence—with the exception of trying to keep her quiet—neither David nor Rosemary so much as acknowledge Judy's existence; she simply sits in the back of the car, clutching her teddy bear and reading a children's edition of *Hansel and Gretel*. Judy's choice of reading material hints at *Dolls'* fairy tale quality, with its antiquated setting, fantastical narrative and stern moralism. But it is also a planted intertextual reference designed to function as both a symbol of the film's own subtextual meaning and a biting metaphor for David and Rosemary's terrible parenting. After all, *Hansel and Gretel* is a tale about children who are "taken into the woods and abandoned by parents who cannot and will not care for them" (Ashliman 41).

With their car stranded in thick mud, the dysfunctional family decide to walk to a house looming dreadfully in the distance, much to the chagrin of the over-privileged Rosemary ("you want me to walk?"). In an act of pure spitefulness and malice, Rosemary engineers a reason to torment Judy by claiming that carrying her teddy bear is slowing the child down; she takes her stepdaughter's prized possession—simply "Teddy" to Judy—and throws him into the undergrowth. In the dream sequence that follows, Judy imagines that Teddy grows to a monstrous size and returns from the bushes to punish David and Rosemary for being so cruel to her; at first he appears as a much larger—perhaps seven or eight feet tall—replica of the toy cast into the rain, before a grotesque, vicious bear bursts through Teddy's skin and begins to eat David and Rosemary alive. Shortly before she awakens from her daydream, Judy chastises Teddy for his rash actions; in one of *Dolls'* many comedic touches, the monstrous bear simply shrugs apologetically in return.

As well as introducing the film's playful tone, this dream sequence is a foreshadowing of what is to come and hints that Judy will never truly be in any danger for the rest of the film's running time. After all, *Dolls'* toys are both monsters *and* heroes: the avengers of innocence and childhood. This scene represents Judy's fantasy that her beloved bear will enact revenge on her behalf and, as Reynold Humphries points out, "throughout the film the doll-maker and his wife will act out such desires and turn them into reality" (97). Teddy may not really dispose of Judy's obnoxious parents, but the Hartwickes' creations certainly will.

It is when the Bowers enter the Hartwickes' home that they encounter Gabriel's toys. Judy first catches a glimpse of a living doll in the mansion's darkened cellar; of course, she is the only one who sees it. Shortly afterwards, Gabriel shows Judy a room filled with his hand-made toys: dolls, cars, automatons, soldiers and animals made of porcelain, wood and tin. We linger on his creations, clearly encouraged to admire his craftsmanship. As Gabriel leads Judy away from the room, a decapitated doll head smiles of its own accord, an image which is undoubtedly designed to be horrifying; after all, it is undeniably disconcerting to see a change of facial expression on what should be an inanimate object. Considered in the context of the film's larger thematic concerns, though, the doll's smile is clearly one of joy: she is simply pleased to have been noticed, admired and appreciated. Such a sentiment is echoed by Gabriel as he introduces himself at dinner: "I am a doll-maker. I make the most wonderful toys: dolls, puppets, soldiers, ballerinas. But nowadays, people seem to want their playthings mass-produced. Nobody wants dolls that are special anymore, that are one of a kind."

Lennard suggests that the antiquated style of *Dolls'* toys is quite incongruous with the film's 1980s setting, especially when viewed with knowledge of what was to come in *Child's Play*, its sequels and imitators: "the terrible toys of *Dolls* (wooden dolls, grenadier guards, etc.) strike one as curiously outdated alongside the novel, talking and slob imbibing dolls of the 1980s." However, as the writer goes on to recognize, this is rather the driving point of the film. He continues, "In fact, these lovingly crafted anachronisms clearly represent childhood as imagined by an adult, a nostalgic, romanticized, and fundamentally subordinate identity, even as they brutalize perceived opponents of that ideal (punk rock hussies, careerist mothers, wimpy fathers)" (133). Though Lennard's conclusions are essentially sound, the "curiously outdated" toys featured in *Dolls* are not necessarily representative of an adult's perception of childhood—rather, they are purposely designed to resemble playthings common in the early twentieth century. Gabriel's creations are relics from a specific point in time—after toys had passed into the realm of children's play but, importantly, before they were the subject of commoditization and mass-production—when childhood was culturally valorized and toys were widely seen to symbolize the precious innocence of youth. The feeling tied up in *Dolls*' depiction of playthings *is* one of nostalgia, but not just an adult nostalgia for a generic "childhood." It is a longing for a particular perception of childhood and play that existed for a brief period of time during the transition from the nineteenth to twentieth centuries, before the mass industrialization of toy making and commercialization of playthings as commodities had contributed heavily to the invention of the child consumer.

In fact, *Dolls* is designed to create a palpable sense of nostalgia for days gone by from its very beginning. In order to strengthen the sense of nostalgic longing attached to its titular toys, the very narrative of the film—of a group of strangers stranded together in a darkened mansion during a raging storm—is clearly designed to evoke memories of James Whale's *The Old Dark House* (1932) and its many imitators, while the Hartwickes' home and even the owners themselves seem to have scarcely changed since the nineteenth century; the mansion is illuminated by candlelight and is adorned with nineteenth-century fittings, while Gabriel and Hilary both wear nightwear more befitting of the 1890s than the 1980s. The casting of Guy Rolfe and Hilary Mason, too, heightens the film's archaic tone by recalling their earlier roles in horror films that had come to be seen as "old fashioned" by 1987, in the wake of the invention of "New Horror" as typified by the works of George A. Romero, Wes Craven, Tobe Hooper and so on. Rolfe had played the title role in William Castle's gimmicky *Mr. Sardonicus* (1961), during which—in true Castle style—audience members were famously asked during a brief interlude to vote on whether the film's despicable villain should live or die, and had appeared in gothic horror *And Now the Screaming Starts!* (1973) for the defunct British production company Amicus Productions, while Mason had famously played the blind seer Heather in Nicolas Roeg's dark psychological thriller *Don't Look Now* (1973). Even the film's stereotypically English setting is crafted to lend it a quaint, antiquated quality by drawing on Britain's heritage and its association with a rich pre-industrial history. All of these elements are designed in combination to create an overarching sense of nostalgia for a time before capitalist modernity and, importantly, to make the visitors to the Hartwickes' home seem out of place within their surroundings rather than vice versa. This is a place frozen in time where antique toys seem at home. It is the punks and yuppies who are the invaders to be repelled; and the toys are more than willing to repel them by force.

And what of those punks and yuppies: why do Gabriel's toys choose to kill them and why are they rendered heroic for doing so? In the case of the punks, they are killed more for what they represent than for anything they do. When they attack Isabel and Enid, the toys are not protecting or avenging Judy as they will later in the narrative. The punks never do anything to threaten her directly, though they are guilty of sexually harassing Ralph, carelessly throwing Gabriel's antique dolls around and generally treating the Hartwickes' possessions with contempt (before attempting to steal them). Humphries suggests that the toys punish them simply because they "dismiss the dolls as old-fashioned as they do not correspond to the current fabrication of toys" (98). While this is a valid reading, on a deeper level Isabel and Enid are also killed for embodying another unfortunate and crass facet of 1980s society: the commercialization of punk, a sub-culture that had originally been built on the countercultural and anti-establishment ideals of individualism and anti-capitalism but that, by the mid-1980s, had been largely subsumed into mainstream consumer culture (Zuschlag 449).

It is not surprising that Gordon recalls that Isabel's visual style was purposely based on pop icon Madonna (Gordon and Naha). Madonna contributed to the popularization of punk fashions as she rose to fame in the early 1980s. In 1984 her song "Like a Virgin" became a chart-topper all over the world and she became a global superstar. Just as mass-production and television marketing led to the exploitation of children's playthings, the assimilation of punk fashion into pop music eroded its true meaning and turned punk into a commodity ripe for turning a profit. We cheer for the dolls as they claim their first victim because they are avenging a noble ideal destroyed by capitalism; just as the Cabbage Patch Kid is an expensive, obnoxious bastardization of a toy's true meaning and purpose, Isabel's brand of punk is built on nothing more profound than her consumer preferences. Enid later finds Isabel not alive nor dead, midway through her transformation into a hideous doll—an allegory for her fakery in life—and is killed not long afterwards, executed by firing squad for her own false identification with the hijacked subculture. A squad of wooden soldiers gun her down in one of the mansion's many lonely hallways. We are not encouraged to feel saddened when either of them meets their end; rather their deaths are played for comedy rather than horror.

But the true villains of *Dolls* are Judy's father and stepmother, and the dolls' heroic status is confirmed when they dispose of them to better the child's life. In an updated vision of *Hansel and Gretel*'s terminally selfish parents, David and Rosemary are the quintessential caricatures of Reagan's America: obscenely rich, habitually self-involved, cold and uncaring. Beyond a clear link to *Hansel and Gretel*, Gordon reveals that Rosemary is also heavily influenced by Cruella De Vil of Dodie Smith's 1956 novel *The Hundred and One Dalmatians* (Gordon and Naha), something that is apparent from her costume alone and which firmly underlines her indifference and cruelty towards children. Thus Rosemary is rendered a representation of the very worst attitudes born of capitalism; Cruella De Vil, of course, is a woman who believes there is nothing money can't buy. David, on the other hand, is clearly new to this aspirational lifestyle, a man who left his family—Judy's real mother is at home in the United States and, with the exception of the summer months, raises her child without David—so that he could marry for money, power and influence. At one point in the narrative, while discussing their hedonistic way of life, David remarks to Rosemary, "We're rich." Her rebuttal is swift: "I'm rich."

Both David and Rosemary are depicted negatively from the film's outset and become increasingly abusive to Judy as the narrative continues. They begin by simply ignoring her, before Rosemary takes her most treasured item from her and throws it away. Later, when Judy repeatedly tries to warn her father that something—at the film's outset, Judy believes them to be "elves"—has killed Isabel, he accuses her of lying and comes close to striking her. He only hesitates because Rosemary reminds him that he will be forced to pay more of their precious money to Judy's biological mother were she to find evidence of physical abuse. Humphries argues that because they wish to discard her, Judy is "treated as a toy by her parents" (98), which seems like a neat and fitting metaphor. However, it is actually more accurate to conclude that David and Rosemary treat Judy as if she were a fully-grown adult; they are constantly chastising her for telling stories of ghosts and goblins, they deplore her childish qualities—imagination, wonder and awe—and want her to "grow up" so that she can function without them. They are, of course, more interested in spending their money. In a further allusion to *Hansel and Gretel*, then, David and Rosemary would love nothing more than to abandon their daughter and let her fend for herself, and they effectively do so by refusing to listen to her cries for help: routinely dismissed by her parents as nothing more than irritating tall tales. At just seven years old, Judy is encouraged—no, forced—by her father to suppress her youth and innocence and become a part of the adult world, a metaphor for the crushing pressures of conformity exerted upon the child consumer. Furthermore, to treat Judy as a toy Rosemary and David would need to take ownership of her; for all their materialistic desires, the one thing Judy's parents are reluctant to possess is their child.

When the heroic toys attack the film's villains, then, they are both avenging Judy's awful treatment by the adults who should be most committed to caring for her and exerting her right to a childhood. It is no coincidence that *Dolls*' most violent death sequence is reserved for the malicious Rosemary. A version of the dream sequence that opens the film—Judy's revenge through her beloved Teddy—is played out in reality when Judy's wicked stepmother finds a vicious pack of porcelain dolls under her bedcovers. There, they stab her repeatedly with small, sharp implements and leave her lying motionless on the mattress, a sheet covering her face. Later, David finds her there and—after briefly attempting to initiate sex with a corpse in another of *Dolls*' blackly comedic moments—removes the sheet to find Rosemary with a hefty portion of her face missing.

When it is David's turn to face the wrath of Judy's toy heroes, he is attacked (twice) by the plaything given to Judy by Gabriel to replace her lost teddy bear: a hideous doll named "Mr. Punch." Of course, Judy's punch is identical in appearance to the infamous puppet used in "Punch and Judy" shows, a tradition dating back to at least the dawn of the seventeenth century (Collier 9–10). Pre-dating *The Great Gabbo* by hundreds of years, Punch is one of the earliest incarnations of a malevolent puppet, usually seen to viciously beat his wife, his baby and others throughout the duration of a typical show. In fact, in an echo of *Dolls*' own narrative, many incarnations of the "Punch and Judy" story see Punch carelessly mistreat his own baby when his wife leaves him in charge of the child. As a well-known cultural representation of a violent and abusive patriarch, then, it is apt that it is Punch who exacts Judy's revenge on her own uncaring father. And, of course, it is no coincidence that together the child and the puppet form "Punch and Judy." Despite his cultural reputation for wanton violence, Judy forms a particularly special bond with Punch; she talks on his behalf and carries him everywhere as she walks the dark corridors of the Hartwickes' house. He replaces Teddy as her principal protector: a talisman to ward off creatures lurking in the dark.

Dolls' Mr. Punch, then, possesses a dual metaphorical meaning—both as a symbolic representation of poor parenting and as Judy's favored toy—and it is perhaps inevitable that it is he who expresses the child's rage against her father in another rerun of Teddy's attack in Judy's daydream. However, David is the only one of the toys' victims who they do not kill. Rather, Gabriel and Hilary intervene after David has managed to successfully destroy Punch, the second of Judy's prized toys to be taken away from her by her parents. The old couple then reveal their true identities: powerful occultists who turn those who have forgotten the virtues of childhood into living dolls. Shortly afterwards, they bewitch David and he begins to gruesomely transform, his nose and chin stretching into hideous hooks and a hump forming on his back as he shrinks to the size of a doll; in an ironic comment on his deplorable attitude to fatherhood, he becomes the new Mr. Punch. Furthermore, his punishment for valuing material goods over his own daughter is to forever be transformed into something to be owned. In fact, by the film's end we learn not only that David has become Punch but that Isabel, Enid and Rosemary have all been fashioned into dolls crafted in their own likenesses. As they sit on the Hartwickes' mantelpiece, we know that in death they are forever doomed to live as material possessions as comeuppance for their consumerist greed, hedonism and selfishness in life. Presumably, however, they will have the chance to redeem themselves by joining Gabriel's horde of hero toys and bringing a twisted sense of justice to the next group of unfortunates to find themselves on the Hartwickes' doorstep.

The only visitor to the mansion who is not harmed by either the toys or the Hartwickes during the storm is Ralph, the mild-mannered American who arrives with Isabel and Enid. He is spared for three reasons: firstly, because he is not a materialistic, selfish or money-orientated individual—rather he is kind, caring and selfless, going so far as to bring the punks to shelter without ever losing his composure even when Isabel and Enid take delight in making him feel uncomfortable with ironic sexual advances. Secondly, despite having known the child for only a matter of hours, Ralph is a better parent to Judy than either her father or stepmother: he listens to her, humors her fantastical claims and, importantly, treats her like the seven-year-old child that she is (though Judy does have to remind him of her age once, when they become lost in the mansion and her sense of direction fails her). This is something Judy's father completely fails to understand; when his daughter refers to Ralph as her "friend," it is heavily implied that David suspects him of paedophilia because he cannot fathom the notion of being friends with any child and certainly not Judy. Finally, Ralph is unharmed because he is childlike himself: he finds Gabriel's creations enchanting and—even if he is initially embarrassed to do so—recalls his own childhood toys fondly; they were not disposable items to be discarded and replaced at the whims of toy companies and advertisers, but treasured and sorely missed friends and guardians.

There is a scene, however, in which we are led to believe Ralph may become the toys' next victim. Shortly before the film's climax, Judy leads him into a room filled with hundreds of dolls who come to life before his eyes. Frightened, Ralph lashes out and the playthings become angered and attack. Judy pleads with them to stop and—somewhat surprisingly—they comply. After some deliberation, they decide to let Ralph go. It is implied by his positive portrayal throughout the rest of the film that it is principally for the three reasons listed above that they choose to spare him, though there is also a fourth: simply because Judy asks them to. Until this point in the film's narrative, there still appears to be a slight possibility that the toys might hurt Judy; when they yield to her pleas for them not to harm her friend, this scene explicitly confirms their function as her loyal protectors and we understand that the rest of their murderous rampage has been in the service of shielding her from the horrors of adulthood, here equated with capitalist modernity.

At the film's climax, only Judy and Ralph have survived the night: the two individuals who appreciate the loving craftsmanship poured into Gabriel's toys. Gabriel and Hilary choose to completely ignore the previous night's events, allowing Judy and a very confused Ralph to believe they have imagined everything. They produce an elaborate story in which David, Rosemary, Isabel and Enid took flight during the night, telling the child that her father eventually came to the conclusion that she would have a better life with her mother; conveniently, he has left enough money to pay for both Judy and

Ralph to fly back to the United States. In the film's final scene, Judy finds her lost teddy bear on the seat of Ralph's car and chooses to give him to the Hartwickes, so he might spend the rest of his days amongst toys. Humphries interprets the child's final action as an extension of Judy's relationship with her father and stepmother, arguing that she gives up Teddy because she knows how it feels to be treated only as a toy (98–99). Again, Humphries' interpretation of Judy's relationship with her parents seems neat but ultimately unsupported; though Judy's final action is significant. In giving Teddy to the Hartwickes, she is rejecting her assumed status as a child consumer; her bloodthirsty toy guardians have taught her that it is her personal relationships, rather than the things she owns, that define her. As they drive away from the Hartwickes' house, Judy begins to convince Ralph to come home and meet her real mother.

Humphries' brief analysis of *Dolls* is one of the few available scholarly works on the film. In tandem with the argument presented here, he comes to the conclusion that the film's message is one of anti-consumerism, starting: "the film becomes an extended allegory of an inversion of conservative family values, where children are either fetishized or repressed and parents unconsciously act out society's economic values, based on endless consumption and the repetition of the same" (98). Though these conclusions are generally sound, I would take issue with them on two principal points.

Firstly, *Dolls* actively fetishes childhood as an innocent time before individuals are irreversibly subsumed into the capitalist system. It laments the unfortunate cultural shift that took place over the course of the twentieth century, culminating in a society that attempts to convert children into valuable consumers at younger and younger ages. It does not, as Humphries suggests, satirize or condemn the valorization of childhood, but rather endorses it. *Dolls* endorses childhood as a period—in fact, the only period—during which an individual is free to exist outside of the crushing pressures of consumer culture: a time of imagination, awe and innocence. Furthermore, through its allusions to the cold abandonment of young children by their mother and father in *Hansel and Gretel*, the film suggests that modern parents are guilty of forcing their children to grow up too fast, effectively eroding their childhood years by assisting in their premature assimilation into the capitalist system.

Secondly, Humphries does not recognize the importance of the films' eponymous dolls in expressing the film's anti-capitalist meaning. It is worth repeating that *Dolls* is an anomaly in the "killer toy" sub-genre, in which puppets and toys are generally represented as evil, malevolent beings for children to fear, their sentient animation a dreadful portent of doom. In *Dolls*, this typical representation is subverted and murderous toys become heroic: the guardians, protectors and avengers of mistreated children. Gabriel's toys are specifically designed to recall a time before the mass commercialization of the toy industry: lovingly handmade items to be treasured in direct opposition to the exploitative and aspirational toys of the 1980s. While Chucky— a serial killer formed of plastic and latex—is every child's worst nightmare, *Dolls'* playthings only pose a threat to adults who have forgotten the magic of childhood. Judy finds the Hartwickes' creations fascinating; it is her parents who come to find how frightening they can be. They are, therefore, items associated with excitement *and* fear, enchantment *and* dread; monsters to the adults who have embraced modernity and forgotten the wonders of a time before their introduction to capitalist society, but heroes to the children who rely on them to exert their right to childhood.

WORKS CITED

Ashliman, D.L. *Folk and Fairy Tales: A Handbook*. Westport, CT: Greenwood Press, 2004.
Buckingham, David. *The Material Child: Growing Up in Consumer Culture*. Cambridge: Polity Press, 2011.
Collier, J.P. *Punch and Judy: A Short History with Original Dialogue*. Mineola, NY: Dover Publications, 2006.
Cross, Gary. *Kids' Stuff: Toys and Changing World of American Childhood*. Cambridge: Harvard University Press, 1997.
Gordon, S., and E. Naha. Commentary track. *Dolls*. Directed by Stuart Gordon. 1987. Brighton: 101 Films, 2014. Blu-ray.
Hamilton, N.A. *The 1970's*. New York: Facts on File, 2006.
Humphries, Reynold. *The American Horror Film: An Introduction*. Edinburgh: Edinburgh University Press, 2002.
King, Geoff. *New Hollywood Cinema: An Introduction*. London: I.B. Tauris, 2002.
Kline, Stephen. *Out of the Garden: Toys, TV and Children's Culture in the Age of Marketing*. London: Verso, 1995.
Lennard, Dominic. *Bad Seeds and Holy Terrors: The Child Villains of Horror Film*. Albany: State University of New York Press, 2014.
Muir, John Kenneth. *Horror Films of the 1980s*. Jefferson, NC: McFarland, 2007.
Pollard, A. "Your Friend 'Til the End...." *Starburst* 393 (2013): 10–13.
Schaller, Michael. *Reckoning with Reagan: America and Its President in the 1980s*. New York: Oxford University Press, 1994.
Scott, Sharon. *Toys and American Culture: An Encyclopedia*. Santa Barbara, CA: Greenwood, 2010.
Zelizer, Viviana A. *Pricing the Priceless Child: The Changing Social Value of Children*. Princeton: Princeton University Press, 1994.
Zuschlag, A. "Punk Rock. *Culture Wars: An Encyclopedia of Issues, Viewpoints and Voices*. Ed. R. Chapman. Armonk, NY: M.E. Sharpe, 2010.

"You are not a live thing. You're a dummy"
The Rights and Hierarchy of the Hero-Creations of Oz

Dina Schiff Massachi

In 1900 L. Frank Baum introduced the world to Oz, a fairyland full of anthropomorphic heroes including a walking, talking Scarecrow. In 1904, Baum's second Oz novel added the magical Powder of Life—a powder with the ability to transforms inanimate objects, such as a pumpkin, into sentient beings like Jack Pumpkinhead, a living jack-o'-lantern. Jack, Scarecrow, and many of the other characters Baum brings to life are heroic, but the vast majority of these created characters do not gain the power and respect that Baum's born heroes receive. When one examines the social hierarchy within Oz, the conclusion seems to be that, for Baum's born heroes, Oz is utopian, where for the creatures created by the Powder of Life, the people of Oz seem to hold an inherent expectation of subservience. Scarecrow, created before the Powder of Life, seems to escape this rule, as does the title character in Baum's *The Patchwork Girl of Oz*. What is it about Baum's Patchwork Girl, a rag doll toy-hero who names herself Scraps, that makes her the only powder created exception, and what does this exception mean for Baum's utopian structure? By establishing the governing rules within Baum's utopian Oz, and then examining the toy-hero, Scraps—her slave status, her commonalities and relationship with Baum's Scarecrow, her created contemporaries in Oz, and the rights that she (and her contemporaries) receives—one can see how the Patchwork Girl, Scraps, and her straw counterpart, Scarecrow, are able to rise above their origins as objects of convenience because their intellectual abilities make them invaluable companions.

Before examining Baum's created heroes, one must first understand the governing rules within Baum's utopian Oz in order to make sense of how the toy-hero fits into the preexisting social structure. While Oz hints at its socialist utopian nature before Baum's sixth novel, it is in *The Emerald City of Oz* that Baum emphasizes his fairyland's utopian ideals by juxtaposing Oz's lack of money and property with the harshness of Kansas's fiscal reality. Baum begins *The Emerald City of Oz* with his familiar child hero, Dorothy, and her family about to lose their Kansas farm: "Uncle Henry grew poorer every year, and the crops [...] only brought food for the family. Therefore, the mortgage could not be paid. At last the banker who had loaned him the money said [...] his farm would be taken away from him" (Baum, *Emerald City of Oz* 118). Baum establishes that, in Kansas, Dorothy's family works as hard as they can, but they still stand to lose their farm. He then tells his readers in great detail about the systems that exist in Oz to avoid situations like foreclosure. In Oz, "there were no poor people [...] because there was no such thing as money, and all property [...] belonged to the Ruler. [...] Each person was given freely by his neighbors whatever he required for his use" (Baum, *Emerald City of Oz* 122). In Baum's Oz, people have all of their needs met regardless of social status or occupation. Oz seems to be an ideal place, a utopia.

Although Baum's Oz provides for the needs of its citizens, it is not perfect. In "Utopian Tension in L. Frank Baum's Oz," Andrew Karp notes two hierarchies existing in this seemingly utopian society: the working versus the leisure class and the monarch versus the ruled people. Although Karp argues that "individuals in Oz are not totally free [...] [as] all property is owned by the benevolent monarch" (110), it is exactly this lack of property that allows for the "elimination of money and poverty" (103) that, according to Karp, made numerous scholars consider Oz a utopia. Karp also notes that "although everyone is supposed to work half the time [...], the primary and privileged characters spend all their time on adventures and parties and little or no time actually working to support the society" (108). This creates a hierarchy between the working and the leisure classes which, I argue, is also seen in the social positions of the characters brought to life. Oz's elite citizens may work, but they are able to leave their jobs to travel and have adventures, while the working class beings pass their lives in unremitting drudgery.

While *The Emerald City of Oz* suggests that Oz has some sort of equal distribution of goods, Baum's following Oz novel, *The Patchwork Girl of Oz*, opens with Ojo, a poor, unlucky (to the point where unlucky is part of his name) Munchkin boy, asking, "Where's the butter, Unc Nunkie?" (Baum, *Patchwork Girl* 19). This begins a line of questions that ends with "Tell me, Unc; why are we so poor?" (Baum, *Patchwork Girl* 20). Despite living in utopian Oz, Ojo and Unc Nunkie do not have their most basic needs met. While Baum explains their status by noting that Ojo and Unc Nunkie live "all alone, in the middle of the forest" (Baum, *Patchwork Girl* 21) far from the Emerald

City, its ruler, and its riches, he also raises the hierarchal issues that a lack of food in Oz creates. Tison Pugh explores this issue in his essay on Oz's use of food and interspecies cannibalism, asking, "[I]f humans eat sentient, intelligent, and anthropomorphized animals in a magical kingdom, are they cannibals?" (Pugh 326). The larger question is if Oz has such food inequalities and a social structure that highlights the differences between its peoples, how can Oz be utopian?

S. J. Sackett explores this very issue in his essay "The Utopia of Oz," noting that "neither Ozma nor anyone else wanted to meddle in the affairs of the citizenry, who were free, within extraordinarily broad limits, to do anything they wanted to" (275). Ultimately, Sackett notes two rules within Oz: "individual communities [...] were not to fight each other [...] [and] no unauthorized person could make use of magic" (276). Baum does not seem to care about hierarchies or how they affect his seemingly utopian Oz, leaving the reader to determine the justness of the system. Sackett notes that, in Oz, "if freedom is essential, but absolute freedom is disastrous, then the solution to the problem of government must be in the *via media* of voluntary acceptance of responsibility. And this, in effect, is the principle which underlies government in Oz" (277). Which returns us to the question: what happens when responsibility isn't voluntary—when a being is brought to life in order to serve?

Although Baum writes other characters that may be classified as toy-heroes, Scraps, a rag doll brought to life, is undeniably the purest example of the trope. Scraps is the title character of Baum's *The Patchwork Girl of Oz*, but she is, arguably, not the central character; Ojo is. The notable fact that Ojo is Baum's hero-quest character within *The Patchwork Girl of Oz* creates an implied inequality between the created and the born before the reader even gets to the plot of the story. Finding they have run out of food, Ojo and his Unc Nunkie decide to visit Unc Nunkie's old friend, a character aptly named the Crooked Magician. Through an unfortunate accident, Unc Nunkie and the Magician's wife, Margolotte, are turned to marble. In order to restore them to life, the Crooked Magician sends Ojo on a quest for five seemingly unattainable spell ingredients: "a drop of oil from a live man's veins; a six-leaf clover; three nice hairs from a Woozy's tail [...], water from a pitch-dark well [and] the yellow wing of a butterfly" (Baum, *Patchwork Girl* 64). It is Ojo, not the eponymous Patchwork Girl, who is the protagonist sent on a quest. Like many of Baum's child-heroes, Ojo does not have to travel alone— as soon as he is handed the task, Scraps volunteers to assist him.

Scraps is constructed to be a servant for Margolotte before the story begins, but the Patchwork Girl is not brought to life until after the appearance of the Munchkin boy. Scraps is meant to be "useful rather than ornamental" (Baum, *Patchwork Girl* 37), and thus is made from "a 'crazy-quilt' [...] [so she would not be proud nor haughty" (Baum, *Patchwork Girl* 32). Margolotte wants a servant who is willing and able to do the household chores, nothing more. Therefore, Margolotte means to give Scraps brains that are "fitten to the station she is to occupy in life" (Baum, *Patchwork Girl* 37). Margolotte wants her patchwork slave to have just enough brains to complete her tasks, but not enough to question her place within the social hierarchy. Ojo "think[s] it both unfair and unkind to deprive [Scraps] of any good qualities that were handy" (Baum, *Patchwork Girl* 40) so, while Margolotte and her husband are not looking, he gives Scraps a little bit of every quality the Crooked Magician can provide. The result is an intelligent character who is "Original, [...] and therefore incomparable. [...] Comic, absurd, rare and amusing [...] the supreme freak" (Baum, *Patchwork Girl* 57). This character, appropriately named Scraps, becomes Ojo's heroic sidekick on his journey to become Ojo "the Lucky" and save Ojo's Unc Nunkie and Margolotte from their petrified, marble state. While the Patchwork Girl volunteers to accompany Ojo, and, in doing so, escapes her would-be oppressors and improves her situation, it is worth noting that Ojo plays a role in The Patchwork Girl's creation. The Patchwork Girl's assistance in Ojo's hero-quest echoes other created characters, each helping their "parent"/maker.

Just as Scraps is constructed from many patterns and fabrics, her personality seems to be an amalgamation of many of Baum's prior hero characters. Like Dorothy, Scraps is a female hero with a feminist bent. While many authors have discussed Dorothy as one of the first American feminist child-heroes, Agnes Curry and Josef Velazquez compare her to Cinderella. While one can see the comparison—Dorothy and Cinderella are both orphan children, both of their adventures feature magical shoes—the Patchwork Girl seems to hold more in common with the servant-turned-princess. Her evil mother figure creates her for servitude, much like Cinderella's step-mother forces her to become a servant. The Patchwork Girl's patchwork nature, designed specifically to be unappealing, is reminiscent of Cinderella covered in ashes. Like Dorothy, Scraps seems to fit within the fairy-tale heroine trope; like Dorothy, the Patchwork Girl subverts this trope by deciding to seek adventure over housework and the Emerald City over Munchkin Country. Curry and Velazquez note that "there is also one major difference: Cinderella finds a Prince, but Dorothy does not" (25), Scraps is described as "no one's sweetheart, no one's wife" (Baum, *Patchwork Girl* 93). Baum's heroines do not wait for a man to help rescue them from their undesirable situation; rather they bravely seek the solutions for themselves.

One of the reasons why neither Dorothy nor Scraps seek out prince/husband saviors is because they are identified as prepubescent child characters—albeit Romantic child characters. In the essay "The Afterlife of the Romantic Child," Frances Ferguson explains that it has [...] long been recognized that children had a special status in the Romantic period [...]. The Romantics [...] created a new economy of respect by seeing children as different from adults. No longer were they deficient adults. Now they were, finally, completely adequate children [215].

In "Queering Age/Sex in Shelly Jackson's Patchwork Girl" Emily Mattingly states that "the Romantic child is an ideal child that never truly existed in the first place, a child that is always already a construction. A figment of the Romantic imagination" (84). The Romantic child is elevated—the perfect, most innocent version of childhood. Although Baum's Dorothy certainly has more adult qualities than your average child, Baum consistently describes her as "an innocent, harmless little girl" (Baum, *Wizard of Oz* 21). This description, along with her heroic, self-reliant actions throughout *The Wonderful Wizard of Oz* reinforce her status as a Romantic child-hero. The Patchwork Girl, brought to life mere minutes before she volunteers to help Ojo on his adventure-quest, certainly classifies as a new, young, child-being. While S. J. Sackett reads Baum's Scarecrow as an example of Locke's "*tabula rasa*, an empty page" (281), and certainly there is a connection between Scarecrow and Scraps, Emily Mattingly places Shelly Jackson's Patchwork Girl within the Romantic child sphere, citing how "the patchwork girl runs through the hills near her home, 'stamping,' hallooing,' 'jumping,' and 'laughing' like she is a Romantic child who is connected to nature" (85). It is almost unnecessary to note that Shelly Jackson's Patchwork Girl, and her actions, derive from Baum's Patchwork Girl, Scraps. Although she is a doll, Scraps similarly fills a Romantic child role. Like Dorothy, the Patchwork Girl's heroic actions elevate her to child-hero status.

Scraps begins to obtain hero status when she declares that she will accompany Ojo on his quest, despite the warning that it will be a long journey and that "those who travel are likely to meet trouble" (Baum, *Patchwork Girl* 77). This warning proves to be true. During the quest, the Patchwork Girl is swallowed by a giant plant, attacked by an overgrown porcupine, and physically thrown by several characters, including: the Tottenhots, Yoop the Giant, and the Champion of Horner Country. These dangers do not deter Scraps, instead she uses her rag doll qualities to protect her (almost exclusively male) companions. When the overgrown porcupine throws its quills at Ojo, Scraps "sprang in front of Ojo and shielded him from the darts, which stuck their points into her own body until she resembled one of those targets they shoot arrows at in archery games" (Baum, *Patchwork Girl* 155). Similarly, Scraps asks Mr. Champion to throw her, as Scarecrow is stuck on a fence. Scraps believes "when [she is] on top the fence [she'll] pull [her] friend off the picket and toss him down" (Baum, *Patchwork Girl* 281). When her friends are in danger, the Patchwork Girl exhibits more regard for her companions than for her own well-being. Like Dorothy, the Patchwork Girl's behavior is classically heroic.

While Scraps shares several of Dorothy's traits, she also shares traits with Baum's earlier created beings. In *The Wonderful Wizard of Oz*, Baum introduces his most famous anthropomorphic characters: Scarecrow, Tin Man, and Lion. While Lion is born a living being, and the Tin Woodman was once a man, but slowly, through amputations and prosthetics, becomes tin, Baum does not explain how Scarecrow came to life, merely that "when the farmer made [the Scarecrow's] head, one of the first things he did was to paint [the Scarecrow's] ears, so that he heard what was going on" (Baum, *Wizard of Oz* 45). Despite his assertion that he is in need of brains, Scarecrow famously uses his problem solving abilities to help his companions along their journey.

From the very beginning of her life, Scraps is able to use her strange assortment of brains to advise and guide Ojo and the Magician toward their mutual goal. Baum makes this point overtly apparent when he has Scraps sing, "Higgledy, piggledy, dee—/What fools magicians be! His head's so thick/He can't think quick, So he takes advice from me" (Baum, *Patchwork Girl* 59). The Patchwork Girl's ability to think her way out of situations is reminiscent of Baum's Scarecrow. Her self-sacrificing, heroic actions also echo the Scarecrow's: he saves his companions throughout *The Wonderful Wizard of Oz*, and also in a chapter of *The Patchwork Girl of Oz* where he allows Yoop the giant to "capture [him], [since] during that instant of delay Dorothy and Ojo had slipped by the Giant and were out of reach" (Baum, *Patchwork Girl* 263). Baum seems to further emphasize the link between Scraps and Scarecrow by allowing other characters to explicitly make comparisons. When the Shaggy Man first meets Scraps, he quickly says, "My dear, you're a wonder. I must introduce you to my friend the Scarecrow" (Baum, *Patchwork Girl* 124). While some have read romantic intent into the interactions between Scarecrow and the Patchwork Girl, it is likely that Baum, who tended to distance himself from romantic plots, was drawing a comparison between the two highly intelligent, brave characters who ignore what is in their own physical best interest in order to help their child-heroes through their quests. One could as easily note the similarities between Scraps and the Tin Woodman, and even read potential romance within their encounter. However, it is the potential for romance between Scraps and Scarecrow that complicates how a reader views the recognition Scraps receives at the end of her novel.

Clearly Baum's Patchwork Girl is a heroic toy, but does she receive the rewards that her tin or straw counterparts receive? At the end of *The Wonderful Wizard of Oz*, the Tin Woodman is given the item of his desire, a (fake) heart, and asked to rule over the Winkie Country; he continues to rule the yellow country of Oz during Ojo's quest. The Scarecrow is, similarly, rewarded with his quested for (albeit fake) brains and made a ruler at the end of *The*

Wonderful Wizard of Oz; although he has relinquished his Emerald City throne to Ozma by the time Ojo and Scraps set out for their adventure, "he has a splendid castle in the Winkie Country, near to the palace of his friend the Tin Woodman, and he is often to be found in the Emerald City, where he visits Dorothy at the royal palace" (Baum, *Patchwork Girl* 130). These characters are allotted the highest honors in Oz—they are members of Ozma's royal court and their opinions are held to be similar in value to the girl ruler's. *The Patchwork Girl of Oz* ends with the Wizard announcing that Scraps "is so remarkable in appearance, and so clever and good tempered, that our Gracious Ruler intends to preserve her carefully, as one of the curiosities of the curious Land of Oz. Scraps may live in the palace, or wherever she pleases, and be nobody's servant but her own" (Baum, *Patchwork Girl* 338); however, the Patchwork Girl's freedom is complicated by her relationship with the Scarecrow. It is easy for the reader to conclude that Ozma values and thus "saves" Scraps for two reasons: she is unique and the Scarecrow is romantically interested in her.

It is disturbing to think Baum, a noted feminist who "became the secretary of the small Aberdeen Equal Suffrage Club" (Loncraine 111), would link a female character's social status to a male character's interest in her, but the textual argument presents itself during the Patchwork Girl's initial appearance in Ozma's palace. Ojo is imprisoned for breaking the law by picking a six-leaf clover (though it is worth noting that prison in utopian Oz is a pleasant experience). Meanwhile, his companions the Glass Cat and the Woozy (an animal-type creature of "all squares and flat surfaces and edges" [Baum, *Patchwork Girl* 102]) are "taken to a nice room" but the Patchwork Girl is singled out: "[Dorothy] kept [Scraps] in one of [Dorothy's] own rooms, for [Dorothy] was much interested in the strange creature" (Baum, *Patchwork Girl* 213). While Scraps is left waiting for to Dorothy's return (and her companions are allowed private spaces in which to rest), Ozma's "old and trusted friends" (Baum, *Patchwork Girl* 216) gather in her banquet hall. Scarecrow quickly steers the conversation toward Scraps, stating, "I met a charming girl on the road and wanted to see more of her, so I hurried back" (Baum, *Patchwork Girl* 217). The other friends weigh in with their opinions, calling Scraps "bewildering, if not strictly beautiful," "queer and—and—uncommon" and "half-crazy," but, ultimately, "seeing that [the Scarecrow] was interested in Scraps they forbore to say anything against her" (Baum, *Patchwork Girl* 217–218). Ozma's court suspend their opinions of the Patchwork Girl because they see that Scarecrow is interested in her. This courtly discussion becomes all the more complex since, at the end of the same chapter, Ozma links the existence of other created characters brought to life with the Powder of Life, Jack Pumpkinhead and Sawhorse, with their ability to "comfort and amuse us" (Baum, *Patchwork Girl* 220)—"us" being Ozma's court. It seems logical that

The Patchwork Girl's imprisonment in Dorothy's room, and her later "freed" status are linked with her ability to comfort and amuse Ozma and her close friends. Scarecrow's interest in Scraps may have saved her from far more than the critiques of Ozma's court.

It can be argued that, like Scarecrow, The Patchwork Girl's unique nature and heroic qualities save her. After all, as Andrew Karp notes, "Baum's characters express [...] a desire for self-reliance and autonomy, a need to assert one's distinctness in the face of social pressures for conformity and uniformity, an urge to be free from society's efforts to inculcate specific mores, a 'yearning for leisure and freedom'" (106); but Karp also notes the tensions that Baum's unique characters present, as they "suggest a devaluation of the group" (106) and some "express [...] elitism" (107) ultimately creating "a dramatic difference between the distinct individuals and the faceless, working masses" (109). Setting aside the hierarchal issues that exist within a society that elevates the individual, is Scraps granted the right to "live in the palace, or wherever she pleases, and be nobody's servant but her own" (Baum, *Patchwork Girl* 338) because she is part of a unique elite, because she is a heroic toy that amuses those in power, or for another reason? In order to answer this, we must consider the Patchwork Girl's contemporaries—the other characters brought to life via the Powder of Life.

The Patchwork Girl of Oz presents five characters animated via the Powder of Life: Scraps, Bungle the Glass Cat, Jack Pumpkinhead, the Sawhorse, and the Phonograph Player. Each character was created as an object of convenience with a purpose that somehow benefit their maker. While Jack Pumpkinhead and the Sawhorse were brought to life in Baum's *The Marvelous Land of Oz*, and not within *The Patchwork Girl of Oz*, Baum chooses to retell the tale when Ozma and her court gather in her banquet hall and discuss Scraps. Clearly there is a parallel meant to be drawn, or there would be no purpose in recapping prior events. Ozma recounts how she "had made a pumpkin-headed man [...] to frighten [Mombi the Witch's] [...] but [the Witch] knew what the figure was and to test her Powder of Life she sprinkled some of it on the man [...]. It came to life and is now [her] dear friend Jack Pumpkinhead" (Baum, *Patchwork Girl* 220). Since these events are recapped during a discussion about Scraps, it seems that Baum wants his readers to draw connections between Scraps and Jack Pumpkinhead. Like Scraps, Jack's initial purpose was service—he was meant to scare the witch. Though Jack's inanimate body fails at this task, Ozma and Jack arrive at a deal—"[Jack] owes [Ozma] obedience [...] and [she] owe[s] [him]—support" (Baum, *Land of Oz* 34). Jack, like Scraps, accompanies his parent/creator on her adventure, heroically helping Ozma to escape her life with Mombi and regain her place as the rightful ruler of Oz. While "Ozma loved the stupid fellow [Jack], who had been her earliest companion" (Baum, *Patchwork Girl* 235), and while Jack lives in a pumpkin house of his choosing, he is still, ultimately, Omza's obedient creation. Scraps helps Ojo; she "recognize[d] the fact that Ojo was her first friend" (Baum, *Patchwork Girl* 212) and frequently risks herself to save him, but she is neither obedient to him (although he gave Scraps her brains) nor to Margolotte (who sewed her into existence).

Sawhorse, another character from *The Marvelous Land of Oz*, is also mentioned in this banquet hall discussion. Ozma recounts how, as she and Jack Pumpkinhead escaped from Mombi, they "came upon a wooden Sawhorse standing by the road and [she] used the magic powder to bring it to life. The Sawhorse has been with [her] ever since" (Baum, *Patchwork Girl* 220). Just as one may conclude that Baum wanted a comparison between Scraps and Jack, one can see how a Powder of Life hierarchy is formed within this scene. The Sawhorse, even more so than Jack, is Ozma's obedient servant—he does not leave her. Although he is another heroic creation, he holds a status similar to a living animal, where Jack's status is closer to that of Ozma's not-too-bright son. Where Jack may not have Scarecrow's famous brains, he is able to live on his own, away from Ozma, until he is needed by the child ruler.

Jack Pumpkinhead and Sawhorse are characters carried over from an earlier Oz story who play a minor role within *The Patchwork Girl of Oz*. Scraps, Bungle the Glass Cat, and the Phonograph Player are brought to life within this tale, and are thus allotted more space within the narrative. Bungle and the Phonograph illustrate the mentality of a created character who, through a lack of obedience, fails to serve a purpose. Bungle and Phonograph each regret the pointlessness of their existence. Andrew Karp refers to this misery as the "unfortunate consequences [of unfettered individualism] on select beings in Oz" (Karp 114). Bungle and the Phonograph seem caught between their nature as objects meant for their makers' pleasure, and their own desires. When examined closely, the reader can see that Bungle and Phonograph's inability to reason their way through this existential crisis and find purpose separates them from achieving the usefulness of Baum's toy-hero Scraps.

Bungle's very name implies that her existence is a mistake or a failure. While the Crooked Magician created Bungle, "it was a poor job because [Bungle was] useless and a bother to [him] […]" (Baum, *Patchwork Girl* 48). The magician's wife calls the Glass Cat "Bungle" because she does not serve her intended purpose. Instead of catching mice, Bungle admires her beauty and wanders through the garden. By ignoring her cat-like nature, Bungle has taken on the life of a collectable toy—her purpose is more decorative than functional. Bungle overcompensates for her chosen function by admiring her beauty to the point of narcissism, leading others to describe her as a "saucy, inconsiderate Glass Cat, with pink brains and a hard ruby heart"

(Baum, *Patchwork Girl* 48). As an ornament, Bungle is unloved and unhappy. She both acknowledges that her existence is a mistake and her misery when she tells the Crooked Magician, "no one can regret more than I the fact that you made me" (Baum, *Patchwork Girl* 48). Though the Glass Cat is as reluctant to serve as Scraps is, she regrets that she was brought to life. While one can empathize with her desire to be more than a servant, by ignoring her purpose—catching mice—she becomes useless and self-centered.

Scraps models for Bungle a way to reject being an objects meant for their makers' pleasure while still retaining a purpose; Scraps is no servant, but she does help her human companions. When Bungle sees Scraps about to undertake an adventure to help Ojo, the Glass Cat bravely offers to join the journey. Though the Crooked Magician endorsed The Patchwork Girl's journey, stating that she "may be able to help the boy, for [her] head seems to contain some thoughts [the Magician] did not expect to find in it" (Baum, *Patchwork Girl* 65), he does not offer the Glass Cat the same encouragement. The Magician publicly states that "[the Glass Cat will] get broken in no time, and [...] couldn't be a bit of use" (Baum, *Patchwork Girl* 65), furthering the notion that Bungle's function has become strictly ornamental; she is the type of toy that sits on a shelf and is admired, but should not be played with. Bungle refutes this notion when she bravely replies, "Three heads are better than two, and my pink brains are beautiful. You can see 'em work" (Baum, *Patchwork Girl* 65). While haughty, the Glass Cat shares the Patchwork Girl's bravery. She has the desire to be useful. The Patchwork Girl, Scraps is able to "enjoy [...] life" (Baum, *Patchwork Girl* 68) almost from the very moment of creation; the Glass Cat, caught between her nature as an object meant for her maker's pleasure and her own desires, has to learn how to take pleasure in her heroic actions.

Though she is brave enough to join Ojo's journey, the Glass Cat is unable to escape the beliefs her makers enforced upon her. Bungle's perception of her ornamental nature keeps her from the types of bravery displayed by Scraps. When Scraps is tossed about by an unseen hand, Bungle suggests she and Ojo "go to sleep, or something will happen to us" (Baum, *Patchwork Girl* 80). She does not rescue her friend, as Scraps would. She limits herself by reinforcing the message of the Magician—the world is a dangerous place for a pretty glass cat. Toward the end of the novel, Bungle's conceited nature is improved upon when the Wizard "took the pink brains and replaced them with transparent ones, and now the Glass Cat is so modest and well behaved that Ozma has decided to keep her in the palace as a pet" (Baum, *Patchwork Girl* 338). It is interesting to note that Oz only becomes utopian for Bungle when her nature is adapted. The belief that she has no purpose beyond beauty must forcibly be removed from her head in order for her to fully rise above her selfish nature. In order to live within a truly utopian Oz, Bungle must sacrifice the very things that make her a unique individual—the ruby brains that enhance her glass beauty.

Bungle was purposely brought to life, even if the Magician "bungled" it. The Phonograph, another Powder of Life character struck by the "unfortunate consequences [of unfettered individualism] on select beings in Oz" (Karp 114), is brought to life through a series of unfortunate events: the phonograph (which Baum does not consider a proper noun until after it becomes sentient) was playing when the Magician took the bottle of the Powder of Life out to animate the Patchwork Girl. The Patchwork girl jerks awake, causing the powder to fly. The powder is accidentally sprinkled on the phonograph, causing him to become sentient. Like Bungle, the Phonograph seem caught between his nature as objects meant for his maker's pleasure, and his own desires. As the Phonograph is not purposely created, he is not given the kind of brains that would allow him to navigate this existential crisis.

The Phonograph Player is unable to produce an action that the other characters value. While it seems his job is to create music, no one appreciates what he plays. He runs from the Crooked Magician after "he threatened to smash [the Player] to pieces" (Baum, *Patchwork Girl* 87); only then does he attempt to join Ojo's quest. The Phonograph Player is not motivated by bravery or a desire to contribute to the greater good of the group, but by loneliness. He wants to join Ojo and Scraps so he can "talk and play tunes all [he] wants to" (Baum, *Patchwork Girl* 87), regardless of whether or not his fellow travelers enjoy his noise (which they do not). The Phonograph Player insists that the others are required to like the music he produces, "and if you don't the proper thing is to look as if you did" (Baum, *Patchwork Girl* 88). Since the Phonograph does not self-regulate, and the others do not have a way to turn him off (as he is now living), the Phonograph becomes an inconvenience rather than an enjoyable distraction. This leads Ojo to reject his offer of friendship; Ojo asks the Player to leave, denying him the ability to join the journey and possibly become a hero.

Ojo tells the Phonograph that "we've no objection to you as a machine [...] but as a music-maker we hate you" (Baum, *Patchwork Girl* 136). In order to join on the journey, the Phonograph would have to sacrifice the very things that make him a unique individual—his very nature as a music player. The Phonograph responds with the question, "then why was I ever invented?" (Baum, *Patchwork Girl* 136), suggesting that he regrets his sentient nature. When he is asked to leave, he does not go quietly. The Phonograph Player continues to follow the group and play music that no one seems to like, Ojo threatens to "smash [his] record" (Baum, *Patchwork Girl* 89). It is remarkably unusual for a heroic Oz character to threaten another character physically, but the Shaggy Man, another member of Ozma's court that crosses paths with Ojo and Scraps, makes a similar threat when he tells the Phonograph that he will "take [the Player] all apart [...] and scatter [the] pieces far and wide over the country" (Baum, *Patchwork Girl* 137). The Phonograph's lack of ability to understand the needs of others causes him to be useless. Without purpose, he regrets his life and everyone he comes in contact with despises his futility to the point where they threaten his very existence.

Where the Phonograph Player runs off and is not heard from again, and Bungle ultimately elevates herself to a prized collectable, Scraps ends the novel with the right to "live in the palace, or wherever she pleases, and be nobody's servant but her own" (Baum, *Patchwork Girl* 338). Scraps is allowed to retain her colorful, unique ways; she does not have to conform to the standards of her makers. Is there anything—apart from her gendered role as a potential love interest for Scarecrow—that separates Scraps from Baum's other creation characters—thus justifying her seemingly special treatment? In their essay "The Ethics and Epistemology of Emancipation in Oz" Jason M. Bell and Jessica Bell argue the "anti-racist and anti-slavery symbolism in [*The Patchwork Girl of Oz*] is thickly layered. Scraps, the intended slave, is made of cotton, [...] and her hairstyle evokes cornrows [...]" (Bell and Bell 232). Is The Patchwork Girl's freedom granted as social commentary? And, if so, what is the larger commentary of the place of freedom in a utopia where other created creatures are not granted the same freedoms? Bell and Bell link Ojo's journey from unlucky to lucky to knowledge: "Even Margolotte knows that 'knowledge is the greatest gift in life' and that knowledge will prove the key to finding Ojo's luck" (Bell and Bell 231). If we set aside potential romantic interest, Scraps and Scarecrow share two very important similarities—they are self-sacrificingly brave for their friends, and they have brains that make them invaluable companions. Similarly, several of Baum's subjugated characters, including the Glass Cat, Jack Pumpkinhead, and the Phonograph, have brains that cause them to be functionally useless. By returning to the hierarchal issues existing within Oz's seeming utopian society, we can better understand how the Patchwork Girl's ability to think (and not her potential romantic standing) that differentiates her from the other created beings within Oz.

In the same manner that Scraps is Scarecrow's literary counterpart, Tiktok, introduced in Baum's *Ozma of Oz*, is Tin Man's counterpart. Tiktok, an anthropomorphic wind-up toy, is described: "like a man [...]. He was only about as tall as Dorothy herself, and his body was round as a ball and made out of burnished copper. Also his head and limbs were copper" (Baum, *Ozma of Oz* 39). Dorothy's animal companion, a chicken named Billina, points out that Tiktok "isn't alive" (Baum, *Ozma of Oz* 39), and Dorothy tells Billina about the Tin Woodman, immediately linking the two metal men in the reader's mind. Dorothy reads the directions printed on him: "For THINK-ING:—Wind the Clock-work Man under his left arm, (marked No. 1) For

SPEAKING:—Wind the Clock-work Man under his right arm, (marked No. 2) For WALKING and ACTION:—Wind Clock-work in the middle of his back, (marked No. 3)" (Baum, *Ozma of Oz* 42). Tiktok is not merely a created being, he is a constructed in a manner that makes him incapable of emulating life without constant maintenance by the living creatures around him. When he is wound, he is able to use his thoughts and actions to help Dorothy solve the problems that arise along her journey; like Scraps and Scarecrow, a wound Tiktok is capable of being an independent hero. When he is run down, he is of no help to the little girl. He is nothing more than a dependent, oversized toy.

It is in Tiktok's nature to run down, making him unable to consistently help his human companions. This may seem similar to the Tin Man's rusting, but Baum makes sure his readers understand the difference between the tin and copper men when the two characters discuss which is superior. The Tin Man states that Tiktok is "greatly inferior to my friend the Scarecrow, and to myself. For we are both alive, and he has brains which do not need to be wound up, while I have an excellent heart" and Tiktok concedes that he "cannot help be-ing [the Tin Man's] in-fer-i-or for I [Tiktok] a, a mere ma-chine" (Baum, *Ozma of Oz* 99). Later in the novel, when Tin Man is temporary left behind, Tiktok suggests that the Tin Man's "ma-ter-i-al was not ve-ry du-ra-ble" and Scarecrow replies, "Oh, tin is an excellent material [...] and if anything ever happened to poor Nick Chopper he was always easily soldered. Besides, he did not have to be wound up, and was not liable to get out of order" (Baum, *Ozma of Oz* 224). Baum points out, again and again, the superiority of the born, thinking, self-reliant Tin Man over the created, dependent Tiktok. The point is emphasized one final time when, in the end, "Tiktok, claiming to be Dorothy's faithful follower because he belonged to her, had been permitted to join [Ozma's] party" (Baum, *Ozma of Oz* 232). Tiktok is not permitted access to Ozma's court based on his own heroic merits (though he has as many as any of the other created heroes), but because he is Dorothy's possession.

It may be easy for a reader to dismiss the slave-like nature of this ever growing cast of created beings, as so many fit into the toy, robotic, or otherwise non-human category, if Baum did not pen similar humanoid characters that further complicate this hierarchy. Chopfyt, another foil to the Tin Woodman, is a man built from the human parts from the former bodies of Tin Woodman and Captain Fyter, a Tin Soldier similarly turned into a Tin Man. Both the Tin Woodman and Captain Fyter were engaged to the Munchkin girl Nimmie Amee before their tin transformations. In *The Tin Woodman of Oz*, the two Tin Men set out on a quest to find Nimmie Amee in order to make good on their promise of marriage. They discover that Nimmie Amee has already married Chopfyt. She tells her former suitors that Chopfyt "is now trained to draw the water and carry in the wood and hoe the cabbages and weed the flower-beds and dust the furniture and perform many tasks of a like character" and she happy because she is "mistress of all [she] survey[s]—the queen of [her] little domain" (Baum, *The Tin Woodman* 245). Despite being assembled from human parts, Chopfyt is doomed to the same existence that Scraps escaped—household slavery; he is clearly subservient to his mistress/wife. While he does not seem to regret this existence the way Scraps does, the Tin Woodman and the Tin Soldier explicitly state how much they would regret living a life like Chopfyt's—reminding the reader how undesirable a life of servitude is.

In *The Utopia of Oz*, S. J. Sackett examines the Scarecrow and Tin Woodman and hypothesizes that Baum used them to unite "the intellect and the emotion[al] in a harmonious relationship" (287). Sackett also notes how Baum, and Oz, clearly values intelligence, as "the Scarecrow himself once remarked, 'I consider brains far superior to money [...]. You may have noticed that if one has money without brains, he cannot use it to advantage; but that if one has brains without money, they will enable him to live comfortable to the end of all his days" (287); presumably this statement works because one with brains will have the ability to use their intelligence to find the resources they need to gain comfort. Going on that assumption, if one were to replace the word "money" with the idea of freedom, the statement seems to serve as a guide for how Baum's beings, created or not, gain rights within Oz.

Oz's creatures without brains, or with inferior brains, are subservient to those with brains because those with brains can use them to their advantage—to change from unlucky to lucky or to gain freedom from servitude. Chopfyt, described as having a "cold and indifferent stare that was almost insolent" (Baum, *The Tin Woodman* 241), can then be interpreted as a slave because he is indifferent (and insolent), not merely because he is created. Similarly, Tiktok, Sawhorse, The Phonograph, and other created beings that fall within a seemingly lower social status in Oz are lower not merely because of their creation status, but because they cannot think themselves out of their hierarchal situation. Baum brings this to the reader's attention when, after recounting the tale of Jack Pumpkinhead, Ozma's earliest companion, he notes that "Ozma loved the stupid fellow" (Baum, *Patchwork Girl* 235). While Jack is just as brave as Scraps or Scarecrow, he lacks the ability to think through the problems that arise during a journey, thus making him "stupid" and, therefore, inferior. The Glass Cat, granted a place in Ozma's court after her brains are replaced, seems to further illustrate the point that acceptable brains are a requirement in order to rise within Oz's social structures.

In his essay on food in L. Frank Baum's Oz Books, Tison Pugh links social structure within Ozma's court with dietary preferences. Pugh cites how "the animal guests, which Ozma always invited to her banquets and seated at a table by themselves" (336) are separated because, he hypotheses, "he animals are accorded a lower place in the social structure due to their biological forms, as well as due to their appetites" (337). This theory, when extended to Oz's created beings, would suggest that these beings would rank higher than animals, as they do not have appetites that humans would find unappealing. Instead Baum offers textual evidence that created beings tend to be as low, if not lower, than animals within Oz's hierarchal structure. Baum's created characters exist to serve, whether as slaves or as toy-like objects that "comfort and amuse [Ozma's court]" (Baum, *Patchwork Girl* 220). The exceptions to this rule, Scarecrow and Scraps, seem to escape the fate of service because of their brains, their ability to reason their way out of their given status, allow them the freedom to remain unique and autonomous. Andrew Karp notes how Baum "populates the Land of Oz with a plethora of distinct and unique characters and has a number of these characters praise individualism and eccentricity" (106). He also notes "a dramatic difference between the distinct individuals and the faceless, working masses" (109). These differences, this hierarchy, seems to be the same social structure seen among the created beings—those unable to think, serve. Those who think are elevated.

When L. Frank Baum designed the world of Oz, he developed a social structure within his fairyland where humans seem elevated above their anthropomorphic hero counterparts and born seems preferred to created. While nearly all of Baum's named characters that are not villains are heroic, the rewards that they receive seem dependent on their place within Oz's social hierarchy. Scraps, a notable exception to this rule, seems to escape her toy-slave status and gain seemingly unheard of freedom not because of her suspected romance with Scarecrow, but because her unique brains make her an invaluable companion. Her remarkableness, and the suicidal tendencies of some of the other created beings, highlights how Baum's utopian Oz might be less pleasurable for objects brought to life to serve, regardless of their heroic contributions. These creations, lacking brains equip for problem solving, have the choice of blindly obeying or becoming useless objects. If one considers the play on words, then Baum best sums up this point in *Tik-Tok of Oz*, when Quox, a young dragon, and Tik-Tok (my spelling reflects the change in this text) compare themselves. Quox comments, "You are not a live thing. You're a dummy" (Baum, *Tik-Tok* 147). In Baum's Oz, one is not granted the rights of a live thing, regardless of how one came to life, if they lack brains capable of solving the problems that arise within the story—if they are a dummy. Scraps and Scarecrow are much more than stuffed, ornamental toys whose purpose is to serve their masters' bidding. They are elevated among their created contemporaries not because of how they were created, and not because they are useful, but because of how they think.

Works Cited

Baum. L. Frank. *The Marvelous Land of Oz*. New York: Dover, 1969. Print.
_____. *Ozma of Oz*. New York: Del Rey, 1979. Print.
_____. *The Patchwork Girl of Oz*. Mineola: Dover, 1990. Print.
_____. *Tik-Tok of Oz*. New York: William Morrow, 1996. Print.
_____. *The Tin Woodman of Oz*. New York: Ballantine, 1981. Print.
_____. *The Wonderful Wizard of Oz*. New York: HarperCollins, 1987. Print.
Baum, L. Frank, and Jack Zipes. "The Emerald City of Oz." 1910. *The Wonderful World of Oz: The Wizard of Oz: The Emerald City of Oz: Glinda of Oz*. Melbourne: Penguin, 1998. 107–251. Print.
Bell, Jason M., and Jessica Bell. "The Ethics and Epistemology of Emancipation in Oz." *The Universe of Oz*. Ed. Josef Velazquez. Jefferson, NC: McFarland, 2010. 225–245. Print.
Curry, Agnes B. "Dorothy and Cinderella: The Case of the Missing Prince and the Despair of the Fairy Tale." *The Universe of Oz*. Ed. Josef Velazquez. Jefferson, NC: McFarland, 2010. 24–53. Print.
Ferguson, Frances. "The Afterlife of the Romantic Child: Rousseau and Kant Meet Deleuze and Guattari." *South Atlantic Quarterly* 102.1 (2003): 215–234. Print.
Karp, Andrew. "Utopian Tension in L. Frank Baum's Oz." *Utopian Studies* 9.2 (1998): 103–21. *JSTOR*. Penn State University Press. Web. 10 Feb. 2014.
Loncraine, Rebecca. *The Real Wizard of Oz: The Life and Times of L. Frank Baum*. New York: Gotham Books, 2009. Print.
Mattingly, Emily A. "Something Between Higgledy-Piggledy and the Eternal Sphere. Queering Age/Sex in Shelly Jackson's Patchwork Girl. " *The Universe of Oz*. Ed. Josef Velazquez. Jefferson, NC: McFarland, 2010. 77–93. Print.
Pugh, Tison. "'Are We Cannibals, Let Me Ask? Or Are We Faithful Friends': Food, Interspecies Cannibalism, and the Limits of Utopia in L. Frank Baum's Oz Books." *The Lion and the Unicorn* 32.3 (2008): 324–43. *Project Muse*. Web. 10 Feb. 2014.
Sackett, S J. "The Utopia of Oz." *The Georgia Review* 14.3 (1960): 275–291. Print.

Falterity
The Toy as Otherwise Than Hero
Nathan TeBokkel

Falterity: Children, Toys and a Pleaching of Philosophers[1]

 The toy is the locus of a child's imagination, the icon for the transposition of her ego and agency, the idol of her disparate dreams, of her fragments and figments of memories, experiences, thoughts, actions, and relations—and therefore of her self. It is through the toy that the child creates worlds and others. Because of the roles it plays, and the roles in which it is played with, the toy is cast as a hero in plastic and on screen. But to the child, this heroism is not so clear.

 Toy Story (1995) and *Wreck-It Ralph* (2012), two animated Disney films about toys and videogame avatars, are our means to grasp this falterity. We study Buzz Lightyear, Woody, the toys of Sid Phillips, Wreck-It Ralph, and Vanellope to listen to what they have to tell us about falterity. We play with these toys in an eccentric set of theories, and we play with these theories in Andy's room and Litwak's Arcade. We meekly feel the need to be childlike in our lives and loves, to neither feel nor reason, but both and more.

 To claim that the toy is *either* a hero *or* a villain, to claim that the toy is *both* a hero *and* a villain, or to harmonize these claims—"either *both-and* or *either-or*"—is to reify binaries which are false, though often convenient shorthand. To make claims along any of these lines is to elevate the binary to a transcendental position. As such, the binary, the philosopheme of post- and -structuralism, is nominally, and only nominally, analyzed and excised from its position as dictator of discourse, and therefore able to retain its stranglehold on thought and being. Following Giles Deleuze, we may think that conjunction—*And-Then, Both-And*—might be enough to escape binaries, but it merely papers over fissures.[2]

Cleaving to binaries leads to oversimplification, apathy, and oppression.[3] Alternatively, we ought to enmesh ourselves empathically rather than to define ourselves by right and might. When someone speaks to us, "we have been cautioned that he is not speaking with his own voice but speaking the language of his gender, his family, his class, his education, his culture, his economic and political interests, his unconscious drives, indeed his state of physical health and alertness" (Lingis, *Trust* viii). But these layers, while real all together, are split until they are irreal and alone. To love, we must "go beyond what [we] know and hold on to the real individual" (ix). We must try to perceive the Deleuzian conjunction in *its* transcendental position: the toy is *both* "both hero and villain" *and* "either hero or villain"; the speaker is all of these perceived layers and more.

When conjunction is so perceived, we encounter paradox. We become like the child and the toy in a world of intuition and play, which is why they are the paradigm for this theoretical move. The transcendental conjunction is only transcendental because it is most immanent; it seems so far beyond us only because it is so deep within. And it is only perceptible through the more indeterminate "neither-nor." The toy is *neither* hero *nor* villain, *neither* "both hero and villain" *nor* "either hero or villain." The toy is *otherwise*, in Emmanuel Levinas's sense: toward, like, of the other. It plays different parts; it is played with in different parts.

As Levinas says, "I myself can feel myself to be the other of the other" (*Totality* 84). I am no "I" *per se*; I am no aseity, no ipseity, no haecceity without the irreducible others who constitute me and whom I constitute. I am no agent, no prime mover, but an *agencement* of alters.[4] I am absolutely *contingent*—irrevocably subject to chance, irrecuperably dependent on specific circumstances, and irrecusably part of a greater whole, which is itself a part of a whole, and so on in a near-infinite recursion. Falterity, therefore, is a faltering alterity, an altering falter. It is the uncertainty of flesh, plastic, blood, and code, the entanglement of chromosomes and metaphors. It is the superposition of selves and others, children and toys, as *alters*.

"Falling with style": Indeterminacy and Buzz Lightyear

Buzz Lightyear traverses a pseudo-dialectic. He believes he is a Space Ranger, then believes he is a toy, but never really comes to believe he is both. There is no binary to be discovered, overturned, suspended, or privileged in

Buzz, but the simple fact that neither "Space Ranger" nor "toy" adequately encompasses who he may be. He may be both and more; carer and cared-for, player and played-with. These possibilities are conjured from the alters that he almost already[5] is: the cast and seam of his plastic body, the glue of his stickers, the chirp of his voicebox, his backstory and packaging, his voice and character, Andy's imaginings, the audience's perceptions. To try to feel how we and Buzz are otherwise than our radications and ratiocinations, we will focus on the metaphor of "falling with style" in the film *Toy Story*.

Buzz thinks he is a Space Ranger "temporarily marooned during a crucial mission" (Ebert "Toy Story"). Hailing from Sector Four rather than Playskool, he messages Star Command and tries to repair his cardboard ship (Stanton 26–33). While the other toys are impressed, Woody is exasperated: "These [wings] are plastic. He can't fly!" Buzz corrects him—"They are a terillium-carbonic alloy and I *can* fly"—and demonstrates by diving from the bed, bouncing off a rubber ball, shooting off a Hotwheels ramp, and spinning around on a plane mobile before landing perfectly in front of Woody. "That wasn't flying!" cries Woody. "That was falling with style!" (33–35).

To catalyze their conflict, Woody knocks Buzz out the window after luring him there with the promise of saving an endangered toy. If Buzz truly believes he is a Space Ranger, why does he agree to help a mere toy? Why does he not try to fly when knocked from the window? It is as if Buzz almost already thinks he is a toy who cannot fly. After a series of protracted arguments about whether Buzz is on his way to Star Command or is "a child's plaything," Woody and he find themselves at Sid's house, where they will likely be destroyed (46–70).

During their first escape attempt, Buzz runs into a den, where the television—a pseudo-Lacanian mirror—awaits. The TV announces "Calling Buzz Lightyear!" Buzz, thinking it is Star Command, opens his wrist communicator. He is interrupted by the voice-over of a child, who says, "Buzz Lightyear responding!" Confused, Buzz walks toward the TV, which proclaims, "The world's greatest superhero is now the world's greatest TOY!" The announcer presses a button on the Buzz doll and its sampled voice declares, "It's a secret mission in uncharted space!" Buzz then presses his own button and hears the same sampled phrase (84–86).

In Lacanian theory, here *the* subject becomes *a* subject, in the act of discerning the difference between its ideal self and itself, between subject-center-whole and object-periphery-part. But here falterity diverges from psychoanalysis. Buzz does not quite recognize that he is a toy. Imaginary and Real conflict because both are false impositions onto the falterity that he is, a superposition more complicated than either Imaginary, Real, or both could render.

As the commercial ends, the words "NOT A FLYING TOY flash across the bottom of the screen" (86–87). Stricken, Buzz looks up through the stairs' railing at a small window and the blue sky beyond. "The taunting voice of Woody echoes in his head," so he climbs the railing, opens his wings, leaps, falls, and crashes (87–88). This moment contrasts starkly with his flight around Andy's room. First, a snapshot of Buzz as a flying Space Ranger, like Schrödinger's cat observed alive, and second, an out-of-focus glance at Buzz as a falling toy, like Schrödinger's cat observed dead. But all along, unlike Buzz, we feel that things are more complicated than one or the other, that things are otherwise even if we can glimpse one or the other at a certain place and time. And we feel that this glimpse falters with that which precedes it, like Schrödinger's cat unglimpsed in its chamber[6] and Buzz unopened in his spaceship on Andy's bed (26).

"I'm not a Space Ranger," says a resigned Buzz to Woody. "I'm just a toy." Woody counters: "Being a toy is a lot better than being a Space Ranger. [...] Look, over in that house is a kid who thinks you are the greatest, and it's not because you're a Space Ranger, pal, it's because you're a *toy*! You are *his* toy" (106). Buzz realizes himself here; he becomes aware of who he is, and he makes who he is real. He is more than flying and falling, toy and Ranger. "There's a kid over in that house who needs us," he affirms, and the two leave Sid's for Andy's house (105–09).

The moving truck has just left, so they give chase. Woody lights the rocket Sid strapped to Buzz's back and the two are launched toward the truck. The rocket ascends, peaks, "Buzz confidently presses the button on his chest" and his wings jut out, "severing the tape that holds him to the rocket." Holding Woody, he separates from the rocket seconds before it explodes. They begin to fall, and Woody covers his eyes, but Buzz "banks under some power lines and soars upward again." "Hey, Buzz! You're flying!" Woody shouts. Buzz replies, calmly, "This isn't flying. This is falling—with style" (131–34).

Buzz is falterity. He realizes this, and thus comes to care and be cared for. This realization is neither a transcendence where he must lift himself above earthly distinctions (Kierkegaard, *Works* 72), nor an immanent movement through those distinctions, but almost always both. Each alter lives[7] and loves each alter—whom Søren Kierkegaard calls the *neighbor*—uncertainly:

> He *neither* cravenly avoids the more powerful but loves the neighbor, *nor* superiorly avoids the more lowly but loves the neighbor and wishes *essentially* to *exist* equally for all people, whether in actuality he is known by many or not. This is undeniably a considerable span of the wings, but it is not a proud flight that soars above the world; it is self-denial's humble and difficult flight along the ground [84, emphasis mine].

Buzz neither avoids being a Space Ranger and flying, nor being a toy and falling, but finds that he may fall with style. His essence is to exist for Andy, the kid who needs him, and for others, as others exist for him. He is

Schrödinger's cat in its chamber, in all its terrible precarity, and it is our job not to decide whether he is dead or alive, not to observe him and make him one or the other, but to feel how he is not quite either. And he is thus able to be rescued from that chamber, to be cared for, and reciprocally, to care. No certainty girds moral action—it depends on indeterminacy. In the words of Levinas,

> Love aims at the Other [...] in his frailty. Frailty does not here figure the inferior degree of any attribute, the relative deficiency of a determination common to me and the other. Prior to the manifestation of attributes, it qualifies alterity itself. To care is to fear for another, to come to the assistance of his frailty [*Totality* 256].

The task—for Kierkegaard and Levinas, for the child, for the faltering $^{sub}_{ob}$ject—"is not to find the lovable object, but [...] to find the once given or chosen object lovable, and to be able to continue to find him lovable no matter how he is changed" (*Works* 159). Buzz is more than a toy and a Space Ranger by being neither of them. Buzz does not soar above, nor does he fall beneath, our withering, deciding, deciduous observations.[8] Instead, he falters, he falls with style directly into the moving box, his own Schrödingerian chamber in the back seat of Andy's car, where he had been all along (Stanton 134–35).

The Impression of Sky: Contingency, Sheriff Woody and King Candy

Toy Story opens with Andy playing in his bedroom. The camera pans down his walls, "lined with cloud wallpaper giving the impression of sky," and over boxes "drawn up in crayon to look like a miniature Western town" (2). There are several important features in Andy's play. It is highly organized and meticulously planned. The room is carefully arranged, the imagined gives us the impression of the real and vice versa, the time it took to set up the play is probably much greater than the time of play itself. Andy plays with his toys "out of character": Mr. Potato Head is a wanted thief; Slinky is a force-field (2–4). To Andy, the toy is a constellation of possibilities. The relationship of child and toy reveals the falterity that is the toy and the falterity that is the child.

Andy wears a cowboy hat as he and Woody play together, which is not simply Andy (subject) playing with Woody (object), nor Andy as object of Woody's affection (4–5). The ambiguity about who is the subject and who is the object suffuses the soundscape as they play, providing an eloquent transition from Buzz's falling with style—the "I" of Randy Newman's theme song may be both Andy and Woody. In Buzz, we tried to feel the falterity from which emerge all selves and self-perceptions. In Andy and Woody's song and play, we infer falterity on a seemingly different level: the falterity inherent in the attempt to distinguish the self from the other.

The impression of sky in Andy's room is contingent upon impressions of the real sky, and the impression of real sky is in turn shaped by Andy's walls and other representations like them. This falterity of impressions mimes Woody's impression of favoritism, contingent upon Andy's favoritism, and both reveal to us the myriad contingencies of falterity. What we thought was the self, what Woody thought was himself-as-favorite-toy, proves to be no agent, no individual, but an agencement of alters, of (non)heroes and (non)favorites, contingent on them all.

By contingent we mean neither of chance, nor dependent on certain conditions, nor part of a near-infinite recursion of parts and wholes, but all of these and more. We also mean contingent in Quentin Meillassoux's sense[9]: contingency is non-reason, inexplicability, "irreducib[ility] to all preregistered possibilities" (Meillassoux 108).[10] Through it, we perceive that we are not just demi-divine decision-makers, but also mundane and decision-made.

Woody's being favorite is contingent in all these senses. Where Buzz's falterity is *within* himself, his essence and his existence, Woody's falterity is *without* himself—in Andy's favoritism, in the admiration of the toys. Woody is Andy's hero and friend, his "favorite since kindergarten," and leader of the other toys. Andy's room is cowboy-themed, and Woody sits on Andy's bed, while the other toys sit under it or in the toy chest (2–14).

But Buzz becomes Andy's new favorite toy, and the audience observes this transition during a montage: Andy plays with Woody, then sets him on the floor and shoots him with Buzz's laser; wearing his cowboy hat, Andy runs into his closet and runs out wearing "a homemade spaceman's helmet"; "the posters, the drawings on the wall, the pillow, the bedspread" all gradually change from cowboys to spacemen. Andy chooses to sleep with Buzz in his bed, now, and "Woody peeks out at them from the toybox." Woody also ceases to be the toys' favorite: Buzz helps Rex roar, has Etch-A-Sketch draw him, does Troll Doll's hair, and works out with Tinkertoys. Even the name ANDY on the sole of Buzz's foot gives the impression of inevitability, of reified certainty: it is written in permanent marker, whereas ANDY on Woody's foot has a backward N, is "in a much more childish scrawl, and is largely faded" (35–38).

Woody first tries to retain Andy's favor by belittling Buzz, and then by pushing Buzz out the window (25–28, 46–49). But his plan backfires. Andy searches for Buzz as Woody "painfully watches," and Andy eventually, sadly, chooses Woody as his favorite (52). Forcing others to observe you a certain way, to claim you as favorite or to reject you, is painful and unjust. Caring for the (non)favorite, for the cat in the unobserved chamber, is not. Woody flails against the inexorability of the determinisms and determinations of others and of himself. He finds that he is not some kind of binary or biunivocal agent that can freely act, but an agencement that is contingent on others.

Toward the end of the film, Woody realizes that even if he is not Andy's and the toys' favorite, he is not rejected by them. When Buzz and Woody are falling with style, trying to catch up to Andy, they soar over the moving truck. Woody shouts, "We missed the truck!" Buzz replies, "We're not aiming for the truck!" and the two drop into Andy's van's sun roof, into a box right beside Andy. A moment before Andy lifts them out, the audience observes the inside of the box: Woody has fallen into Andy's cowboy hat, and Buzz into his spaceship (134). Andy has brought both his favorites. We are able to feel, for a frail moment, the kind of indeterminacy Schrödinger scoffs at and that our observations preclude. There is no reason without contingency; there is no logic without attuned intuition. In the box, there is neither favorite nor hero, reject nor villain, dead nor alive, but the indissoluble possibilities of both and either, of many favorites, of otherwise than favoritism.

Similarly, in *Wreck-It Ralph*,[11] the characters warn each other of the dangers of "going Turbo," which means to try and transcend their position and programming, to leave their games and be "out of order." To "go Turbo" is to mistake sky for the impression of sky, to mistake our observations of the cat for how it must be and must have been. It is Turbo who presages the phrase (Lee 17, 48). Turbo's game, *Turbo Time*, used to be the most popular game in the arcade. Like Woody, *Turbo Time* was soon replaced—by *RoadBlasters*, an updated racing game that "stole Turbo's thunder" and made him envious enough to abandon his game and cross into the new one. He enters the screen of *RoadBlasters*, shouting his catchphrase "Turbo-tastic!" and glitching out, causing the racers to crash, and eventually "putting both games and himself out of order, for good" (56–58). The toy, avatar, or child carelessly rationalizes and taxonomizes when she thinks in terms of me against you, white against black, favorite against reject, and hero against villain. She fails to see the host of alters, shades of gray, beloveds, and (non)heroes, and simultaneously fails to care for them and be cared for by them. This is a failure not only of ontology, but of morality.

Fix-It Felix and the others believe Turbo is dead, but we learn that he is King Candy, the zany ruler of the newest racing game, *Sugar Rush*. He has repeated the takeover of *RoadBlasters* by taking over *Sugar Rush*, to keep himself the favorite. King Candy is jealous of Vanellope, the rightful ruler of *Sugar Rush*, now a glitch whose code he had attempted to delete (43–44, 68, 76–87). At the climax of the film, King Candy and Vanellope race each other, wrestling and glitching, and the audience sees Turbo's face flicker through King Candy's. Vanellope asks him who he is, and he shouts back, "I'm Turbo! I'm the greatest racer in this arcade! And I didn't escape *RoadBlasters*, learn code, and reprogram this game to let you [...] take it away from me!" (92–101).

King Candy, neé Turbo, is eaten by a cy-bug and merges with it, becoming "the most powerful virus in the arcade" who "can take over any game." However, he fails at this, too. Unable to circumvent his contingency and unable to feel his falterity, he "flies into the light and is zapped" (105–07).

To Infinity and Beyond: Nonsublimation, Sid's Toys and Princess Vanellope

Buzz, Woody, and King Candy are computer animations, collections of codes and commands, in a very literal sense. In a representational sense, they are plastic toys and video-game characters comprising paint and dyes, plastic and hydrocarbons, circuitry and currents, stickers and glue, rubber, cloth, stuffing, speakers, and springs. All these parts falter among themselves, and falter beneath the other-from-other distinctions that may be made. The physical and imagined toy also falter and remind the child, in a playfully abject way, that he too is a faltering agencement of alters and objects.[12] The child is a falterity not only of the metaphors he shapes and is shaped by, of his socioeconomic development, but of chromosomes, flesh, and physical laws.[13] The falterity we felt in Buzz was beneath determinations of his self, and the falterity we felt in Woody and King Candy was beneath determinations of self apart from others. Now, we turn to the falterity of deciding between others, which we will observe in Sid's Toys and Vanellope. We will sense how falterity asks us to love, and what kind of love may emerge.

In *Toy Story*, Sid brings Woody and Buzz to his house, and they watch him replace a Janie doll's head with a pterodactyl's before they are locked in a room with his macabre toy creations: "a one-eyed doll head atop a spider-like body made of erector set pieces, [...] a toy fishing pole with fashion doll legs, a skateboard with a combat soldier's torso screwed to the front end, a jack-in-the-box with a rubber hand for a head," "a duck head Pez dispenser with baby doll torso and plunger base," "a Hotwheels car with baby arms, [and] a tin wind-up frog with monster truck wheels instead of legs" (Stanton 72–76, 112–13).

Woody and Buzz reason that these mutants are cannibals and flee. But Sid's toys, mismatched and broken falterities, are vulnerable and able to care more than anyone else in the film. They drag the Janie doll and the pterodactyl beneath the bed not to eat them, but to tape their heads "back on the correct bodies" (76). After Buzz's fall from the stairs, they reattach his arm (100). Skittish, they seem to *know* little, and they are mute, which emblematizes their ability to *listen*, which is not to hear and understand sense, but to strain to care, to allow another to be as indeterminacy beyond meaning.[14] It requires a tuned and attuned ear, a care that goes beyond simply caring-for, and recognizes that it too is cared-for. To listen is to be open, child-like, to be broken for the cares of others—a glance will not do, an observation will fail (Nancy *Listening* 39–42).

Shattered, Sid's toys are whole. This is integrity, the nonsublimation of parts for wholes and vice versa.[15] It cares little for recuperability not because it transcends recuperability, but because it accepts what it cannot control and does not think about what it cannot change at all—it is beyond infinity because it is beneath infinity. It is acceptance of falterity, neither nihilistic resignation nor agential agitation for one binary opposite. The toys and Woody, however, do impart a message to Sid as they rescue Buzz: "From now on, you must take good care of your toys" (Stanton 110–20). The child comes to feel through play; through his toys and avatars, he experiences breakdowns and glitches, and he loves, for "it is the Rust we value, not the Gold" (Pope 36).

We also witness this nonsublimation in *Wreck-It Ralph*. Vanellope is whole in her brokenness. Like Sid's toys, she, once princess of *Sugar Rush*, has been transformed by forces beyond her control. She is bullied, ostracized, and unstable. She wants to race, but King Candy prevents her (Lee 39, 52–53). He explains that if she races and glitches, the game will be out of order and removed from the arcade, and that while the other citizens of *Sugar Rush* may escape, Vanellope will die because glitches cannot leave their games. But the real reason King Candy prohibits Vanellope from racing is "because if she crosses the finish line, the game will reset and she won't be a glitch anymore" (83–85, 92–93).

During the final race, Vanellope controls her glitch and uses it to her advantage. She is no longer the object of glitching, nor is she quite a subject who glitches, but she has felt the falterity that antedates both (101–03). She, like Sid's toys, is a careful listener, and she uses her glitch to save Ralph. She crosses the finish line, resets the landscape, restores her code, and transforms into "the Rightful Ruler of *Sugar Rush*." However, she "concentrates and glitches right out of the dress and crown" and says that she is not a princess or a glitch, but "a racer with the greatest superpower ever" (106–10), a falterity that precedes weakness and strength, glitchiness and princessdom. As Ralph watches the Moppet Girl play *Sugar Rush* and glitch Vanellope through two karts to the finish line, he concludes that the players love her, "glitch and all" (114).

This is the child's love for the toy, the so-called self's love for the so-called other, which cares for falterity. Imagine a child who would only play with a perfect, clean doll, or on a mistake-free game. This child does not exist or would soon not exist. The toys of children are otherwise-than-heroically dirtied and worn; this wear arises from their being loved and calls for that love.

In *Wreck-It Ralph*, it is not only Vanellope whose falterity is to infinity and beyond, but the mismatched and incomplete objects around her. First, the kart that she and Ralph make in the Kart Bakery mini-game is a jumble of ingredients and garbage. On the door at the end of the mini-game is "a beautiful image of a perfect cart. The garage door opens, revealing their abomination beneath it" (65). The perfect projection and perception of the whole belies real, faltering parts; the distinct self belies indeterminate others.[16] Knowing they have not found the perfect, lovable object, Ralph begins to apologize, but Vanellope, feeling that they can make the object they have lovable, kisses and hugs the kart, "I love it. I LOVE IT! I LOVE IT!" (61–66). Second, Vanellope's home is "some sort of unfinished bonus level" in a volcano. As she learns to drive, we see the unfinished track spiraling up and crossing the diet cola lava on a broken bridge made of pink sugar wafers. The level may be incomplete, and Vanellope's lean-to may be made of discarded candies and wrappers, but it is her home, its track her training course (70–76).

Sid's toys and Vanellope love and are loved not because of their incompleteness or despite it, but through embracing it, for "the only things that can be valued or treasured are things that are mortal, finite, transient, and temporal, their very impermanence being the condition under which we hold them dear" (Caputo, *Insistence* 227). They are not infinite or flying, but to infinity and beyond, falling with style. Their mismatched parts stick out and their codes flicker through, but so do the alters we are.[17]

Levinas approximated our pseudo-Schrödingerian position when he noted that "subjectivity is structured as the other in the same," that it "is the restlessness of the same disturbed by the other."[18] But he neglected that this restlessness *precedes* distinctions of same and other, that *tehom* is not quite *nihil*,[19] that if subjectivity is intersubjectivity, it is interobjectivity, too. Levinas's same disturbed by the other is really others disturbed by others—alters. The same is alienated because it was never really the same to begin with, but something else entirely, something like Sid's toys and Vanellope.

Now, it is neither essence nor existence that must come first, but an alteration of Levinas's phenomenological ethics, which he considered a first philosophy. What comes first is the cat in the chamber, falterity, and therefore not a reasoned ethical law, but a proto-phenomenology of sorts,[20] which consists in listening to imperatives of those things around and within us, in imagination, in attunement and attention.

The child at play does not seek to know facts about her world, but intuits its fictiveness. She does not seek to find the perfect toy, but feels the toy she has is nonsublime in its own way, a falterity. If she knows, thinks, and decides, she also listens, feels, and cares. Her need is not to reason whether Buzz is a toy or a Space Ranger, whether Woody is the favorite or the reject, whether King Candy is still the greatest racer in the arcade, whether Sid's toys are broken or whole, or whether Vanellope is a glitch or a princess. Her need is not "to be able to love a person despite his weaknesses and defects and imperfections [...], but rather this, to be able to find him lovable despite *and with* his weaknesses and defects and imperfections" (Kierkegaard, *Works* 158, emphasis mine). Her need is not of laws, rules, or truths, but of their faltering, in the idea of the body and the grimy fact of the flesh, in hi-def perfection and grainy eight-bit. Her love is not a love that needs certainty, but a love that feels the needs, cracks, errors, and indeterminacy of alters—and embraces them.[21] As Levinas says, "a being without needs would not be happier than a needy being, but outside of happiness and unhappiness" (*Totality* 146).

Every time Buzz leaps, he shouts "To Infinity and Beyond." Not quite like Kierkegaard's knight who leaps past uncertainty to absurd certainty, Buzz leaps past sublimations and falls with style toward (un)certainty. Love—of the child, the love of Sid's toys and Vanellope—"does not sublimate itself, even when it is 'sublime'" (Nancy, *Shattered* 254). By listening to falterity, love is beyond sublimity—to infinity and beyond, beyond *beneath*—and it does not sublimate itself. It does not seek to become perfect, to affirm some binary, to be socially acceptable, to be refined or quintessential. If a chemical or geological sublimation is an extraction of purities, then this love leaves "pure" and "impure" alone and tries to understand otherwise, in brokenness.

And That's Not Bad: Free Play and Wreck-It Ralph

Falterity is the indeterminate agencement that Buzz and Woody are, that we are. It is the neither-nors, the otherwise; we need to attend to it by loving nonsublimely. We can learn all this from the child at play. In fact (and in fiction), this may be the only place to learn it.[22] And it is difficult to discern fact and fiction, even for adults, who are unable to define or distinguish between instances of Activity play, which is literal, locomotive play, and instances of Pretend play, which is non-literal, imaginative play (Turnbull). In her famous study, "Social Play Among Preschool Children," Mildred Parten noted that play is inherently social, even when it is solitary. Her contemporary, Lev Vygotsky, argued against the Piagetian paradigm of fixed developmental stages and instead elaborated a social theory that identified the influences of others as determinative of a child's development (Alves). The child is almost always immersed in such falterity, in neither the pretend nor the literal, but in both and more—in alters of all kinds. And so, with Wreck-It Ralph, we must uncertainly question the free play of the interstices of life and love.

Free play is the falterity of free will and determinism, illustrated by the comedic conflict between Woody's pullstring and voice. When he and Buzz first try to escape Sid, his pullstring "gets caught on one of the curls of the wrought iron railing" and makes his voicebox shout its catchphrases despite his attempts to stifle it (Stanton 83). We may say that Woody is determined by forces, by others beyond his control. However, during Buzz's rescue, Woody uses his pullstring's catchphrases to get Sid's attention. Then he uses his pullstring's voicebox to say phrases other than those in his programming, which causes Sid to nervously check the pullstring until Woody speaks in his "regular voice" and terrifies Sid—"so play *nice*" (117-19). Woody is neither his pullstring nor his voice, but that which preexists these distinctions: the free play of an animated pullstring, a live toy. Free play always comes with strings attached: strings of care and feeling. It is the idea that we are humble bricolages of forces, and that since we cannot always decide which is which, we had better play nice.

Both pullstring and voice, free will and free choice, emerge from the falterity that is free play. This play is not compatibilism, but presupposes it, too. This play is a falterity explored through the entanglement of will and law, of post- and -structuralism. *Free will* is the ability to act regardless of everything; *free choice* is being forced to act because of everything.[23] *Free play* is not quite both: it is determining things and being determined by things. To the child psychologists, free play is internally motivated, unstructured, and chosen play-time. There are no rules—other than social development, audience credulity, and the laws of physics—that constrain the child. Andy is free to pretend Woody is real, and Woody is free to pretend not to be.

In the Derridean sense, *play* preexists binaries and structure, like falterity. But it does so because Jacques Derrida has oversimplified linguistics, splitting the Saussurean sign into sign and referent, signifier and signified, and suggesting these parts are interchangeable.[24] This split focuses on the parts, and precludes the Peircean sign, or the center. Derrida is thus left with play: the infinite substitution of false centers because of the "absence of a center" (363). Claiming there is no center *at all* is like claiming there is *no cat* in Schrödinger's chamber. It is not true that there are no origins, but rather that origins may be so old and chaotic that we may not know them. Not knowing and not being able to know are all the more reason for feeling.

Deconstruction assumes that if metaphysics is broken, it ought not exist. But falterity would have us perceive that metaphysics, thus deconstructed, can be reconstructed lovingly via physics, through 'pataphysics.[25] Deconstruction does not oppose reconstruction, as we've been led to believe, but the two are contingent on each other and on some kind of (non)struction. We listen in the gaps of determinism, structure, and signs and find that free will is missing. We feel the paradoxes and inconsistencies of free will and find that determinism is missing.

These definitions of free play—Parten, Vygotsky, Derrida—accrete if we splice Luis de Molina's theory of middle knowledge with 'pataphysics. Secularizing this medieval Christian theology, *'pataphysical molinism* reconciles free will and determinism by proposing that *circumstances* determine actions, but that circumstances are determined and may or may not exist.[26] Wreck-It Ralph would choose to smash the Niceland windows during game mode, and would choose not to smash the windows outside game mode, and whether or not he is in game mode is up in the air. It is clear that a $^{sub}_{ob}$ject does not have free will with no strings attached, nor does it have strings attached to nothing. There may, however, be strings attached to more strings, like Woody's knit body and his pullstring, like string theory's universe.

$^{Sub}_{Ob}$jects are agencements attuning within circumstantial determinations, creating determinative circumstances themselves. If this free play becomes ineffably complex, as it may, it is like Derrida's center—not "nonexistent," but simply not explicable. We feel that it is impossible to decide whether an agencement acted because it was determined that it would act that way, or because it chose to act that way. More importantly, we see that the distinction between these is moot. There is no sense in either the claim that "everything made it so that I could not act differently" or in the claim that "my act was independent of everything."

In *Wreck-It Ralph*, videogame avatars are "the cold-blooded (or maybe code-blooded) inhabitants of rigidly deterministic worlds" (Scott). Every avatar is determined by his game, and simultaneously every avatar determines his game—*this* is free play. Ralph is the bad guy, he wrecks things, he lives in the dump. Felix fixes what Ralph wrecks, and since "fixing is the name of the game," Felix gets all the glory. Felix is the so-called hero; Ralph is the villain (Lee 1).

On the thirtieth anniversary of his game, Ralph visits BadAnon, where a group of bad guys meet under the banner "One Game at a Time." There, Zombie explains that "labels not make you happy—good, bad.... You must love you." Clyde, a Pac-Man ghost, warns Ralph not to "mess with the program," and that "we can't change who we are, and the sooner you accept that the better off your game and your life will be." They close with the Bad Guy Affirmation: "I'm bad. And that's good. I will never be good. And that's not bad. There's no one I'd rather be than me" (5–8). Though the bad guys stress determinism, this affirmation explores the indeterminacy of free play, the entanglement of will and law.

Ralph struggles with his identity, ultimately coming to feel that he is not fixed wholly by his game and its laws, nor by others' perceptions of him, nor by his own self-perceptions, but by all these and more. When he returns from BadAnon, he crashes the Nicelanders' anniversary party, which excludes him even though he is one of the game's main characters. He leaves in a fury, vowing to win a medal like Fix-It Felix, so that he may be other than "just the bad guy who wrecks the building" (11–19). He knows he is more than a villain, than Zombie's "bad," and the film reveals his pseudo-dialectical journey from being a circumstantial villain, to being a superficial hero, to realizing that he is neither and so can be both and more.

When Litwak's Arcade reopens in the morning, the Moppet Girl starts to play *Fix-It Felix, Jr.* "The intro music plays. Nicelanders take to their positions. But Ralph does not. A quote bubble pops up [above a Ralph-shaped space], reading: 'I'm gonna wreck it!'" (28). What should fill that space can be determined from everything already there: Ralph in the game, Ralph the villain. But Ralph himself, the real Ralph gone Turbo to win a medal, cannot be determined from what remains. All that can be determined is what he would likely be in that circumstance. Determinism and free will are contingent on each other and on circumstance. René Daumal's proportionality—to know x = to know (Everything—x)—must be molinistically rephrased: to know x = to know (Circumstance—x). From the absence of Ralph at one moment, we cannot determine Ralph at all moments, but only in that one, almost.[27] All the Moppet Girl and Litwak can decide is that "the game's busted," and all the Nicelanders can do is "stick with the program." And so Litwak hangs an "OUT OF ORDER" sign on the screen (28–29).

By leaving his game, Ralph has abandoned his role as simply a part of a whole, as an entry in a matrix, but he has realized multiple roles, a part-whole recursion. He is not only the empty space he left in Fix-It Felix; he is not only a villain. As a child is more than Mr. So-and-So's daughter, the avatar is more than their place in the game, the toy more than their spot on the pillow. Ralph journeys to *Hero's Duty*, "interfere[s] with the first person shooter," and instead of facing the cy-bugs again, journeys to the final level and takes the medal for himself. After acting against the program of his game and this one, he is ejected in an escape pod (27–33).

The pod launches through Game Central Station and crashes in *Sugar Rush*, where Ralph meets Vanellope. It is through their relationship that he begins to discover more about what he is. He learns that he is not determined by his code—at least, not entirely. Determinations and free will emerge from indeterminate play, and their effects are still real, though not as conclusive, certain, right, and mighty as they once appeared.[28]

Ralph moves from determined to determiner to indeterminate, a backward stumbling through molinist metaphysics to return to physics, to 'pataphysics that was there all along. Ralph says in his opening lines that he's "a wrecker" who wrecks professionally, but in the Kart Bakery, Vanellope cajoles him into creating a kart (10, 62–66). Here he realizes not his inner hero, but senses that the many determinations, wills, nodes, codes, and roles that he is are at play with one another. He is an agencement and so he attunes rather than acts agentially; the free play that facilitates this is, like nonsublimating love, "not a principle of unity but the un-principle which sees to it that unity is transient or impossible" (Caputo, *Against* 211).

As the cy-bug plague and King Candy destroy *Sugar Rush*, Ralph nearly destroys himself to create the light that eventually zaps all the bugs. As he plummets from King Candy's grasp toward Diet Cola Mountain, he recites the Bad Guy Affirmation to himself. Just as he is about to fall into the lava, Vanellope speeds across the broken bridge of the unfinished bonus level and catches him (Lee 106–07). The film cuts from a restored *Sugar Rush* to the Moppet Girl playing *Fix-It Felix, Jr.*, where Ralph happily wrecks the Niceland apartments (112). He has accepted his role in the game, intuiting the contingencies of himself and others, but he accepts this role otherwise than he had before—and freely playing, he creates new roles. He reveals a new bonus level in which homeless, out-of-order characters such as Q*bert help him wreck the apartments. He and Felix have made his dump into "East Niceland," full of homes for him and the others (113). Acceptance of his falterity leads Ralph to caring and to being cared for, to listening and being listened to. At the end of the game, when he is lifted up to be thrown off the roof by the Nicelanders, he "smiles and looks pretty darned content." From their shoulders, he can watch Vanellope racing in *Sugar Rush*, and he says, "Turns out, I don't need a medal to tell me I'm a good guy. 'Cause if that little kid likes me, how bad can I be?" (114).

Through Buzz Lightyear, we explicate indeterminacy, our inability to properly decide and truly know; through Woody and others, we complicate contingency, our $_{ex}^{in}$rinsic dependencies on others; through Vanellope and Sid's toys, we implicate the shattered agencements we are and the nonsublimation we need to listen to and care for them, rather than glance at and observe them; through Wreck-It Ralph, we play with these circumstances and eke a world from hard determinisms and quixotic wills. The toy shows us the falterities we are, and the child, how to respond to these falterities.

The child in his play, in her games, shows us who we are, and then shows us how to care for ourselves, which means showing us how to care for others and how to be cared for by others. We learn that philosophy need not stop at thinking, but move to feel, like Alcibiades listening to Socrates and vowing to change his life (Zwicky 285). We learn that we are broken and mismatched, between and among, despite and with and because of, contingent, vulnerable, and irreducibly indeterminate, not apart, agential, or autonomous. Falterity is of dreams, memories, experiences, thoughts, actions, and relations in every circumstance. The toy is otherwise than a hero, the child otherwise than a subject or object, and the world of alters to be lived in, cared for, and listened to.

Notes

1. A "pleaching" is an interlacing of dead and live branches, arbors, and shaped trees—"arbortecture." Our use of the gerund replaces traditional terms for groups of philosophers, such as "school" or "ponder." It alludes to the many philosophers entwined in this essay, to the idea that philosophy must accurately represent the world, and to the reality that philosophy often artificially shapes the world to conform to its ideas, a turn that this essay will play with and attempt to reverse. Aurally, it connotes "preaching" and "impeaching."
2. cf. Deleuze, *Thousand Plateaus* 4–6, 12, 36; *Anti-Oedipus* 3–25.
3. We witness the detriment of binaries in everyday life: human-animal, government-citizen, immigrant-resident, black-white, male-female, straight-queer, rich-poor, smart-stupid. Sometimes they help us act, but almost always, if uncritically assumed, they incite conflict and inflict hurt.
4. "An agencement replaces the traditional notion of agency as "intentional, rational, and premeditated." It is Deleuze's original French word, translated by Brian Massumi into "assemblage," which is an error according to Vinciane Despret. "Assemblage" suggests an abiotic fixedness, but agencement is "an active process of attunement that is never fixed once and for all," a "rapport of forces that makes some beings capable of making other beings capable, in a plurivocal manner," and incessant distribution and redistribution of constitutive entities (Despret 29, 38).
5. To recover indeterminacy in philosophy, to feel while we think, we propose replacing the Yale School's certain refrain of "always already" with the uncertain phrases "almost already" and "almost always."
6. "A cat is penned up in a steel chamber, along with the following diabolical device (which must be secured against direct interference by the cat): in a Geiger counter there is a tiny bit of radioactive substance, *so* small, that *perhaps* in the course of one hour one of the atoms decays, but also, with equal probability, perhaps none; if it happens, the counter tube discharges and through a relay releases a hammer which shatters a small flask of hydrocyanic acid. If one has left this entire system to itself for an hour, one would say that the cat still lives *if* meanwhile no atom has decayed. The first atomic decay would have poisoned it. The ψ-function of the entire system would express this by having in it the living and the dead cat (pardon the expression) mixed or smeared out in equal parts. [...] An indeterminacy [...] can then be *resolved* by direct observation. That prevents us from so naively accepting as valid a 'blurred model' for representing reality. In itself it would not embody anything unclear or contradictory. There is a difference between a shaky or out-of-focus photograph and a snapshot of clouds and fog banks" (Schrödinger 156–57). This analogy does not advocate complacency in regard to suffering, nor the prohibition of binaries, but feeling and thinking otherwise. All analogy is such imperfection, a sort of infelicitous felicity, a shaky snapshot of clouds.
7. "To live is a sort of transitive verb" (Levinas, *Totality* 111).
8. By "deciduous" we etymologically play with "decide," and allude to and illude with Deleuze's notion of Western thought as "arborescent," or predicated upon binary thinking, branching like a tree, a "fake multiplicity" (*Thousand Plateaus* 15–17). Deleuze errs, for a tree too is a multiplicity with many genomes, symbioses, and communities of insects, fungi, flowers, mosses, rodents, and birds.
9. Meillassoux and his fellow object-oriented ontologists, in attempting to understand things as they are, make the human error of splitting the world into subjects and objects, and damning the connection between the two as "correlationism" (Meillassoux 13; cf. Pettman). But correlationism need not be a relation that a subject adds to an object, which facilitates the subject's inevitably biased view of the object, but can be a possibility that predates the distinctions between subject and object entirely. "We *are* already this 'natural chiasm' [...]. We do not need to negotiate and enter into one" (Caputo, *Insistence* 176); and "the lack of some theory of correlation reduces thinking, perceiving, and the like to magic, in which objects simply drop from the sky" (198). It thereby negates the science it seeks to advocate, and reduces the world to uncomplicated parsimony. "Correlationism" is a straw man.

10. We use *contingency* because of its etymology and contemporaneity, but this idea has been around for millennia: the Tao (Lao Tzu), haecceity (Scotus), gestalt (Wertheimer), inscape (Hopkins), epiphany (Joyce), luminous detail (Pound), form of life, internal relations (Wittgenstein), blik (Hare), the undeconstructible (Derrida), holobiont (Margulis), and ineffability, resonance (Zwicky).

11. The film has been called the *Toy Story* "of Generation X arcade play" (Scott), with its throwbacks to Pac-Man, Centipede, and Donkey Kong analogous to *Toy Story*'s throwbacks to the classics of the Baby Boomers. *Wreck-It Ralph* is the story of a videogame villain, Ralph, who wrecks stuff so the hero, Felix, can fix it and win a medal. Ralph abandons his game in search of his own medal in other games; he wants to be a hero too. He ends up befriending a racing-game glitch, Vanellope, and realizing himself as he helps her realize herself.

12. We depend on photosynthesis for oxygen, on plants and animals for nourishment, on gut flora for digestion, on macrophages and antibodies that kill viruses and bacteria in our blood, and on bacteria in our mouths which neutralize plant toxins (Lingis, *Animal* 166). We are constituted by hundreds of endogenous retroviruses in our genomes (Ryan 220–31), by what were aerobic prokaryotes for our mitochondria (Sagan), by what were spirochetes for our nuclear membranes and cellular structures (Margulis, "Imperfections"), by what may have been archaebacteria for our peroxisomes (de Duve), and by gut bacteria that may independently pass genetic material to our offspring (Moon).

13. Microcosmically, biologists may study the individual as a multiplicity of symbioses—a holobiont with a holobiome (Margulis, "Endosymbiosis," Guerrero, "Symbiogenesis"). Macrocosmically, stars and planets evolve from the accretion of stardust, a process that may have created Earth. It is a sintering of innumerable alters, as are we (Johansen).

14. cf. Nancy, *Listening* 6–9, 31. Sid's Babyface toy taps out a quiet code on the bedframe to call the others to Woody's aid, but none speak (Stanton 110).

15. "No heart is as whole as a broken heart" (Nancy, *Shattered* 255). "There are no parts, moments, types, or stages of love. There is only an infinity of shatters: love is wholly complete in one sole embrace or in the history of a life" (266).

16. These broken toys defy philosophy's sublime "body." They are "malformed, disfigured, diseased, disabled, miscegenated, and transvestic" (Caputo, *Against* 195–96); they are flesh because they are beneath the "active, athletic, healthy, erect, white male body, sexually able and unambiguously gendered, well-born, well-bred, and well-buried, a *corpus sanum* cut to fit a *mens sana*" (194). "The flesh [...] is always being organized and lifted up into a body" (208).

17. We are archives of vestigial features: the appendix, tonsils, sinuses, tailbone, goosebumps, and ear-muscles. We are collections of design flaws, too: our genitals are reproductive and excretory; our birth canals are too narrow; our eyes have a blind spot; our pharynx is for eating and breathing, and therefore causes us to choke; our lower backs and knees cannot painlessly support bipedalism; our brains gravitate toward confirmation biases, availability biases, and the status quo. We are hosts of other life-forms, as mentioned above, but also hosts of other things: glasses to see; hearing aids to hear; crutches, wheelchairs, bikes, cars to move; drugs to heal, digest, escape, and think; prosthetic biomechanical devices, Lego hands, pacemakers, gauzy, 3D-printed heart valves to regain functions; cell-phones, which are now merely external, to communicate; computers to write and remember.

18. cf. Levinas, *Totality* 38–39, 194; *Otherwise* 25, 68–69.

19. Originary profundity (*tehom*) is not quite nothingness (*nihil*). cf. Keller 155–238.

20. A poetics of obligation. cf. Caputo, *Against*.

21. "The humans who appear in *Toy Story* are intentionally rendered to look artificial. In this movie, people are 'unreal'; all the vividness [...] is saved for the toys" (Berardinelli "Toy Story"). We are taught in *Toy Story* to empathize like a child with "mass-produced, inanimate playthings," and in *Wreck-It Ralph* with pixelated avatars (Scott). Another example of a child's nonsublime love: "This toy is, for Lenni, [a] *truck* [like] those 'real' trucks that drive down the 'real' highways—indeed, for him, it's probably more central than those are. Ironically, for Lenni, it's *real* trucks that are metaphorical" (Hofstadter, *Surfaces* 43).

22. We say "fact and fiction" to note that the two are cognate; following Bachelard, *un fait est fait*, a fact is forged, a fact is a fiction (Caputo, *Against* 204).

23. From this determinism comes Daumal's proportionality, a sort of 'pataphysical negative theology: "to know x = to know (Everything—x)" (Daumal 7-9).
24. cf. Tallis.
25. "What we philosophers used to call 'metaphysics' is fast giving way to the macrophysics of the imaginably large scope of the universe (if there is but one) and the microphysics of the unimaginably small. What we used to call 'metaphysics' in philosophy, theories of being as such in terms of the forms, substance, essence and existence, monads, Spirit, and so on, amounts to highly imaginative and impressionistic accounts—and hence a kind of 'poetics'—of the main features of the medium-sized things we meet up with in ordinary experience" (Caputo, *Insistence* 192). 'Pataphysics is the science of exceptions, of imaginary solutions. cf. Jarry.
26. Essentially, Molina claimed that God knows what would happen in every possible circumstance, but not which circumstance will occur—this latter is a result of human free will. cf. MacGregor.
27. Daumal overreaches: "From the complete knowledge of Mr. So-and-So, one could deduce the knowledge of the rest of the universe by virtue of the principles of causality [...]. Similarly, remove in thought So-and-So from the world without changing anything else: you still imagine him right where he was, because from the knowledge of the universe minus So-and-So it is possible to deduce knowledge of So-and-So" (7-8). *Contextualized universe* becomes *circumstance*.
28. In the Station, we learn of one such determination, announced by a hologram of Sonic the Hedgehog: "If you die outside your own game . . . you don't regenerate. Ever. Game Over" (Lee 10).

Works Cited

Alves, Pedro Ferreira. "Vygotsky and Piaget: Scientific Concepts." *Psychology in Russia: State of the Art* 7.3 (2014): 24–34. Web. 24 Sept. 2015.
Bardini, Thierry. *Junkware*. Minneapolis: Minnesota University Press, 2011. Print.
Berardinelli, James. "Toy Story." *Reelviews*. 1995. Web. 2 Apr. 2015.
———. "Wreck-It Ralph." *Reelviews*. 31 Oct. 2012. Web. 2 Apr. 2015.
Bök, Christian. *'Pataphysics: The Poetics of an Imaginary Science*. Evanston: Northwestern University Press, 2002. Print.
Caputo, John D. *Against Ethics: Contributions to a Poetics of Obligation with Constant Reference to Deconstruction*. Bloomington: Indiana University Press, 1993. Print.
———. *The Insistence of God: A Theology of Perhaps*. Bloomington: Indiana University Press, 2013. Print.
Chapman, Michael J., Michael F. Dolan, and Lynn Margulis. "Centrioles and Kinetosomes: Form, Function, and Evolution." *The Quarterly Review of Biology* 75.4 (Dec. 2000): 409–29. Web. 24 Sept. 2015.
Daumal, René. *Pataphysical Essays*. Trans. Thomas Vosteen. Cambridge: Wakefield, 2012. Print.
de Duve, Christian. "The Origin of Eukaryotes: A Reappraisal." *Nature Reviews Genetics* 8 (2007): 395–403. Web. 24 Sept. 2015.
Deleuze, Gilles, and Felix Guattari. *A Thousand Plateaus: Capitalism and Schizophrenia*. Trans. Brian Massumi. Minneapolis: Minnesota University Press, 1983 [1972]. Print.
———. *Anti-Oedipus: Capitalism and Schizophrenia*. Trans. Robert Hurley, Mark Seem, and Helen R. Lane. Minneapolis: Minnesota University Press, 1987 [1980]. Print.
Derrida, Jacques. "Structure, Sign and Play in the Discourse of the Human Sciences." *Writing and Difference*. Trans. Alan Bass. New York: Routledge, 1978 [1967]. Print.
Despret, Vinciane. "From Secret Agents to Interagency." *History and Theory* 52 (Dec. 2013): 29–44. Web. 1 Apr. 2014.
Douglas, Angela E. *Symbiotic Interactions*. New York: Oxford University Press, 1994. Print.
Ebert, Roger. "Toy Story." RogerEbert.com. 22 Nov. 1995. Web. 2 Apr 2015.
———. "Wreck-It Ralph." RogerEbert.com. 31 Oct. 2012. Web. 2 Apr 2015.

ENCODE Project Consortium. "An Integrated Encyclopedia of DNA Elements in the Human Genome." *Nature* 489.7414 (Sept. 2012): 57–74. Web. 24 Sept. 2015.

Fleer, Marilyn. "Kindergartens in Cognitive Times: Imagination as a Dialectical Relation Between Play and Learning." *International Journal of Early Childhood* 43.3 (Nov. 2011): 245–59. Web. 24 Sept. 2015.

Guerrero, Ricardo et al. "Predatory Prokaryotes: Predation and Primary Consumption Evolved in Bacteria." *PNAS* 83.7 (Apr. 1986): 2138–42. Web. 24 Sept. 2015.

———. "Symbiogenesis: The Holobiont as a Unit of Evolution." *International Microbiology* 16 (2013): 133–43. Web. 24 Sept. 2015.

Hofstadter, Douglas, and Emmanuel Sander. *Gödel, Escher, Bach: an Eternal Golden Braid*. New York: Basic, 1999 [1979]. Print.

———. *I Am a Strange Loop*. New York: Basic, 2007. Print.

———. *Surfaces and Essences: Analogy as the Fuel and Fire of Thinking*. New York: Basic, 2013. Print.

Hugill, Andrew. *Pataphysics: A Useless Guide*. Cambridge: MIT, 2012. Print.

Jarry, Alfred. *Exploits & Opinions of Doctor Faustroll, Pataphysician: A Neo-scientific Novel*. Trans. Simon Watson Taylor. Boston: Exact Change, 1996 [1898]. Print.

Johansen, Anders, Mordecai-Mark Mac Low, Pedro Lacerda, and Martin Bizzarro. "Growth of Asteroids, Planetary Embryos, and Kuiper Belt Objects by Chondrule Accretion." *Science Advances* 1.3 (2015): 1–11. Web. 24 Sept. 2015.

Keller, Catherine. *Face of the Deep: A Theology of Becoming*. New York: Routledge, 2003. Print.

Kierkegaard, Søren. *Fear and Trembling*. Ed. and trans. Howard V. Hong and Edna H. Hong. Princeton: Princeton University Press, 1983 [1843]. Print.

———. *Works of Love*. Ed. and trans. Howard V. Hong and Edna H. Hong. Princeton: Princeton University Press, 1995 [1847]. Print.

King, Christine E., et al. "The Feasibility of a Brain-Computer Interface Functional Electrical Stimulation System for the Restoration of Overground Walking After Paraplegia." *Journal of NeuroEngineering and Rehabilitation* 12.80 (2015). Web. 24 Sept. 2015.

Lazcano, A., R. Guerrero, L. Margulis, and J. Oró. "The Evolutionary Transition from RNA to DNA in Early Cells." *Journal of Molecular Evolution* 27 (1988): 283–90. Web. 24 Sept. 2015.

Levinas, Emmanuel. *Otherwise than Being: or Beyond Essence*. Trans. Alphonso Lingis. Pittsburgh: Duquesne University Press, 1998 [1974]. Print.

———. *Totality and Infinity: An Essay on Exteriority*. Trans. Alphonso Lingis. Pittsburgh: Duquesne University Press, 1969 [1961]. Print.

Lingis, Alphonso. "Animal Body, Inhuman Face." *Zoontologies: The Question of the Animal*. Ed. Cary Wolfe. Minneapolis: Minnesota University Press, 2003. 165–82. Print.

———. *The Imperative*. Indianapolis: Indiana University Press, 1998. Print.

———. *Trust*. Minneapolis: Minnesota University Press, 2004. Print.

MacGregor, Kirk. *Luis de Molina: The Life and Theology of the Founder of Middle Knowledge*. Grand Rapids: Zondervan, 2015. Print.

Margulis, Lynn, and Michael J. Chapman. "The *Arthromitus* Stage of *Bacillus cereus*: Intestinal Symbionts of Animals." *PNAS* 95.3 (Feb. 1998): 1236–41. Web. 24 Sept. 2015.

———. "The Chimeric Eukaryote: Origin of the Nucleus from the Karyomastigont in Amitochondriate Protists." *PNAS* 97.13 (June 2000): 6954–59. Web. 24 Sept. 2015.

———. "Endosymbiosis: Cyclical and Permanent in Evolution." *Trends in Microbiology* 6.9 (Sept. 1998): 342–45. Web. 24 Sept. 2015.

———. "'Imperfections and Oddities' in the Origin of the Nucleus." *Paleobiology* 31.2 (2005): 175–91. Web. 24 Sept. 2015.

———. "Semes for Analysis of Evolution: de Duve's Peroxisomes and Meyer's Hydrogenases in the Sulphurous Proterozoic Eon." *Nature Reviews Genetics* 8 (Nov. 2007). Web. 24 Sept. 2015.

Meillassoux, Quentin. *After Finitude: An Essay on the Necessity of Contingency*. Trans. Ray Brassier. New York: Bloomsbury, 2008. Print.

Moon, Clara et al. "Vertically Transmitted Faecal IgA Levels Determine Extra-Chromosomal Phenotypic Variation." *Nature* 521.7550 (May 2015): 90–106. Web. 24 Sept. 2015.

Nancy, Jean-Luc. *On Listening*. Trans. Charlotte Mandell. New York: Fordham University Press, 2007. Web. 20 Dec. 2013.
_____. "Shattered Love." *A Finite Thinking*. Ed. Simon Sparks. Stanford: Stanford University Press, 2003. 245-74. Print.
O'Connor, Timothy. *Theism and Ultimate Explanation: The Necessary Shape of Contingency*. Malden: Blackwell, 2008. Print.
Parfit, Derek. *Reasons and Persons*. Oxford: Clarendon, 1984. Print.
Parten, Mildred B. "Social Play Among Preschool Children." *Institute of Child Welfare*, 1933. 136-47. Web. 24 Sept. 2015.
Pettman, Dominic. *Human Error: Species-Being and Media Machines*. Minneapolis: Minnesota University Press, 2011. Print.
Pope, Alexander. "The First Epistle of the Second Book of Horace." *Complete Poetical Works*. Ed. Henry Walcott Boynton. New York: Houghton, Mifflin, 1903 [1737]. Web. 21 Sept. 2015.
Ryan, Frank. *Darwin's Blind Spot: Evolution Beyond Natural Selection*. New York: Houghton Mifflin, 2002. Print.
Sagan, Lynn. "On the Origin of Mitosing Cells." *Journal of Theoretical Biology* 14 (1967): 225-74. Web. 24 Sept. 2015.
Schrödinger, Erwin. "The Present Situation in Quantum Mechanics." *Quantum Theory and Measurement*. Ed. J. A. Wheeler and W. H. Zurek. Princeton: Princeton University Press, 2006 [1935]. 152-67. Print.
Scott, A. O. "Bad-Guy Avatar Seeks Midlife Career Change: 'Wreck-It Ralph,' with John C. Reilly and Sarah Silverman." *New York Times*. 1 Nov. 2012. Web. 2 Apr. 2015.
Tallis, Raymond. *Theorrhoea and After*. London: Macmillan, 1999. Print.
Toy Story. Screenplay by Andrew Stanton, Joss Whedon, Joel Cohen, and Alec Sokolow. Disney-Pixar, 1995. Web. 7 Apr. 2015.
Toy Story. John Lasseter. Disney-Pixar, 1995. Film.
Turnbull, J., and V. B. Jenvey. "Criteria Used by Adults and Children to Categorize Subtypes of Play." *Early Child Development and Care* 176.5 (July 2004): 539-51. Web. 24 Sept. 2015.
Willingham, Aarron T., and Thomas R. Gingeras. "TUF Love for 'Junk' DNA." *Cell* 125.7 (June 2006): 1215-20. Web. 24 Sept. 2015.
Wreck-It Ralph. Rich Moore. Disney, 2012. Film.
Wreck-It Ralph. Screenplay by Jennifer Lee and Phil Johnston. Disney, 2012. Web. 7 Apr. 2015.
Zwicky, Jan. *Alkibiades' Love: Essays in Philosophy*. Kingston: McGill-Queen's, 2015.

"You made the journey, the Long Journey!"
Performances of Race, Nation and Toyhood in Paddle-to-the-Sea

THADDEUS ANDRACKI

In Holling Clancy Holling's 1942 Caldecott Honor picture book *Paddle-to-the-Sea*, readers are introduced to Paddle, the toy hero of the story, soon after his creation. Paddle is an "Indian" man sitting in a canoe, carved from wood by a young First Nations boy.[1] Neither Paddle nor the "Indian" boy—as he is called—have nations that are actually determined in the text, although they would presumably be of one of the Ojibwe First Nations, based on the story's origin in the Lake Nipigon region of northern Ontario. The book describes Paddle's harrowing journey from Nipigon, through the Great Lakes and the St. Lawrence River, to the Atlantic Ocean, meeting along the way sawmills, fishermen, a shipwreck, a forest fire, factories, Niagara Falls, and finally, the sea.

Though *Paddle-to-the-Sea* is often considered creative nonfiction, a text whose primary intent is teaching children about the physical and human geography of the Great Lakes through an interesting and engaging story, this chapter will instead suggest that, by reading this text with a focus on Paddle's toyhood, readers may find instead information about power and repression. By paying attention to the narrative of Paddle as a heroic toy, audiences are offered insight into particular performances of race and nation in the United States during the World War II era.

First/Native Nations responses to *Paddle-to-the-Sea* have varied. Debbie Reese, a Nambé Pueblo scholar of American Indian imagery in children's literature, has noted that the boy who carves Paddle is given neither a tribal/First Nation identification nor a name, as well as the fact that Paddle is called by the slur "Injun." She questions in particular what an educator reading this

"You made the journey, the Long Journey!" (Andracki) 115

book to young people would do with this term (Reese, "Thoughts"). Others, under consultation with elders and Native community members, have incorporated *Paddle-to-the-Sea* into culture-based arts education curricula for First/Native Nations young people—particularly Ojibwe in Minnesota—using critical pedagogy to interrogate the use of "Injun" in the text (Bequette and Hrenko 103-4). The author, as a White settler himself, does not intend to act as a definitive arbiter of the book's First/Native Nations content and its "authenticity," stereotype, or offensiveness, but will use this chapter to trace the circuits of White settler colonialism in which Paddle finds himself and the showcase ways that those circuits deny him "real" toyhood.[2] By following these traces, one can see that Paddle reveals a great deal about the ways that racialization and colonization of First/Native Nations people played out in the context of the midcentury United States.

The boy who creates Paddle promises that Paddle's journey will make him "real": "The time has come for you to sit on this snowbank and wait for the Sun Spirit to set you free. Then you will be a real Paddle Person, a real Paddle-to-the-Sea" (Holling 4). Indeed, Barbara Bader, in her landmark, comprehensive study of the American picturebook has this to say: "Paddle-to-the-Sea is one of those inanimate figures, that, like the Steadfast Tin Soldier, quickly take on life; the words 'Please put me back in the water' are carved on his bottom, and you find yourself hoping for him—hoping ... that somehow he'll survive fire and ice and Niagara Falls" (Bader 411). Paddle does indeed take on a bit of "real life" throughout his story. Repeatedly, Paddle's actions are described using terms that most people would likely consider agential. He "is never alone"; he "sees no land" and "plays his old game of loop-the-loop"; he "explores" and "travels"; he "misses the paper excitement [a newspaper story about his journey] for some real excitement of his own" (Holling 22, 26, 36, 40). In every step along his expedition, Paddle seems to have a sort of liveliness.

Yet in spite of his creator's claim that reaching the ocean will make him "real"—and in spite of his heroic success in that quest—Paddle's narrative framing never quite grants him true sentience, animation, or "realness." This chapter will read Paddle as a toy and object of material culture and, drawing from a promiscuous archive of Indigenous studies, posthumanist thought, and children's literature scholarship to argue that *Paddle-to-the-Sea* gives us a way of seeing what kinds of toys are "allowed" to become real under conditions of White settler colonialism and the ways in which "realness" is denied to the colonized. It focuses on the primacy of the question of what it means to be "real," because, as Lois Kuznets has argued, it is a fundamental thematic motif of toy narratives—particularly toy quests, like Paddle's (Kuznets 2). Any examination of Paddle contextualized within the history of children's literature must grapple with these anxieties.

And yet, Paddle is still a toy, just a "thing." In order to understand Paddle's toyhood, this chapter takes up Robin Bernstein's concept of a *scriptive thing*, which she defines as "an item of material culture that prompts meaningful bodily behaviors" (Bernstein 71). Toys, as many other cultural artifacts, consist not only of their material form, but also a dense network of social and cultural scripts that invite those with whom they come into contact to perform in certain, historically constructed ways. For example, Bernstein explains how soft, cotton dolls—both Black and White—came to be precisely to "accommodate" cuddling interposed with violence, violence that was more particularly scripted toward Black dolls (118). This essay reads Paddle as a scriptive thing whose portrayal within his story invites those who come into contact with him along the way to perform in ways that secure White settler colonialism. This essay asks: What scripts does Paddle have? What gestures does he incite? And how do those scripts, gestures, and performances shape the ways in which race, nation, and colonization are understood?

Situating Paddle *in Time and Place*

To understand the scripts that Paddle hands to those with whom he comes into contact, he and his book must be situated within their particular time and place. Holling wrote *Paddle-to-the-Sea* at a time just before the advent of World War II, in a nation reckoning with the looming threat of international conflict on the horizon, as well as with the "modernization" of everyday life. Nathalie op de Beeck characterizes picture books of the time period between the World Wars—of which *Paddle-to-the-Sea* is an optimal example—as spinning a "fairy tale of modernity." In these fairy tales, the citizen-subject for whom the book was intended, the (White, settler) American child, is given a script for "time-sensitive concepts of class, race, ethnicity, gender, childhood, and nation—unstable categories that essentialist picture-book caricatures and definitions very often seek to stabilize" (op de Beeck, xiv). These picture books, though imperfectly (performers don't always stick to the script), intend to indoctrinate children into what it means to be "modern."

Gary D. Schmidt, similarly, views children's literature of this time period as a project of "making Americans"—that children's literature of the time leading up to and immediately following World War II was deeply invested in shifting away from a European children's literary tradition and focusing on defining what being a child in "modern" America meant—or at least what the "ideal" child in "modern" America would look like (Schmidt xxvii). According to Schmidt, this "modern" America is centered on building a "democracy that enabled unique cultures to survive and thrive even as they lived side by side," a democracy of inclusion (83). Questions about America, as a cohesive, geographic unit with a particular set of social values, came to be central to the project of children's publishing, particularly as much children's literature prior to the midcentury had arrived from Britain or other parts of Europe. These questions led to books focused on American landscapes and creating a liberal, multicultural democracy.

Part of this project of making Americans in children's literature was a tendency toward regionalism. *Paddle-to-the-Sea* is a book that is distinctly Upper Midwestern in nature. After crossing the national border from Canada into the United States, a process that takes a third of the book, much of the focus of Paddle's journey is on Lake Superior (another six chapters take place on the U.S. side of the Lake) and the waters surrounding Minnesota, Wisconsin, and Michigan. By the time Paddle reaches Lake Erie and Ohio, the book is two-thirds of the way to completion, and the other landmarks of the book are told through what amounts to a laundry list: Toledo, Sandusky, Cleveland, Erie. The book clearly focuses on the geography and the culture of the Upper Midwest. And yet, it is also, in some ways, a Canadian story. Upon going over the Niagara Falls, Paddle crosses back into Canada and ends up reaching the sea near Newfoundland and returns home to Nipigon. Priscilla Ord and Carole Henderson Carpenter have noted the particularly Canadian nature of the book in their 1977 overview of Canadian children's literature—in which they also note the tendency for children's literature about and produced in Canada toward "realistic topics such as the natural or cultural milieux ... and accounts of the settlement and development of the country" (Ord and Carpenter 4). *Paddle-to-the-Sea* is a book that is preoccupied with the realism of the Upper Midwest and Canada. Furthermore, Paddle is a liminal toy, existing between two places (places whose geography is in fact the product of settler colonialism) and often crossing borders.

Paddle is also a sort of "Indian doll," and to understand what scripts he might hand to those he meets on his journey, it is useful to understand the kinds of toy First/Native Nations people who might have existed at the time. In her explication of the history of racialized dolls in the United States, Robin Berstein astutely observes that First/Native Nations dolls—and other non–Black people of color dolls—were conspicuously absent from catalogs and toy stores in the early twentieth century. Dollmakers during this time period cultivated communities in which Black and White dolls were expected to persist, fulfilling racial expectations of "enduring mammies," but First/Native Nations dolls ceased to exist in these "doll-lands," clearing the imagination of "vanishing Indians" for proper colonization (Bernstein 156). Instead, children were more likely to encounter "toy Indians" in hard, miniaturized, warring figurines—toy soldiers used for what H.G. Wells famously called "floor games." As Bernstein notes, "these games enacted stories of empire, of civilization and savagery, of war and death, and of the wonderland of the American frontier. In white children's play, hard Indian dolls battled and died on the frontier wonderland of the nursery floor" (157). Lois Kuznets explains, through examination of incidences of toy soldiers and other miniature manipulatives in children's literature that figures such as Paddle inspire feelings of both vulnerability, in empathy with their plight, and liveliness, in the sense that "they have an elusive life of their own" (Kuznets 80). Paddle, in his intended readers' imaginations, likely is found at a nexus of the disappearance of his people, violent play, and the independent life that he may have on his own.

It is also, perhaps, no accident that Paddle is a canoe/person. Paddle cannot be separated from his canoe—he is literally carved into it. Misao Dean has written on the figure of the canoe and canoeing in Canadian cultural memory:

> While canoes and canoeing were adopted by non-indigenous traders and settlers as practical and necessary tools for the exploitation of First Nations lands and peoples, since the advent of the engine canoeing has become a fetishized activity [and the canoe a fetishized symbol] … an activity that no longer has use value and instead appears to have, in itself, the power to heal the split between Canada, as an idea and an ideological construct, and the real, physical land it occupies [17].

Paddle and his canoe are fused together into one thing, a metonym of indigeneity itself, eliding Indigenous or First Nations personhood into a signifier of sheer Otherness. In this distinctly Canadian and Upper Midwestern book, the canoe/person toy of Paddle is electrified across his surface with meanings and signifiers of the land upon which he travels. The scripts of Paddle are affected by the canoe-ness of his toy-ness. He is more distinctly and recognizably "Indian" in his canoe, and his canoe is both a fundamental signifier of his Canadian-ness and his indigeneity.

It is unlikely the unnamed "Indian" boy had any of these scripts in mind when he says, "I made you, Paddle Person, because I had a dream. A little wooden man smiled at me. He sat in a canoe on a snowbank on this hill" (Holling 4). However, situating Paddle within his time and place, it is clear that he, as a toy Indian/canoe is overfull with meaning. It is on this snowbank where readers begin with Paddle, and his quest to become "a real Paddle Person, a real Paddle-to-the-Sea" (Holling 4).

Paddle Meets a Sawmill: To Be Real, Taken and Brave

After Paddle's snowbank melts and he first embarks on his journey, he makes his way through a brook and a pond into the river. Powering through the river, north of Lake Superior, as it thaws and the spring breakup forces logs into the sawmill, Paddle leaves the world of "nature" and encounters the first non–First/Native Nations people of his voyage. However, this "first contact" is mediated through brute machinery. The log chute, bull chain, and spiked chain of the sawmill provide the context through which Paddle first meets people after his journey has begun. Nathalie op de Beeck describes how picture books of the mid-twentieth century often heavily feature machines, revealing anxieties about the increasingly industrialized terrain of the "modern" United States. The machinery of the sawmill provides a tableau of the mechanized world so fetishized and feared during this time.[3] Paddle enters the sawmill atop a log, and is pulled towards the saw in an exciting and frightening scene.

The people Paddle encounters are, of course, the men who work at the sawmill, French Canadian lumberjacks. Here, audiences are introduced to one of the first performances of nation in the story: the lumberjacks' stereotypical performance of French Canada. In his analysis of the endurance of French Canadian stereotypes in the national narrative of Canada, historian José E. Igartua describes the stereotype known at the time of *Paddle-to-the-Sea* as one of a gregarious, laid-back, simple, and excessively vibrant personality (Igartua 121).[4] "By Jo!" yells the lumberjack when he first sees Paddle, and taking him up from the log tells him, "Sit there, my fran" (Holling 14). In addition to the lumberjack's obviously marked dialect through elisions of letters, the lumberjacks perform their national and ethnic identities through an unruly expressiveness, an overly surprised and friendly overture. In a culture that reads ethnic difference through excess of affect or "animatedness" such as the United States (Muñoz 69, Ngai 93), the lumberjack's performance in relation to Paddle acts as a signifier of their different nationalities and ethnicities. Though Paddle and the lumberjack are technically both Canadians, Paddle's First Nation and the lumberjack's French Canadian identity—as would have been considered quite distinct from British Canadian—are performed to separate them.

Paddle comes into contact with the men first by coming up toward the saw on top of a log. "The rivermen shouted with surprise as Paddle rode his log up the bull-chain" (Holling 12), and later they "laughed at the way he had ridden the log into the sawmill" (14). Like a hero, daring and brave, Paddle enters the scene of machinery as the White man's Indian, a fearless "warrior" willing to take on the modern machinery (foolishly, as their laughter indicates). This hero is then plucked and rescued from his fate by the French Canadian lumberjacks. Though he is not real, he must be saved. There is something about Paddle's appearance that invites taking him in hand. Not only is Paddle grasped, but also the French Canadian lumberman knows that his son would feel ownership of Paddle prior to even knowing his existence:

"Henri would cry," when it was time for Paddle to go back into the water, he says (Holling 14).

As a scriptive thing, the script that Paddle offers is one of taking and possession. Goenpul scholar Aileen Moreton-Robinson describes the relationship between White people and Indigenous people in contemporary settler societies through the concept of "the white possessive," the "excessive desire [of white people] to invest in reproducing and affirming the nation-state's ownership, control, and domination" (Moreton-Robinson xii). For Moreton-Robinson, colonization—an effect of the nation—is inextricably bound up with racialization. Whiteness as a racialization is tied to the possession of lands taken from Indigenous peoples and the disavowal of Indigenous sovereignty; Indigenous peoples are racialized so that they may be "known" and disavowed in the racial hierarchy. Paddle, in the White imagination, invites others to take and possess him—that is what White people are "supposed" to do with First/Native Nation personhood and property.

There is a particular friction in this situation in which Paddle's first encounters are with French Canadians, in that the Quebecois had/have been fighting sovereignty battles of their own. Though French Canadians are obviously White, Quebecois, even at the time of publication of *Paddle-to-the-Sea*, questioned their own sense of belonging to the Canadian nation (Turcotte 118). (Of course, questions of Quebecois sovereignty take on a particular irony when one considers that the "sovereign" land on which Quebec now stands was invaded, stolen from First Nations peoples, and occupied by White settlers.) To stake a claim of belonging to this place that Paddle is passing through, a gesture that indicates the white possessive is necessary. The lumberjack secures his own sovereignty in Canada—a sovereignty often felt denied to French Canada—by taking hold of an Indigenous toy. By seizing the toy, the lumberjack is performing the script of taking, the settler claiming the land.

A Fish Story

After leaving the sawmill, Paddle spends a great deal of time without again encountering people, although evidence of humans abounds. Paddle crosses the Canadian-U.S. border twice and makes his way through Duluth, Minnesota and Superior, Wisconsin, where iron mining cast ore into the water, turning it brick red. Paddle picks up some of this red ore and carries it with him to his next human-toy encounter, with fisherman near the Apostle Islands, in Lake Superior.

"Best catch in weeks!" say these men. "And that's not all—look! we're even netting red Injuns in canoes!" (Holling 24). The natural world—the red ore that Paddle has travelled through—only serves to reinforce Paddle's ethnic difference, his "Indian redness" to these White fishermen. When painted "redder," the script that Paddle issues becomes more noticeable. "The men paused only for a moment to look at Paddle" (Holling 24), but pause they do. Upon noticing Paddle's difference, the men perform an exaggeration of their race: they use a racial slur to identify Paddle. Through their announcement of Paddle's racial difference, the fishermen separate themselves as not-"Injun," and thus perform their own whiteness. This gesture is intended to secure their own belonging on stolen land. As with the lumberjacks at the sawmill, the fishermen take the script offered within their context with Paddle and use him as a means to affirm settler colonialism.

Here, audiences also see the beginnings of the potential for Paddle's realness. Paddle comes into view for the fishermen and causes him to "[pause] only for a moment to look at Paddle" (Holling 24). Robin Bernstein describes how the things that may be described as "scriptive" act analogously to Roland Barthes's conception of the *punctum* in a photograph: "A thing, like a *punctum*, demands that people confront it on its own terms; thus a thing forces a person into an awareness of the self in material relation to the thing" (73). Paddle acts as the *punctum* of this scene, coming sharply into view because of his exaggerated "Indian redness" and forcing the fishermen to confront him on his terms. They do this by reinforcing his toyhood and inferiority with their slur. Yet, Paddle obviously has the ability to affect the men's movement and attention. Jane Bennett usefully terms this ability for things, like the scriptive things that Bernstein introduces, to produce an effect "thing-power." She writes that the term "draws attention to an efficacy of objects in excess of the human meanings, designs, or purpose they express or serve" (Bennett 20). By seeing things as lively, in the way that Bennett does, it is possible to begin to see that Paddle is given the promise of "coming to life" or becoming "real." However, rather than remaining engaged in liveliness, the story forecloses this encounter, and Paddle slips away again, back in the water and to his quest.

Settler Multicultural Inclusion on the Soo

As Paddle continues on his journey through Lake Superior, he observes a winter shipwreck as a violent storm rends a freighter in two. In the ship's wreckage, as the men of the ship are saved, Paddle washes up at a Coast Guard Station alongside them (Holling 28). There, a Coast Guard officer named Bill picks Paddle up, spruces up his paint, improves his rudder, and adds to the message printed on Paddle's underside.

After Bill finishes his project of improving Paddle's condition, he calls his friend at "The Soo"—a nickname for Sault Ste. Marie—"twin cities that lie one in Canada, one in Michigan," bridged in part by a series of locks that make travelling down the St. Mary's River far less dangerous (chap. 16). In order to help Paddle reach the sea, Bill asks his friend, Maloney, to carry Paddle to Buffalo, New York, through an elaborate put-on:

> "Hello, Maloney? This is Bill. Say, after that last wreck we picked up an Indian in a canoe. Yeah. Came two thousand miles from Nipigon," and Bill swung the receiver so his pals could listen.
> "JUM-ping WHITE-fish!" boomed a voice. "HOW did he EVER—"
> "YEAH," Bill continued, "and he doesn't speak English. Now, sometime you'll be running to Buffalo. You're to take him and his canoe with you—"
> "*HEY!*" The yell could be heard across the room. "My freighter doesn't take passengers! *INDian—caNOE—ARE YOU CRAZY?*" [32].

Paddle gets sent to Maloney by way of Pierre, "the trapper [he's] acquainted with" (Holling 32). When Pierre arrives, Maloney shouts for him to "GET OUT! AND TAKE THAT INDIAN WITH YOU!" Pierre places Paddle on Maloney's desk and with a drawl, insists that Paddle travel to Buffalo. Seeing that Paddle is a toy, Maloney quickly changes his tune and says, "Paddle goes to Buffalo with me, safe and sound!" (34).

Here, in Maloney, readers see the traces of a formation here named "settler multicultural inclusion." Maloney declares that his freighter does not have "room" for an "Indian in a canoe" who "doesn't speak English." At the same time, though, Pierre, the French Canadian trapper "you're acquainted with" is indeed welcome to come. The freighter acts as a site where the kind of settler multicultural inclusion that Gary D. Schmidt describes in *Making Americans*, in which children's books showed to their readers the kind of world they ought to create, one in which "America ... enabled unique cultures to survive and thrive even as they lived side by side" (83). This vision participates in the creation of a literature that Clare Bradford critiques as a "settled," inclusionary vision for Indigenous peoples in settler societies, rather than a decolonized literature (Bradford 16). Pierre, with his French Canadian (stereotypical) drawl, is part of this multicultural America/Canada that Holling is creating aboard the freighter. However, Paddle, when believed to be an "actual Indian"—that is, a human being—is not.

Paddle-the-imagined-person is the sort of Indian that disrupts the vision of multicultural inclusion that Maloney espouses. As Chickasaw scholar Jodi Byrd notes, "Indigeneity remains troubling, I think, for the very reason that those colonial conditions disrupt—often exponentially in relation to the violences done to Indigenous peoples—the notions of liberalism, democracy, and humanism in large part because such concepts have all too often depended on the eradication of indigeneity" (Byrd 16). Because the concepts of inclusion and democracy Maloney is imagining (and that Schmidt maintains that children's literature was producing during this time) rest on nation-states founded through the genocide of First/Native Nations, it is a *settler* multicultural inclusion, in which First/Native Nations play no part. The appearance of Paddle-the-imagined-person is unacceptable, because even though Maloney "knows" that First/Native Nations people exist, they "ought" not to.

However, when Paddle is rendered as inanimate, through the simple act of placing him on the desk, Maloney's tone quickly changes. Rather than acting as a disrupter to Maloney's vision of his "settled" freighter, Paddle becomes a symbol of inclusion that is welcomed into that modern space. Once Paddle is frozen and inanimate and able to be easily manipulated by White settlers (as his improvements in Bill's hands evidence), he becomes the "Indian" who may be included in settler multicultural inclusion. As an inanimate object, Paddle will make no claims for sovereignty, tradition, or self-determination. Instead, he is merely an ethnic Other on a heroic mission easily recognizable under the conditions of settler multicultural inclusion, a mission that Maloney is happy to abet. Paddle offers Maloney the script of being easily manipulated and "played with" in a geographic game against the wilderness. Maloney happily performs once Paddle's threatening ("real") indigeneity is rendered un-real.

Local History on the St. Lawrence

One of Paddle's last encounters before actually reaching the sea comes when he is on the St. Lawrence River, near Montréal. The chapter opens with the explanation that "Paddle spent that winter in Canada with a little old lady.... Paddle joined her collection of Indian, French and British curios of early Canada" (Holling 48). The story continues as the woman relates the local history of the Montréal-St. Lawrence region to a young American boy. She begins with the "Indian name for the River," Canada. At this point, though, the "Indian" quickly vanishes, as she says, "nowadays ... some of the biggest ships come a thousand miles from the sea to Montreal. This is skyscraper city today." However, the woman returns to the matter of First/Native Nations when describing the "Indian canoes with many paddlers" that brought beaver pelts to trade with the French at Quebec trading posts. She also describes how Champlain, the "father of New France," "fought the Iroquois. The Hurons loved him, but the Iroquois hated all Frenchmen" (48).

In the woman's story of local history, Paddle is quickly subsumed into the bric-a-brac of a bygone past, simply a disappeared part of the multicultural history of the settler state. Under Paddle's banishment to the shelf, the woman is able to narrate a local history in which First/Native Nations people begin with deep connections to nature—naming the river and trading beaver pelts—

move quickly to violent encounters with the French invaders of the region, and, finally, are absent from the modern landscape of the "skyscraper city."

White Earth Ojibwe ethnohistorian Jean M. O'Brien has argued that local histories have been central to the ways that settlers positioned themselves as inheritors of modernity, while effacing First/Native Nations' ability to "become modern," and, through that effacement, their claims to their lands (O'Brien xxi). Although O'Brien's extensive research covers particularly nineteenth-century local histories from the region of southern New England, her framework is useful for understanding how the histories settlers circulate among themselves work to create the conditions for their settlement. By narrating the history of the land on which she sits, this woman is able to place Paddle within a script (a word O'Brien uses) of local history that is obsessed with "the issue of purification—of distinguishing between nature [the River] and culture [skyscrapers] … wars are typically scripted as savage and heathen, initiated by furious assaults by Indians on innocent 'settlers'" (27). Within that script, First/Native Nations people are made finally to disappear, and Paddle, one of the trading "Indians," is firmly established as part of the "natural world" and unmodern, despite his recent date of production, and vanished to the shelf of historic curios. In doing so, she is able to reaffirm her and Quebec's claim to sovereignty over their land (even as questions of French Canada's sovereignty vis-à-vis British Canada loom in the distance). The script of Paddle in the context of local history is merely one of being, as O'Brien would say, "written out of existence," so that French settlers may be the "first" to lay claim to the land.

Reaching the Sea and France

Shortly after the woman makes good on her promise and returns Paddle to the river so that he may reach the sea, he, in fact, succeeds in his quest. Passing through the Gulf of St. Lawrence, he catches the Gulf Stream, carrying him out to Newfoundland, where he reaches the Atlantic Ocean for the first time. From there, he is picked up by a French ship carrying fish and is taken across the Atlantic to France. In France, his story, told through the names of places he has reached carved on his underside, becomes popular enough that a newspaper writes an article about his "long journey." That news article makes its way back to Nipigon County in the hands of the French Canadian lumberjack after being sent a copy by a cousin: "Us Frenchmans, we get lonesome for mail that speak French" (Holling 54). The lumberjack is in Nipigon to fish trout and has brought his mail with him. Upon reaching the article about Paddle, he notices him and exclaims: "*I* am the one who saved him from the saws! By all the Saints, I did it! *Me*! Years back I put him in the river! Oh! I mus' tell my Henri! By Jo, *you* talk 'bout long journey!" (54).

By coincidence, another person standing on the dock is the nameless "Indian" boy who created Paddle, who observes, "'You put him back in the river and sent him on? Good. I made that one,' he said softly, and turned away" (55). Stepping down into his canoe, the young man reflects on Paddle's journey, at the book's end:

> In the canoe, the Indian smiled. Once he paused in a stroke, and rested his blade. For that instant he looked like his own Paddle. There was a song in his heart. It crept to his lips, but only the water and the wind could hear.
> "You, Little Traveler! You made the journey, the Long Journey. You now know the things I have yet to know. You, Little Traveler! You were given a name, a true name in my father's lodge. Good Medicine, Little Traveler! You are truly a Paddle Person, a Paddle-to-the-Sea!" [55].

Paddle has heroically finished his journey (although where he finally ends up, we have no idea), and through his journey, readers might expect that he become "real." Instead, they find the French lumberjack claiming responsibility for his journey (in which, to be fair, he did play a large part). Instead of recognizing Paddle's heroism, instead we again find the Quebecois man espousing a white possessive, claiming Paddle's journey as his own, effacing Paddle's real role in the journey and securing his own place in the settler state. Paddle again scripts the action of settler taking.

Paddle does not become "real" in any sense that we might recognize; he certainly never speaks, moves his arms, paddles his own canoe, or grows any larger. Instead, we find that his young creator retreats into himself. His affirmation of the lumberjack's generosity is not heard or understood by the others on the dock. He turns away, and becomes "his own Paddle." The illustration accompanying this text shows a stylized and indistinct boy kneeling in his canoe, echoing the figure of Paddle in the background, both set against a setting sun. Rather than Paddle becoming real, his creator is instead subsumed into Paddle's toyhood and figurehood. The "Indian" boy speaks in stereotypical language, making nouns proper and using exclamations like "Good Medicine!" devoid of any context. He is denied a place in modernity and is instead made less real himself. In spite of his claim that Paddle is "truly a Paddle Person," it appears that they are both denied realness as the scripts of settler colonialism play out.

The Empty Promise of Becoming "Real": Indigenous Resistance and Unsettling Readings

Throughout his journey, we are told, "Paddle never showed surprise. For four years he had been what he was supposed to be, a Paddle-to-the-Sea.

And he had done what he was supposed to do. And so he showed no surprise, even at crossing the ocean" (Holling 52). Paddle evidences no emotion of his own, and, as has been shown, is consistently reinscribed as a non-alive toy. Instead, Paddle merely achieves what Mel Y. Chen might call "animacy," having the ability to affect those he encounters while absent of consciousness. Chen's concept of animacy, which they prefer not to define precisely, but carries with it the concepts of "liveliness," "the ability to affect," and some semblance of "sentience," is useful to describe Paddle's condition throughout the story, because Chen finds animacy in animals, lead, and mercury, things we would often consider "inanimate" (Chen 2).

Unlike the Velveteen Rabbit, who is promised "realness" when he is well-loved, and Pinocchio, who will be a "real" boy when he proves himself as brave, heroic, and truthful, Paddle is promised his "realness" as a function of his success in his Long Journey. Paddle is not real, though. Paddle is "animate," in Chen's sense of the word. He certainly has the ability to affect those around him, and, as discussed, he carries within him the "thing-power" described by Bennett. He is both beloved, and heroic, as so many other animate toys are. And yet he is never "real."

Dakota scholar Philip J. Deloria describes how the "authentic," especially in terms of First/Native Nations people, is a culturally constructed category, in which settlers can "image and idealize the real, the traditional, and the organic" (Deloira 101). For Deloria, the drive for a fetishized "authentic Indian" is a "characteristically modern phenomenon" for settlers to remedy the unsettling feeling of being alienated from stolen land (ibid.). Throughout the book, the scripts that Paddle offers to the settlers encounter rely on his "authenticity" as a First/Native Nations canoe-person-toy. However, since he also comes under the authority, seizure, and possession of White settlers across his voyage, his "authenticity" becomes not a tool of his own, but a means in which he comes to serve as a tool to secure settlers' own sense of self and belonging. This echoes multiple Indigenous authors' skepticism toward the ability for "authenticity" to be an effective goal for Indigenous policy or theory (Barker 19, Garroutte 78). If Paddle is "authentic," he should be "real," because his quest has intended to make him a "real Paddle Person," but white possession denies him his realness. The "authentic" is a trap.

Unlike Disney's Pinocchio, Field's Hitty, and scores of other "real" dolls from the midcentury period, Paddle is denied the opportunity to become real. Lenape (Delaware) scholar Joanne Barker discusses in her book *Native Acts* the ways in which claims to tribal authenticity and recognition function not in opposition to colonialism, but often precisely within "racialized discourses that serve the national interests of the United States in maintaining colonial and imperial relations with Native peoples" (Barker 6). In the same ways that O'Brien describes American Indians' denial into modernity, Paddle is denied "realness" in a settler colonial effort to efface the disruption that indigeneity presents to settler multicultural inclusion.

This essay has suggested that Paddle acts as a scriptive thing that, from a settler optic, incites gestures that secure colonial, racial schemes with the effect of excluding Paddle from "realness." However, viewing settler colonialism in a totalizing way can obscure First/Native Nations resistance and decolonization efforts. Settler colonialism is not settled; First/Native Nations people have resisted colonialism since settlers first invaded and continue to work towards decolonization. Viewing the racial and colonial schemes that Paddle reveals as complete can efface the "realness" of this resistance through the lens of settler colonial studies itself. In order to recognize this, this essay will conclude with a troubling of its own arguments, turning them on their ear: Paddle is heroic in that, in addition to being denied realness, he also *refuses* realness, and in doing so, illuminates the contingencies that present settler colonialism as a settled matter.

It is not that Paddle is a hero in spite of being denied realness. It is that, though he is denied realness in spite of his heroic success, his *true* heroism is in his refusal to appeal to realness. In doing so, Paddle reveals the ways in which Canada and the United States, in their continuing claims for multicultural, liberal democracy, require the destruction, disappearance, and inanimacy of their Indigenous peoples. Paddle does indeed reach the sea, and he is a hero in that quest. But he is also a hero in that he lays bare the violence of the colonial system in which he is produced.

The toys of midcentury United States children's media—Pinocchio, the Velveteen Rabbit, Hitty—when they are promised the chance to be "real," in fact are or become real. Realness is the normative position of toyhood in children's texts. Across his entire journey, Paddle acts without the normative conditions of toyhood in children's literature—becoming real—and instead, refuses to be recognized. In doing so, Paddle remains merely a scriptive thing. The scripts Paddle produces, as an "Indian" canoe-person-toy, perhaps, make him all the more real, even though he is not "real." Those scripts that Paddle unearths for us shine light on the ways that colonization and racialization affected and continue to affect First/Native Nations people, and his commitment to refusing recognition is in fact a de-colonial effort. By denying the legitimacy of recognition (though he is also denied that recognition as "real"), Paddle works to show how settler colonialism must present itself as a settled matter.

Debbie Reese lays forth a vision for "indigenizing children's literature" in an article of the same name, centered on the project of "carving a space where Indigenous values and knowledge are respected" by "displacing the stereotypes and erroneous ideas that many people 'know' about American Indians," and "being honest about the place of Indigenous people in American history" (Reese, "Indigenizing" 61). Reading the scripts that Paddle suggests is a project that, perhaps not quite the same as the methodology of Reese's concept, at least dovetails with it. By centering indigeneity in our analyses of children's texts, we not only can expose stereotype and erasure, but also understand the ways that settler colonialism works to deny its violent and ongoing nature.

As we follow our toy hero and see how he is denied "realness," we also see the messages that children's texts send to their intended audiences about the "realness" of colonized peoples. The scripts of race and nation, themselves wrapped up in Paddle's toyhood, give us insight into the ongoing nature of racism and colonialism. In reading Paddle in this way, I hope that we may begin to "carve out space" for Indigenous nation-building and work towards a de-colonial view of children's literature.

Notes

1. I place Indian in quotes in this sentence, because, though Indian is the descriptor used to describe both the nameless boy and Paddle, it is rarely used to describe First Nations people in Canada today. I take this opportunity explain language I use in this chapter, noting that language used to describe Indigenous peoples is always political and is essay fluid, complex, and contingent. I will use the terms "First/Native Nations" to refer to people and peoples indigenous to North America and "Indigenous" to refer to autochthonous people within a global context. "American Indian" and "First Nations" refer to people with a tribal base in the geographic regions that are currently called the United States and Canada, respectively. Whenever possible, I will use tribal or First Nation affiliations to refer to individuals.
2. Throughout, this essay uses "settler" to particularly mean "White settler," following the lead of Chickasaw scholar Jodi Byrd.
3. It is interesting to note that op de Beeck is particularly concerned with the ways that machines, either explicitly or implicitly, are granted sentience within picture books of this time period. The machines of the sawmill have nearly as much anthropomorphism as Paddle himself, with the log chute described as a "giant tongue, licking into the water," with an "open mouth" into which logs are fed into a "hungry" saw with a "buzzing noise which sometimes became a shriek" (Holling 12).
4. Igartua characterizes these as positive aspects of a French-Canadian stereotype, while negative aspects include: laziness, ignorance, vindictiveness, and content with "lot in life." Neither "positive" nor "negative" stereotypes, however, help provide context for thinking about the complexities of a group of people.

Works Cited

Bader, Barbara. *American Picturebooks from Noah's Ark to the Beast Within*. London: Macmillan, 1976.
Barker, Joanne. *Native Acts: Law, Recognition, and Cultural Authenticity*. Durham: Duke University Press, 2011.
Bennett, Jane. *Vibrant Matter: A Political Ecology of Things*. Durham: Duke University Press, 2010.
Bequette, James W., and Kelly Hrenko. "Culture-Based Arts Education." *Honoring Our Heritage: Culturally Appropriate Approaches for Teaching Indigenous Students*, edited by Jon Reyhner, Willard Saskiestewa Gilbert, and Louise Lockard. Northern Arizona University Press, 2011. *Dr. Jon Reyhner*, jan.ucc.nau.edu/jar/HOH/HOH-6.pdf.
Bernstein, Robin. *Racial Innocence: Performing American Childhood from Slavery to Civil Rights*. New York: New York University Press, 2011.

Bradford, Clare. *Unsettling Narratives: Postcolonial Readings of Children's Literature*. Waterloo, Ontario: Wilfred Laurier University Press, 2007.
Byrd, Jodi A. "'In the City of Blinding Lights': Indigeneity, Cultural Studies, and the Errants of Colonial Nostalgia." *Cultural Studies Review* 15, no. 2 (2009). *Directory of Open Access Journals*, doi:10.5130/csr.v15i2.2035.
Chen, Mel Y. *Animacies: Biopolitics, Racial Mattering, and Queer Affect*. Durham: Duke University Press, 2012.
Dean, Misao. *Inheriting a Canoe Paddle: The Canoe in Discourses of English-Canadian Nationalism*. Toronto: University of Toronto Press, 2013.
Deloria, Philip J. *Playing Indian*. New Haven: Yale University Press, 1998.
Garroutte, Eva Marie. *Real Indians: Identity and the Survival of Native America*. Oakland: University of California Press, 2003.
Holling, Holling Clancy. *Paddle-to-the-Sea*. New York: Houghton Mifflin, 1941.
Igartua, José E. "The Genealogy of Stereotypes: French Canadians in Two English-Language Canadian History Textbooks." *Journal of Canadian Studies/Revue d'études canadiennes* 42, no. 3 (2008): 106–132. *Project Muse*, muse.jhu.edu/article/367040.
Kuznets, Lois Rostow. *When Toys Come Alive: Narratives of Animation, Metamorphosis, and Development*. New Haven: Yale University Press, 1994.
Moreton-Robinson, Aileen. *The White Possessive: Property, Power, and Indigenous Sovereignty*. Minneapolis: University of Minnesota Press, 2015.
Muñoz, José Esteban. "Feeling Brown: Ethnicity and Affect in Ricardo Bracho's *The Sweetest Hangover (And Other STDs)*." *Theatre Journal* 52, no. 1 (March 2000): 67–79. *Project Muse*, doi:10.1353/tj.2000.0020.
Ngai, Sianne. *Ugly Feelings*. Cambridge: Harvard University Press, 2005.
O'Brien, Jean M. *Firsting and Lasting: Writing Indians Out of Existence in New England*. Minneapolis: University of Minnesota Press, 2010.
op de Beeck, Nathalie. *Suspended Animation: Children's Picture Books and the Fairy Tale of Modernity*. Minneapolis: University of Minnesota Press, 2010.
Ord, Priscilla, and Carole Henderson Carpenter. "Canadian Children's Literature: A Cultural Mirror." *Children's Literature Association Quarterly* 2, no. 3 (1977): 3–6. *Project Muse*, doi:10.1353/chq.0.1519.
Reese, Debbie. "Indigenizing Children's Literature." *Journal of Language and Literacy Education* 4, no. 2 (2008): 59–72. *JoLLE@UGA*, jolle.coe.uga.edu/archive/2008/indigenizing.pdf.
———. "Thoughts on Sharon Creech's WALK TWO MOONS." *American Indians in Children's Literature*, 25 Feb. 2010, americanindiansinchildrensliterature.blogspot.com/2010/02/thoughts-on-sharon-creechs-walk-two.html.
Turcotte, Edmond. "As Seen by a French-Speaking Canadian." *University of Toronto Quarterly* 14, no. 2 (January 1945): 117–123. *Project Muse*, doi:10.1353/utq.1945.0027.

"Even if you can't see something, it doesn't mean it isn't there"
Toys as Heroic Agents of Creativity and Cultural Criticism in Small Soldiers

Michael Brodski

An interesting aspect concerning the release of Joe Dante's underestimated and commercially rather unsuccessful *Small Soldiers* (1998) can be seen in the treatment of the fact that Dante, formerly known for original and subversive works such as *Gremlins* (1984) and *Innerspace* (1987), seemed to be forced by his producers to create a generic children's film. The director himself complained that originally he was told to "make an edgy picture for teenagers, but when the sponsor tie-ins came in the new mandate was to soften it up as a kiddie movie" (Brew). And even one of the movie's central acclaimers—the film critic Jonathan Rosenbaum—stresses the position that the important aspect concerning *Small Soldiers* lies beneath its rather childish surface, calling it a "trenchant satire masquerading as a summer kids' movie" (Rosenbaum "Cutting Heroes Down to Size"). Rosenbaum therefore affirms the film's blunt criticism by openly relating the film's pop culture with violence while simultaneously neglecting the employed extent of childhood and children's culture as an essential role in said proclaimed intention.

On the contrary, this raises the question why the abovementioned elements of *Small Soldiers* are not treated seriously enough, especially given that both the film's villains and the protagonists are toys technically brought to life. On top of this, a significant narrative storyline portrays a central problem of childhood and growing up by depicting the generational conflict between the teenage boy Alan (Gregory Smith) and his father. How can one read the film's satiric ingredients that Rosenbaum points out in the main context of its qualities concerning childhood and especially one of its pivotal, actually iconic signifiers, the toy, as its plot-defining and meaningful hero?

First and foremost, it would be important to examine the definition of childhood as a sociocultural and historical concept, thereby enabling a further definition of the herewith connoted specific role of the toy. Since Philippe Ariés's ground-breaking *History of Childhood* (1976), one developing tendency in modern *Childhood Studies* has been to redeem the notion of childhood from a cultural discourse that inextricably ties it to the dominant idea of adulthood, the resulting need, and the requirements of growing up. As one of the leading representatives of this interdisciplinary academic approach, the sociologist Chris Jenks proclaims that children are usually solely seen in the context of a "structured process of becoming, but rarely as a course of action or a coherent social practice" (9). Therefore, being constructed from an adult point of view, the principal goal of childhood lies in becoming one of them: "This adult world is not only assumed to be complete, recognizable and in stasis, but also, and perhaps most significantly, desirable" (ibid.).

Interestingly enough, and in direct relation to this stated discourse on childhood, various analytical approaches to cultural texts tend to regard the toy as an embodiment of a link to the child, which symbolizes its immaturity as well as a yet not reached readiness to face possible problems in a determined "adult" way. In a recent study, Michael Howarth, while analyzing the animation movie *Monster House* (2006) from a media educational perspective, argues that the emotional link of the main protagonist to a stuffed bunny symbolizes his connection to an almost regressive child-status and therefore the obstacles of maturity (200). In order to confirm this, Howarth also draws upon a classical text by the psychoanalyst Bruno Bettelheim (*The Use of Enchantment: The Meaning and Importance of Fairy Tales*, 1978) who remarks that children's toys "are used to embody various aspects of the child's personality which are too complex, unacceptable, and contradictory for him to handle" (qtd. in Horwarth 200). Overcoming the dependence on a toy is consequently being equated with overcoming the contradictory boundaries of childhood to reach a more mature behavior.

Of course, it would seem ridiculous to reject the need of growing up and its media representations completely. At some point, kids stop playing with toys; a fact which one has simply to deal with. However, one can strictly disagree with the stated prevalent conviction by considering the condition of childhood and the toy, one of its central signifiers, as obstacles and, on the contrary, the coming-of-age-trope as the ultimate solution. For this reason, my analysis of *Small Soldiers* shall examine the specific qualities of children's behavior and, drawing upon this premise, especially the significance of the toy and how they reinforce each other. The possibilities of problem-solving as illustrated in the film's plot can therefore be regarded as outcomes of pure childish agency—as well that of the toy embodying this very state of being—instead of rational adult behavior.

On the one hand, it seems important to take into account plausible critical voices as, for instance, James R. Kincaid's noteworthy argument, according to which adults, in the case of *Small Soldiers* the decidedly mature production staff, tend to be "more likely to warm to child's play in a novel or painting than actually to enjoy its repetitive monotony in life" (*Child-Loving* 79). Grown up people therefore seem to favor the creation and reception of pleasurably artificial and potentially vacuous representations of child's play.

However, the potential of cultural texts should not be underestimated due to their undeniable possibility to highlight the qualities of their portrayed subject. In the given case, this might even lead to a reconsideration of the supposed monotony of child's play, thereby, on the contrary, extracting its identity-defining attributes. Even if such genuinely adult productions naturally cannot really reconstruct authentic childish experience,[1] they certainly possess the power to rehabilitate childish perception and play as a profound mode of social experience. Moreover, they also highlight the need to learn to "appreciate kids as active consumers and producers of their own symbolic culture" (Corsaro 91). Consequently, it seems important to underline one of *Small Soldiers* main narrative devices, namely the portrayal of the teenage protagonists and the technically animated toys as active agents. Both the main character Alan and the "good" toys of the film, a group of rather uncommon looking action figures calling themselves the Gorgonites, are introduced as the principal driving forces of the film's plot.

The main argument of this essay is centered on the assumption that the characters do not need to "grow up" by means of a generic coming-of-age plot, but have to rely instead on the qualities of behavior associated with children in order to reach their personal goals. In the case of Alan, it is the wish to be accepted by his father as well as to make his first experiences with a girl, his neighbor Christy (Kirsten Dunst), and, in the case of the Gorgonites, it is their aim to defeat their opponents, a group of antagonistic toys looking like slightly farcical versions of military action figures called the Commando Elite.

The connection between children and toys—particularly concerning play and active behavior—can be in opposition to the stated thesis of Bettelheim, psychoanalytically located by following different clues in various essays by Sigmund Freud. Despite his well-known considerations regarding the perverse and self-defining nature of infant sexual behavior, he also developed other quite fundamental thoughts on the state of childhood. In *Creative Writers and Day-Dreaming* (1907), Freud notes that "every playing child acts like an artist creating his own world" (3), thereby accentuating childish play as an active creative process. Furthermore, concerning the literary trope of the animated toy, he states in his fundamental essay *The Uncanny* (1919), that "the idea of a 'living doll' excites no fear at all" (209). For him, the "source of the feeling of an uncanny thing would not, therefore, be an infantile fear in this case, but rather an infantile wish or even only an infantile belief" (ibid.). The wish to look at toys in an anthropomorphized way could thus be regarded as an aspect of children's tendency to create their own worlds through play. Therefore, one can assume that Freud implicitly combines the idea of child's play and of animated toys, thereby even re-establishing each other. In the case of *Small Soldiers*, this idea of acting between the boy and the toys can be read by analyzing the way Alan and the Gorgonites work together to overcome the obstacles imposed by the narrative.

These aspects will be stressed later in a more detailed manner; at first, one has to consider the meaning and function of the mentioned obstacles. On this level, one can find a parallel, an ontological correspondence between Alan and the Gorgonites as being similarly *Othered* by means of their social standing. At first glance, Alan is introduced as a problem-case, not fitting in his father's rather clichéd notion of a good son. This is specifically shown at the beginning of the movie.

Having been left in authority of his father's toy shop, Alan discovers that the Commando Elite has devastated the location during his absence. Being unable—even with Christy's help—to eliminate every single trace, his returning father claims to regret having placed trust in his son in the first place. Additionally, he also laments that he should have known that it could not have been a good idea to let him be in charge. Moreover, his father's distrust emerges as part of a bigger backstory wound because Alan seems to have been dismissed from different schools, the last of which he apparently—more or less accidentally—set on fire. Therefore, his emotionally easily overwhelmed father completely distrusts and, for this reason, infantilizes him by deeming him unable to take responsibility and become an adult.

Regarding the analytical perspective of this essay, these expectations concerning Alan could therefore be considered as a representation of a repressive, culturally constructed, and top-down driven adult-child relationship. Alan resembles a cultural-historical construction of the child that Kincaid describes as a "hollow category" (Freud *Child-Loving* 12). This implies the child's function as a featureless and thus empty blank space wherein the adult can place his own definitions of childhood. In the given case, Alan's supposed unreliability places his father in the position to project everything he wants, probably his own fears of failure and culturally made-up values, onto the categorization of Alan as childish. In the words of sociologist Jenny Kitzinger, "[N]ot just the *abuse* of power over children […] is the problem but the existence and maintenance of that power itself" (178). Seen as a child, Alan is simply disqualified with regard to his competence of agentic and constructive behavior.

A first connection between Alan and the Gorgonites can thus be found in their similar inferior social status. These toys tend to represent monstrous off-beat freaks determined by their creators, a toy company taken over by a tycoon who originally specialized in producing war technology, to take on an antagonistic role in relation to the actual "bad" toys, the Commando Elite. On account of their inherent programming by a state of the art microtechnology, and the therewith associated automatic adherence to a certain form of warlike role-playing, the Gorgonites serve as a kind of prey for the soldier-like figures. Accordingly, the Gorgonites' appearance is reminiscent of typical characteristics of Western culture's manifestation of the *Other*: This is visualized by means of a pastiche of appalling Gothic-Horror characteristics like bulky, deformed faces, and bodies explicitly referencing Frankenstein's creature. There can even be found an explicit reference, when one of the Gorgonites who had been formerly demolished by the antagonistic toys and afterwards repaired by his comrades and, as a result, is now looking even more grotesque, is seen watching a movie about the famous monster.

Another aspect would be the iconography of the exotic and noble savage, as for instance, the leader of the Gorgonites, Archer (spoken by Frank Langella), besides his animalistic face has the look of a typical hunter of an indigenous tribe. The fact, that he and his friends are terrorized by mainly white looking toys, also inevitably recalls the idea of the colonial oppression of indigenous and therefore *othered* populations. At this point, a parallel can be drawn between this colonialist hint and the treatment of children. As Perry Nodelman writes: "Conventional ideas about childhood appear to be the central model for this sort of colonial thinking about othered groups; it is not surprising that such thinking tends to be represented in parental metaphors like *paternalistic*" (68). Correspondingly, Patricia Holland suggests a broader perspective:

> [T]he dichotomy child/adult parallels other dichotomies which have characterized Western discourse: nature/culture, primitive/civilised, emotion/reason. In each pair the dominant term seeks to understand and control the subordinate, keeping it separate but using it for its own enrichment [15].

Hence, both the boy and the toys are determined and shaped by a binary structured discourse of power, positioning them in inferior roles as the culturally constructed figure of the unreliable and immature child as well as that of the different looking *Other*.

As mentioned above, the possibility of these repressed individuals to overcome the portrayed hindrances and their presumably inferior status recurs to a genuine childish way of problem-solving. Such an aspect can be located in the realms of imagination and creativity. "Should we not look for the first traces of imaginative activity as early as in childhood?" (*On Creative*

Writers and Day-Dreaming 3)—Freud's rhetorical question implies that children are the genuine bearers of shaping the world around them in creative attempts. Carolyn Salvi follows a similar way by stating the child's specific creative potential, quoting a remarkable proposition of Charles Baudelaire who considers the child as a kind of equivalent to a creative genius who sees everything "in the state of newness; he is always drunk. Nothing more resembles what we call inspiration than the delight with which the child absorbs form and colour" (qtd. in Salvi 249). The child thus seems to see things in a special way. A very important aspect of *Small Soldiers* can be observed in providing Alan and the Gorgonites with exactly these possibilities of an agentic access to their environment as a transgressive outburst of childish creativity in the playful interactions between the toys and their owner.

To put it differently, the stated connection between teen and toy and the thereby resulting trope of child's play are presented in an exclusively progressive way, far from being only infantile and inhibiting. The film displays these aspects of creativity from the beginning, starting with the mentioned repair of the Frankenstein-like Gorgonite with different original spare parts such as a transistor radio. Additionally, a recorder plays a significant part in another relevant scene where Alan and the Gorgonites outsmart the Commando Elite who have occupied Christy's neighboring house and kidnapped the girl. In order to distract the evil toy soldiers, they put it in a case taped with the voices of the Gorgonites crying for help together with two bumble balls—a popular 1990s toy—while in the meantime, Archer uses a toy-parachute to glide into the house's chimney. This kind of guerrilla-tactic functions as a profound example of the importance *Small Soldiers* ascribes to the problem-solving quality of child's play. Alan and the Gorgonites interact with each other via a playful intervention, also by using other toys. A very helpful concept that describes how film can portray such particular characteristics of the child's view in relation to a creative agency is also articulated by Karen Lury. Differentiating between the term of *showing* as a rational "adult" way of perceiving things causally and the possibility of *seeing* that she ascribes to the child's view in film, Lury proclaims:

> "Seeing" implies certain qualities and a particular response: it is an unregulated gaze, timeless and ahistorical, it also implies fascination and a sense in which effects (what is seen) are closer to affect (what is felt)...."Showing," in contrast is precisely not this, but is a directed gaze, purposeful; it is also historical, part of a narrative which links cause to effect, it demonstrates, names and classifies [110].

This attitude is also explicitly articulated by the repeated dialogue line "Just because you can't see something doesn't mean it isn't there." The first time, it is spoken by Alan who explains to Archer how the wind moves rustling leaves which the latter misleadingly assumes to be the Commando

Elite hiding in the trees. The second time, in the film's final sequence, it is repeated by Archer himself concerning his aim to find his fictional homeland Gorgon, although it probably may only exist in the Gorgonites' programmed minds. As a result, on a metaphysical level, Alan, the child, opens up the possibility for Archer, the toy, to the abovementioned kind of *seeing* as something more affective than rational. Thus, the toy learns to see things through the eyes of a child, which implies a stubborn clinging to seemingly irrational—in Lury's terms said "timeless and ahistorical"—dreams. On this level, the ontological bound between children and toys is reinforced by a shared perspective.

In the given context of play, the outlined poetic, creative attempt can be particularly described by means of a new and innovative combination and use of things that had originally been produced for other purposes. Both Gorgonites and the Commando Elite—in this respect, the film also subverts the binary Manichean discourse between the two opposing toy fractions—exemplify creative attempts to adapt to their surroundings by inventively combining random everyday items like tools and kitchen equipment into completely new gadgets and even deadly weapons.

Considering this, a very interesting sociological approach that can also be made fruitful for the further analysis of the filmic text is proclaimed by the important childhood sociologist William A. Corsaro. Sharing the position of the already described developing tendency in *Childhood Studies*, Corsaro states that the child's "socialization is not only a matter of adaptation and internalization but also a process of appropriation, reinvention, and reproduction" (*The Sociology of Childhood* 18). Accordingly, children "create and participate in their own unique peer cultures by creatively taking or appropriating information from the adult world to address their own peer concerns" (ibid.). Corsaro calls this specific "childish" approach *Interpretative Reproduction* and in *Small Soldiers*, this term can be applied both to the teens, Alan and Christy, and the toys due to their described innovative and unconventional usage of tools, other toys, and different objects that had been produced by, and mostly, for an adult culture:

> Interpretative reproduction views children's evolving membership in their cultures as *reproductive* rather than linear. According to this reproductive view, children do not simply imitate or internalize the world around them. They strive to interpret or make sense of their culture and to participate in it. In attempting to make sense of the adult world, children come to collectively produce their own peer worlds and cultures [ibid., 24].

When we regard this approach in correlation to an inherently satirical potential in Dante's film, one can consider such an attitude in the stated idea of differentiation between an adult and a childhood-culture, thereby considering the act of transforming belongings from the first to the second. In order to remain on this line, it seems to be important to consider how the shown childlike playful behavior, the state of creatively using objects and dealing with obstacles, can be classified as showing a way of a legitimate cultural, in the given case especially consumerist criticism, and, primarily, the therewith related central role of the toy.

In his chapter on toys in his seminal study *Mythologies* (1954), Roland Barthes stresses a binary construction by portraying the topic of creativity as the most valuable aspect of child's play by actually distinguishing it from the one-sided interaction with mass-produced (and adult-produced) commodity toys:

> The merest set of blocks, provided it is not too refined, implies a very different learning of the world: then, the child does not in any way create meaningful objects, it matters little to him whether they have an adult name; the actions he performs are not those of a user but those of a demiurge [7].

Accordingly, Barthes emphasizes the value of a kind of play driven by one's own creative imaginations and also distinguishes it from an adult-determined prescribed playing which manifests itself in consumerist behavior that requires bought toys (see ibid.). Exactly this distinction between different kinds of play is also portrayed in the film, starting with the premise that all the action figures have been formerly manufactured to make huge profits and adhere to the way they should be played with as is expected by their producers. During the company's business meeting at the beginning of the film, the military tycoon Gil Mars (Denis Leary) defines his expectations in producing toys that ought to "play back" when children start playing with them. In addition to this congenial parallelization of a highly profit-orientated thinking and clichéd military behavior, slogans, and other recurrences, underlined by the film's narrative in several different further tongue-in-cheek situations, such a reference also reinforces different rules as to how children should play and how the ontology of the toy should shape the kind of playing and not, as stated by Barthes, vice versa. In a later symptomatic scene, Christy's younger brother finds the Commando toys intruding into his house and, unaware of the consequences, starts to play with them by imagining a situation where the leader of the soldier toys, Major Chip Hazard, simply dies and one of his inferiors substitutes him. Hardly surprising, the Commandos are not amused by this role playing, tying the child up and taking him hostage.

The resulting question is how the film allows not only to criticize the consumption of creativity inhibiting consumer goods, but also offers a possibility of subverting this capitalistic values in his own narrative, itself connected with creativity and the toy as its main embodiment. For this purpose, a comparison with another movie with anthropomorphized animated toys as its main heroes—John Lasseter's *Toy Story* (1996)—seems to be quite insightful. Speaking about the commercial misfortune of *Small Soldiers*, Martyn Bamber also recurs to the parallel between the two films concerning public expectations, stating the possibility that Dante's movie "alienated audiences because of its cynical stance towards toy merchandising and manufacturing, or maybe they stayed away because they felt that Dante's film was just a rip off of Lasseter's film."

Actually, both of the assumptions underscored by Bamber can be read in a connected way, if one analyzes the manner of portrayal of the toys in *Toy Story*. The presented toy-group that is led by the cowboy figure Woody and the Space Ranger toy Buzz Lightyear are interestingly positioned in a good-bad binary model in terms of the possibilities how to play with them; on the one hand, there is the toy's owner Andy, who, similarly to the producer-intended proposition in *Small Soldiers*, plays with his toys in a regular way according to their look and possibilities of usage inherited via their production design. Contrary to this, the film's antagonist is the vicious neighbor boy Sid who is portrayed by the film's toy-driven perspective as a sadist who destroys toys for fun and also disassembles them to remake them into new grotesque looking forms. The film's alleged intention to proclaim playing with toys as intended by their creators as good while destroying and recreating them as bad—although in a Barthesian sense this possibility could actually be classified as creative and imaginative—stresses the commercially-driven hidden agenda behind the film's storytelling, confirming Rosenbaum's observation of the film as "also in effect a toy catalog." In an essential scene, Woody even urges Sid imperatively to "play nice."

Building upon the fact that Pixar's film was produced on the behalf of the Walt Disney Company, it seems plausible to apply to the film a strategy Disney is actually famous for. Calling it the "Disney effect" (117), Henry A. Giroux and Grace Pollock describe the company's main marketing strategy as an "enormous corporate apparatus that sought to connect the pleasure of film viewing with firmly entrenched habits of consumption" (ibid.) and therefore "to reduce children's identities to the role of consumer" (125). When one compares these evidences with the production background of *Small Soldiers*, it seems important to mention that it is co-produced by the Dreamworks Studios, known for subverting the ideologies connected with the reactionary narratives in many Disney films (Zipes 211). Considering these aspects, it is possible to read *Small Soldiers* as a film that actually challenges the ideological implications presented in *Toy Story*. While Lasseter's movie is primarily interested in portraying the damage done to toys as something quite horrifying, thereby underlining their commercial value in a subtle way that is manifested in a proclaimed "correct" way to play with them, *Small Soldiers* actually embraces this narrative possibility: although all toy figures presented in the film at first glance also seem to be predominantly cinematic representations of franchise toys that can be bought by the children viewers in toyshops afterwards, this assumption is contested by the immense quantity of scenes showing the toys breaking into pieces.

It starts with the "death" of one Commando, Brick Bazooka, who, following the bicycling Alan for spying on him, accidently is cut into pieces. In a following episode, Alan smashes another attacking Commando, a demolition expert named Nick Nitro, into the garbage grinder that shreds his lower body part. Following this increasing tendency, the film almost develops a proper delight in destruction: This is satirically shown in Christy's rage against an animated army of her former Barbie doll collection, as the Commandos duplicate and apply their microchip-technology to bring them to life as a method to hire new recruits. Christy seems to generate a playful lust smashing them with a baseball bat. At this point, the film seems to support both the idea of a kind of creative play *and* the creation of a unique childish approach by not playing with the toys as they are intended to be played with. This intention of the film reaches a culminating point when at the end a whole army of Commando toys is being destroyed by an electric shockwave distorting them completely. In this way, by showing the potential franchise toys either being burned or torn to pieces, the film undermines the portrayed Disney-related generic codes of cinematic marketing which are presented all too evidently in films like *Toy Story* and the portrayal of its toy heroes as utterly alluring for an additional key market. In a very original way, *Small Soldiers* subverts the aestheticization of the toys to make them part of commodity culture while instead highlighting the values of creative child's play as a countermeasure against pure consumption.

By the end of the film, Alan has proved himself to his father and conquered Christy as a love interest without having to necessarily mature, but by exposing the childish qualities of creativity, something atypical of such narratives. The possibility given to him to settle things this way is in turn guaranteed by the Gorgonites. Only with their help and presence, manifested in the simple state of child's play, the symbiosis between a playing teen and his toys, both Alan and the Gorgonites, could master the given obstacles and defeat the Commando Elite. Particularly the restored familiar bond at the end could also be interpreted as a proposed reconciliation, suggesting that adults could try not to dominate by simply finding possibilities to understand childhood and children's culture. It should be remembered that the toy shop of Alan's father is called "The Inner Child." This term was predominantly used in the 1990s in popular psychology to evoke an adult nostalgic longing for a heavily idealized and therefore constructed notion of one's own childhood, thus encouraging the stated use of the idea of the child as a projection screen.[2] One could argue that the film depicts an alternative notion for this term by suggesting that adults value childhood qualities such as play and acknowledge the use of toys as something that used to exist, but now simply does not belong to them anymore which, as a legitimate category, should not be treated from a superior perspective.

Although *Small Soldiers* is a film produced by adults, the outlined narrative structure could therefore be considered as a way to help adults understand the value of play. As a consequence, it is exactly this role of the toy in *Small Soldiers* that provides the possibility of childhood values and serves as a premise for the appraisal of the potential of still being a kid, correlated with a brief critique of mere consumption and determined play by adult culture, which makes the toy in *Small Soldiers* a real hero.

Conclusion

It is common ground in Western culture to place the toy as a pawn of hegemonic discourses. Concerning the definition of the child, toys are mainly treated in the way of "kid stuff." Deemed to be simple reminiscences of the merely ephemeral status of childhood, they are equally regarded only as an extension of the child's limited agentic possibilities. On the other hand, the toy seems to be a dominant signifier of a materialistic commodity culture, a consumer object whose significance and the way of usage and playing are hugely determined by adult interests. In *Small Soldiers,* one can find a subtle remark regarding the connection of both of these discourses when Major Chip Hazard sloganizes the role of his team proclaiming: "We are the Commando Elite, everything else is just a toy!" Devaluating and trivializing the role of a common toy, making it somehow childish in a negative sense, the Commando Elite, in its nature fused with military technology and, accordingly probably one of the most gruesome metaphors for a repressive adult world, is therefore simultaneously a not-toy, something merely grown and not belonging to the world of the child anymore. Simultaneously, *Small Soldiers* offers possibilities how to challenge and subvert exactly these stated discursive constructions, providing satirical implications against consumerism and adult control by exactly relying on the values of children's culture of play and particularly the role of the toy.

As this essay has tried to demonstrate, the proclamation of the film as a child's movie serves not only to camouflage its subversive potential while these values are instead—especially the significance of toys for childish creativity—introduced as countermeasures against adult hegemony. For this reason, the film actually offers possibilities regarding the consideration of the potentially subversive core of children's film in general. Ian Wojcik-Andrews suggests that certain children's films possess a self-reflexive attitude with regard to their unfolding of the narrative's constructed nature and therefore also the made-up character of corresponding inherent ideologies (11). *Small Soldiers* exactly assesses to this possibility by offering the trope of the animated toy. The film presents the toy as a symbol for the creative potential of child's play, thereby also functioning as a subversive counter narrative against adult discourses concerning the state of childhood and the corresponding role of toys as well as consumerism. This method of employing toy figures belongs to a long tradition in art history and would also offer an interesting opportunity for further researches, such as, for instance, a further analysis of its subversive potential in contemporary media texts.

Notes

1. A widely discussed problem that will always remain in media texts made from adults for children follows Jacqueline Rose's famous claim of an impossibility of children's literature as it exclusively produced from the perspective of the adult (Rose).
2. See Kincaid, *Erotic Innocence* 69–72 (the subsection on The Child Within).

Works Cited

Bamber, Martyn. "Joe Dante." *Senses of Cinema*. 01.02.2003. Recovered from http://sensesofcinema.com/2003/great-directors/dante.
Barnets, Roland. "Toys." *The Consumption Reader*. Ed. David B. Clarke and Marcus A. Doel. New York: Routledge University Press, 2003. 27–28.
Brew, Simon. "The Den of Geek Interview: Joe Dante." *Den of Geek!* 21.02.2008. Recovered from http://www.denofgeek.com/movies/gremlins/13227/the-den-of-geek-interview-joe-dante.
Corsaro, William A. *The Sociology of Childhood*. Thousand Oaks: Pine Forge Press, 1997.
_____. *We're Friends Right? Inside Kid's Culture*. Washington, D.C.: Joseph Henry Press, 2003.
Freud, Sigmund. "Creative Writers and Day-Dreaming." *On Creative Writers and Day-Dreaming*. Ed. Ethel Spector Person, Peter Fonagy, Servulo Augusto Figueria. London: Carnac Books, 2013. 2–13.
_____. *Writings on Art and Literature*. Stanford: Stanford University Press, 1997.
Giroux, Henry A., and Gene Pollock. *The Mouse That Roared: Disney and the End of Innocence*. Lanham, MD: Rowman & Littlefield, 2010.
Holland, Patricia. *Picturing Childhood: The Myth of the Child in Popular Imagery*. London: I.B. Tauris, 2004.
Howarth, Michael. "Surreal Estate: Building Self-Identity in *Monster House*." In *Kidding Around: The Child in Film and Media*. Ed. Alexander N. Howe & Wynn Yarbrough. New York/London: Bloomsbury Publishing Inc., 2014.
Jenks, Chris. *Childhood*. London: Routledge, 1996.
Kincaid, James R. *Child-Loving: The Erotic Child and Victorian Culture*. London: Routledge, 1992.
_____. *Erotic Innocence: The Culture of Child Molesting*. Durham: Duke University Press, 1998.
Kitzinger, Jenny. "Who Are You Kidding? Children, Power, and the Struggle Against Sexual Abuse." *Constructing and Reconstructing Childhood: Theory, Policy and Social Practice*. London: Falmer Press, 1996. 157–183.
Kuznets, Lois Rostow. *When Toys Come Alive: Narratives of Animation, Metamorphosis and Development*. New Haven: Yale University Press, 1994.
Lury, Karen. "The Child in Film and Television: Introduction." *Screen*. March 2005, 307–314.
Nodelman, Perry. *The Hidden Adult: Defining Children's Literature*. Baltimore: John Hopkins University Press, 2008.
Rose, Jacqueline. *The Case of Peter Pan, or the Impossibility of Children's Fiction*. Philadelphia: University of Pennsylvania Press, 1992.

Rosenbaum, Jonathan. "Cutting Heroes Down to Size." *Chicago Reader.* 23.07.1998. Recovered from http://www.chicagoreader.com/chicago/cutting-heroes-down-to-size/Content?oid=896882.
_____. "Toy Story." *Chicago Reader.* 01.11.1995. Recovered from http://www.chicagoreader.com/chicago/toy-story/Film?oid=989887.
Salvi, Carolyn. "A Krank's Dream: Espistemology, Aesthetics, and Ideology in *The City of Children.*" *Lost and Othered Children in Contemporary Cinema.* Ed. Debbie Olson and Andrew Scahill. Lanham, MD: Lexington Books, 2012.
Wojcik-Andrews, Ian. *Children's Films: History Ideology, Pedagogy, Theory.* New York: Garland, 2000.
Zipes, Jack. *Fairy Tales and the Art of Subversion.* New York: Routledge, 2012.

The Lonely Doll Series
Fantasy and Fear

MARY BRONSTEIN

"I dream, awake, I dream of falling dolls who need cribs and blankets and pajamas with real feet in them."—Sexton

The doll is a curious thing in the life of a child. At best, a doll is a mute roommate, sharing intimate space while offering infinite possibilities, disappointments and unmet expectations all at once. There are a myriad of types of toys that might fit into under the category of Doll: baby dolls, fashion dolls, miniature dolls, action figures, to name the most common. This chapter focuses on the type of doll that is a representation of little girls, which are typically given to real little girls in early childhood. A doll such as this is an object that is manufactured, purchased, and given with a sole intention: that it will be loved. A doll is a tool of play, built to exist in relation to a child, with a child, for a child and most importantly, of a child. When a doll is played with it becomes a conduit for the narrative texts, desires, dreams,

"Once there was a little doll…. She was very lonely?"—*The Lonely Doll* (All photographs reproduced with permission. Photographs by Dare Wright © Copyright Estate of Dare Wright / Dare Wright Media, LLC. The Lonely Doll® is a registered trademark of Dare Wright Media, LLC).

and pathologies of childhood in ways that other toys do not. Quite simply, doll is a plaything that is made to represent a human being. In play, it transcends mere representation and is able to embody the meaning of an actual being. In fact, it becomes a true companion who is an unquestioningly submissive participant in whatever life the owner decides to create for it. Dolls are gifted, dolls are chosen, dolls are wished for, dolls are collected and dolls are saved. Dolls are also readily abused, resented, destroyed and abandoned. As Lois Rostow Kuznets states, "[T]he doll, created in the unsexed image of the human yet by custom and imagination usually considered female, is, beyond all other playthings the most capable of arousing a child's violent longing or loathing" (95). Because of this the doll can be seen as an object that communicates passivity, inaction, and self-denying servitude, even in the midst of being actively played with. This is illustrated beautifully in Rumer Godden's children's novel, *A Doll's House*, in which a doll explains how it feels to occupy this type of powerless position in the possession of a child: "it is an anxious, sometimes a dangerous thing to be a doll. Dolls cannot choose; they can only be chosen; they cannot 'do'; they can only be done by; children who do not understand this often do wrong things, and then the dolls are hurt and abused and lost; and when this happens the dolls cannot speak" (Kuznets 111). These are articulate words from a doll that understands herself as a non-living entity at the mercy of the children she is meant to serve. Artist Dare Wright introduced a different sort of protagonist doll to young readers in 1957. This doll is Edith: The Lonely Doll.

Dare Wright wrote and photographically illustrated ten books from 1957 to 1981 that chronicle the adventures of a doll named Edith and her companions: two teddy bears named Mr. Bear and Little Bear. *The Lonely Doll* series[1] is intended for young children, but does not use the traditional rhetorical and aesthetic concepts typical to the children's picture book genre. In visual

"She stole quietly out of the house."—*Edith and Mr. Bear*

terms, these books immediately strike the child reader as different from other picture books on their shelf. The main texts of these books are not words, but large, high-contrast black and white photographs that take up the majority of each and every page in each book. The space the photographs occupy is accentuated by the generous size of the books themselves; large enough to fill a child's entire field of vision. Unlike traditionally formatted children's picture books, wherein the illustrations are meant to depict aspects of the primary text of the written narrative, Wright's photographs *are* the books. The written text (typically no more than two sentences on a page) is used in much the way that intertitles are used in silent films, used only when dialog or action cannot be explicitly communicated through the images. Wright does not use her words to explain, describe or expound on the action presented in the photos because this is not necessary. By building the stories with carefully staged and art directed photographic tableaus, the emotional story arc of each book can be fully understood even by those who cannot yet read. Within the differences between Wright's books and other children's literature, one finds the value and significance of these books. The books in Wright's series speak to children in a way that other books do not and cannot.

The books are a meditation on fears of abandonment, confusion of identity, and the conflict between wanting to be cared for and wanting to be independent that children experience on a deeply felt level. Edith is a character who represents the thoughts and anxieties that children cannot articulate with words; thoughts and anxieties that question their place, relevance, and instability in a world made for adults.

The use of black and white photographs is important in relation to Edith's life in the books and the uniqueness of Wright's work. They lend immediacy, legitimacy, a sense of voyeuristic power and an aura of secrecy to the process of engaging with the books.

"**Edith went to bed that night thinking of a pony.**"—*Edith and Midnight*

The photos of Edith and the bears become the point of view of the reader who is peeking at a world that does not know it is on display. The tone of the photographic work is serious; these are images made by a photographer who does not desire to pander to a commercialized idea of what may appeal to the young reader. Wright was a self-taught photographic artist, having learned to photograph and develop film by watching and asking questions during her years as a fashion model (Ashley). The photographs that make up these books were developed by the author's own hand in a closet darkroom in her apartment. The colorless photos are strikingly simple in their frankness and become both object and a living being. On why the use of color is so uniformly associated with children's literature, Julia Kristeva explains, "It is through color—colors—that the subject escapes its alienation within a code (representational, ideological, symbolic, and so forth) that it, as a conscious subject accepts the chromatic apparatus, like rhythm in language, thus involves a shattering of meaning and its subject into a scale of differences" (Nodelman 258). Without any color the subject of the photo is *not* separated from its actual meaning. The photographs require the young reader to slow down and live with the image on each page, which lends a personal and immersive feel to the experience of reading the books. Compared to the visual shorthand, vibrant color and aesthetic noise that are ubiquitous in the adult-produced visual lives of children, these books wash over the young reader with an unprecedented calmness and stillness. Wright extends to the child an opportunity to sit with images that are best read through emotional terms instead of through a more literal representational lens. Because children cannot know her through the language of realistic color, Edith takes on an otherworldliness that adds an uncanny feeling of watching her navigate a world that exists at the tipping point of reality and fantasy.

Edith must be understood as a real toy before she can ever be discussed as a character in Wright's published work. Because Edith is infused with the meaning and purpose of a beloved toy with lived experiences between herself and the author, it is impossible to see her as just a narrative prop. Wright received the actual Edith doll at eight years of age as a gift from her mother (Ashley). Edith is a 22-inch imported Italian doll made in felt by the Lenci Doll Company in 1922, which cost approximately $12.55 at the time of purchase (ibid.). Given that this is the equivalent of $177 in 2015, the doll was an extremely luxurious gift for a young girl at the time. As in Edith's case, dolls of this sort were not brought home casually from the local toy store; they were bought in adult-oriented department stores as objects of status. Children's relationships with them were often limited to seeing them displayed on a shelf or locked in a glass cupboard (Forman-Brunell 225). In the hierarchy of dolls that children intuitively understand, some dolls are to be played with and some are to be looked at and collected. There are dolls that seem to beg the child to use them as tools of play and love without hesitation and others that somehow keep children at bay due to their readable essence as emissaries from the adult world.

Wright used Edith as a play tool throughout her childhood and came to love her as a comfort object (Ashley). A testament to her careful treatment of the doll is the pristine condition Edith's original clothes are in today (ibid.). Through Wright's desire to exist in relation to her as a being instead of an object, Edith transcends her intended role as a delicate object. When Wright re-discovered Edith in her adulthood, she transformed the doll from the baby doll of her youth to a fashionable girl in her own image. Having learned seamstress skills from her mother, Wright designed and sewed all of the costumes Edith wears (ibid.). As an artist, Wright's relationship with Edith became one of creative focus. The photos Wright made with Edith are as much the product of an artistic partnership as any work made possible through the creative symbiosis of two human beings. She exists on the page as a fully intentional being bursting with life. The respect for the toys is apparent in the photographs and becomes so for the child reader. It is through her deeply emotional context as a visitor from childhood that Edith can be such a powerful protagonist in Wright's work. It is also because of Edith's status as a real toy that Wright was able to use her as a subject to full emotional potential. Edith-as-toy is the cooperative, trustworthy, known, risk-taking entity that was, in essence, hired by Wright to play Edith The Lonely Doll.

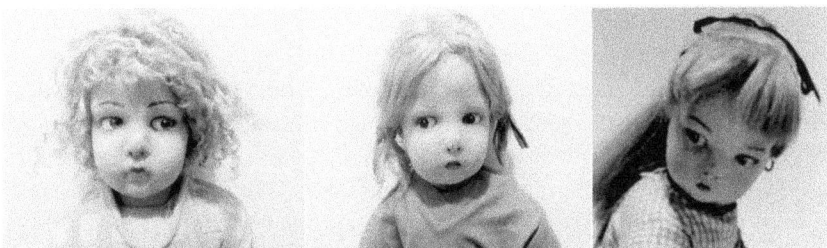

Fig. 1, *left*: A perfectly preserved Lenci 109 series doll manufactured in 1925. This is how Edith would have looked at the time of her purchase, complete with original curly hair. Fig. 2, *center*: A version of the same model doll that was been preserved and was played with and her hair was combed out (Fig. 1 and Fig. 2 photographs by Patricia Hayes). Fig. 3, *right*: The same doll as above, known as Edith from the cover of *The Lonely Doll*. She is photographed after 35 years of play and unpreserved storage and has been restyled by Wright for the books (photograph by Dare Wright).

In Charles Baudelaire's 1853 essay, "The Philosophy of Toys," the writer posits that the first "metaphysical stirring" a child experiences is found in the struggle to find a soul in a beloved toy. He states that children do everything they do with and to a toy as a way to ask "But where is its soul?" (Driscoll 189). Edith has been given a soul by the author. This soul was developed through the years of emotional attachment Edith enjoyed with Wright, but it was given to her in literal terms by the very act of making her the subject in an expansive literary narrative. In fact, a conversation with Lenci doll expert Patricia Hayes (2015) reveals that Edith only exists in her immortalized form because she was so thoroughly loved. The dolls of Lenci's 109 series had faces made entirely from felt. A doll that was purchased in 1922 and then photographed thirty-five years later after years of active play would be altered due to deterioration of the delicate material (Hayes). No one can buy a doll that looks exactly like Edith even if it is the same make and model. Edith is Edith because she is Edith; she is loved, she is used, she is part of life. This gives her identity beyond an anonymous 109 series doll by the Lenci Company. In the books, there is no doubt in the reader that Edith has a soul, or at least is metaphysically connected with humanness is such a way that allows her to feel things deeply. Edith is lonely, after all. In the books, she also is jealous, insecure, excited, proud, hurt, thoughtful, anxious, above all, longing. Being able to endow a doll with a soul is the fantasy of every child who has ever played with one. The power and magic that this would entail is not lost on a child and results in deeply connected and complicated relationships with dolls and other beloved toys.

At the beginning of the first *Lonely Doll* book, the reader is introduced to Edith through her loneliness. She lives in a house that she believes is completely devoid of any other living beings. She perceives herself as living alone and as being alone in the world, with no past and no future. Importantly, it is not a doll-sized house that she inhabits, but a human-sized one. There is strong evidence in the space that this house is not uninhabited by human beings; it is fully furnished, decorated, and filled with belongings. Edith does not tell the reader how she came to be in this house. Importantly, Edith never mentions the absence of people per se, just that she does not wish to be alone anymore. Is Edith unaware of the existence of humans and her inherent connection to them as a doll or is she unaware of her doll status? The reader does not know, but the absence of humans in this domestic space is loud. Most curiously, none of the spaces Edith moves through show signs of a child living in the house. Edith does not come from a child's room. In fact, she comes from no room in the house. Unlike dolls in most homes, there does not seem to be a space where she belongs. She moves through various rooms and into outside space, but she does not lay claim to any particular place. Edith does not know where to go or what to do in these rooms. According to the scholarship of Walter Ong, children's literature as a genre can be defined by its employment of "close reference to the human lifeworld, assimilating the alien, objective world to the more immediate familiar interaction of human beings" (Nodelman 219). Maria Nikolajeva further adds that children's literature focuses on "autonomy of the 'felicitous space' from the rest of the world; a special significance of home; absence of death and sexuality; and, as a result, a general sense of innocence" (ibid.). But Edith lives in a space that is not innocent. It is a space that would be scary to any real child: there is no one to take care of her. Edith is a doll who is not simply lonely; she is actually alone.

In qualifying Edith's loneliness, the third person narrator explains that Edith has everything she needs except for someone to play with. Edith is a doll. As such, she be can defined as that which does *not* need. Edith does not need to eat, sleep, have clothes or shelter. Edith thinks she needs these things because Edith does not know she is a doll. But Edith does not claim to be a human child either. Edith does not know what she is because she is being denied the one actual purpose of any doll: to be played with. Without being useful as a plaything, this doll ceases to fulfill its only intention or reason for being. Edith does recognize a desire to have someone to play with, but her wish and its fulfillment are meaningfully misguided. Her wish is heard by two bears, which arrive at the house to be her friends and ostensibly prevent her from feeling loneliness ever again. But a toy cannot find meaning and life in other toys. A world in which toys spend eternity alone with other toys becomes an allegory for the afterlife fantasy of toys in a garbage heap or dusty attic. Through their union the three toys unconsciously embark on a process of deep denial about their status as unwanted or unused toys. Mr. Bear immediately puts himself in the role of father to both Edith and Little Bear, setting boundaries and rules of behavior. He takes them on trips to places that nice dolls and teddy bears don't often get taken: to the beach, to the farm, for walks on city streets. He scolds them and punishes them for naughty behavior. Edith comes to form an anxious attachment to Mr. Bear, as evidenced by the constant fear she that will disappoint him in such a way that he will leave her alone again. But this is not what Edith wished for. She did not ask for a father and a sibling—she asked for friends to play with. As a toy himself Mr. Bear

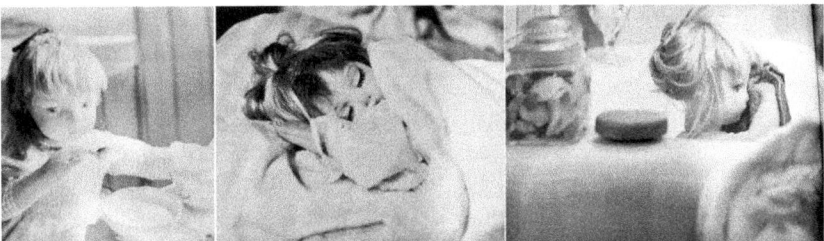

Left: Edith eats alone in *The Lonely Doll*. *Center:* Edith sleeps alone in *Edith and Mr. Bear*. *Right:* Edith takes a bath alone in *Edith and Mr. Bear*.

compounds the reality of Edith's loneliness by wrangling whatever agency and independence she had through her denial of toy-ness into a father-child relationship wrought with uncertainty and emotional manipulation.

A primal fear of all human beings is loneliness. This debilitating feeling signals the actual or perceived lack of connection to others, which signals a panic regarding survival. When children experience loneliness the actual sense of lack that is experienced is complicated by an existential horror: children cannot exist alone. Children fear abandonment and loneliness in a fundamental and visceral way. It is as if children know that if they were truly abandoned and left behind by the world, they he or she will surely die. This truth sits in the depths of the child's mind during and colors the way adults and caregivers are seen and attachments formed. As such, young children know on the deepest level that they can only exist in relation to others. They must be loved or they will disappear. The terrifying reality of the in-relation-to existence of the child is exactly mirrored by a toy's precarious existence in the world. Just as D.W. Winnicott states, "there is no such thing as an infant" (587), it may also be said that there is no such thing as a doll. After all, what is a doll without a person? It only can mean the sum of its artificial parts. It is devoid of emotional or narrative meaning, it is useless and irrelevant. It is in fact nothing at all. Sensing this deeply, Edith longs for someone to play with. While Edith claims to live in an empty home and the reader never sees anyone in the space, it is discovered toward the end of the first book that there is indeed woman who either lives or used to live in this home. Edith and Little Bear find a dressing room in the home and aggressively invade this private space, looking through the woman's shoes, jewelry, clothes, and makeup. Edith and Little Bear sit on the vanity table, knocking things over, spilling water and making a mess out of a previously beautiful and serene arrangement. This dressing room is beautifully kept, extremely feminine, and fantastical in its abundance of lovely items from hegemonic womanhood. It becomes a place in which Edith and Little Bear get very angry about the behavioral constraints imposed by Mr. Bear. They take their rage at him out on the space and even go so far as to vandalize the mirror with insults written in lipstick. When discovered by Mr. Bear his immediate scolding is, "These things do not belong to you!" Who do they belong to? No one asks and no one tells. Of course, the reader intuits that they belong to the woman who lives in this home. The woman who should have been taking care of Edith but who Edith has no access to. The dressing room is the place that illustrates the reason that Edith is the lonely doll: she is in proximity to the possibility of belonging to a person yet does not know where or how to look for this person. This scene is one of missed connections between Edith's life and one shared with someone who loves and cares for her as she desires.

Edith is ostensibly an abandoned toy who struggles to keep herself relevant and in existence. Edith's independence as a doll in a human world cannot be interpreted as a fantasy projection about freedom; it is a lonely trap. Because of this, Edith seeks out living beings over the company of the two bears throughout the entire series. She longs for a connection to things that live, breathe, and need her. Edith finds baby birds, kittens, a myriad of farm animals, and a duck through the course of ten books. She is fascinated by the animals and often wants to possess them, love them, and take them to live at home with her. Mr. Bear forbids most of it, but does allow her to bring a kitten into the home. Edith's love for the kitten becomes so intense that Little Bear becomes violently jealous and Mr. Bear feels the need to scold Edith for showing preference for the kitten over her true friends. Wright uses real animals in the photographs with Edith, to an intriguing result. In pictures without living things, Edith seems very much alive. There is implied movement, energy, and the appearance of varied expressions. However, shown with real animals, the inanimate toy-ness of Edith becomes clear. The animals sometimes blur in the frame while Edith remains in perfect focus. The animals can do harm to Edith, such as when the kitten plays with her hair so much that it becomes a tangled mess. The animals also do not appear to truly look at her. They clearly know that Edith is not alive. This is part of Edith's deep sadness: she wants to be seen, but moreover she wants to be infused with meaning by something that is *really* alive.

That Edith never seeks out or mentions a desire for a human companion is extremely striking. It points to the duality of her consciousness and limits of her existence. In *Edith Learns a Lesson* the doll becomes ill with the measles and passes time by reading *Now We Are Six* by A.A. Milne, a book in which Winnie the Pooh appears. As Edith reads Milne's work is she aware of the similarities and differences between herself and Pooh? Winnie is a toy that comes alive through his relationship with Christopher Robin, a young boy who loves his toys as real beings and thus infuses them with living narratives. Edith is a toy that comes alive through means not clear to her or the reader. Does she wonder where *her* Christopher Robin might be? In these moments Edith is living the everyday life of a human child and is endowed with all the meaning and emotion that this entails. Without humans in her world to act as a reality test Edith cannot sense her own doll-ness and this becomes her biggest struggle toward overcoming her loneliness. The poem "Forgotten" in *Now We Are Six* must be a particularly curious one for Edith to read as it discusses toys lined up on a shelf what for their child to return to his room. It must be assumed that Wright gives this book to Edith in a very purposeful way. This is Wright's invitation for Edith to discover context for her loneliness:

> Here they've been waiting
> All through the day;
> Big Bears and Little Bears [Milne].

A doll is a toy that is designed to be a pretend human being and related to as such. Because of this, Edith has an innate need to be around life that the teddy bears do not have. Wright underscores this by never having the bears show a true understanding of this need and instead show them constantly trying to convince Edith that they are all she needs. The message from both bears is clear: Edith's loyalty should belong to other toys, not creatures from the living world. The world that Wright places Edith in is a deserted island. There are no people on the beaches where the toys vacation, no people on the streets of New York on which they walk, no people in Central Park, no people on the farm that they visit. There are no people for Edith to find even if she wanted to try to connect with them. There are only two photographs in the series that do include actual human beings and those are both in *Edith and Little Bear Lend a Hand*. In both instances, the toys are either ignored entirely or positioned so small in the frame as to render them insignificant. As such, the world that Edith inhabits is quite different than the one a young reader experiences. Because Edith is generally photographed in spaces where people *should* be but are not, Edith-the-character can become uncanny instead of intrinsically comforting. The reader must confront the reality of Edith-as-doll in the processing of her stories. As defined by Sigmund Freud in 1919, uncanniness can be described as "something which is familiar and old—established in the mind and which has become alienated from it only through a process of repression" (241). Wright often positions the reader in potentially comforting and joyful spaces. Yet these spaces have been altered through their emptiness so as to disconnect them from the reader's lived experiences. How many children have played on a completely empty beach? Lived in a home with no adults? Because the reader is shown these images in photographic form, Edith's doll-ness and the toy-ness of the bears are exposed through uncanny violations of the rules of living that a young reader has only recently learned are consistent. The world in the book is real, because it is being shown in photographs, but it is completely foreign from the child's experience in its emptiness, stillness and lack of color. Philosopher Ernst Jentsch discussed a particular aspect of the uncanny that is of use when discussing Edith:

> Among all the psychical uncertainties that can become a cause for the uncanny feeling to arise, there is one in particular that is able to develop a fairly regular, powerful and very general effect: namely, doubt as to whether an apparently living being is really animate and, conversely, doubt as to whether a lifeless object may not in fact be animate [8].

In this case, a double sense of uncanny is present in the books: the reader can feel an unease as to Edith's ambivalent status as a doll who denies her own doll-ness by acting with independent agency in a world that does not include people. But the reader can also take in the uncanny feelings that Edith senses about herself in this world. As the very title *The Lonely Doll* states, Edith is not emotionally comfortable despite being in the form of an object that is symbolic of the joys and comforts of childhood. The double layer of uncanniness in the books provides the intrigue and mystique that draws young readers to these books like moths to a flame. They become a sort of emotional puzzle, which challenge the young mind to decide who or what is real or not real on every page.

In Jentsch's language, Edith cannot be considered living; she is an "apparently living being" (8). Rostow furthers this idea when she states that narratives involving toys that have come to life "resonate with the suffering, confusion, and release of psychic energy that dominate the process of coming to feel independently real, a subject rather than an object" (75). In this description, Rostow unwittingly describes a difficult task of the developing child: coming to terms with what it means to be a living individual who is the subject of an internal experience not shared or governed by others. While developing, children exist on the perpetual brink of real and unreal, of subject and object. When children become aware of the rules that constitute the categories of "alive" and "not alive," a specific kind of existential terror is experienced. The child must contend with their precarious place in the category of "alive." A particularly uneasy realization of young childhood is twofold: the child has not been alive and part of the world for very long at all but has no memory of where they were before. Simultaneous to this is the increased knowledge that the world existed before they did and that their parents lived without them before their birth. This realization comes with confusing and frightening questions: before I was born, where was I? Was I me? When did I start? Who am I in relation to these other people? Who do they want me to be? What am I to them? Is their love and protection of me contingent on what I do? Might they go away if I am not careful? Wright is not afraid to explore these deeply felt but rarely articulated childhood anxieties directly with her young readers. By presenting Edith as a being who is searching for life and meaning but has no past, the young reader cannot help but understand Edith's desire to be in relation with other beings. Edith comes to embody a very particular subconscious fear in the emotional lives of children: how do I know where I belong when everything was already as it will be when I arrived? Do I belong to my parents or do they belong to me? And finally: am I a real person or just an object for adults to control and create purpose from?

Using a doll to explore these themes is an inspired way to make the emotional content of the narratives a step removed from the young reader. Edith comes to represent the child, but since she is actually a manipulated object, the child can meter how close or distanced it is safe to be from her struggle and emotions. Since toys are so centralized in the lives of children, experiencing the narratives enacted by Edith and the bears becomes a kind of extension of their own emotional, narrative-based playwork. Freud states, "in their early games children do not distinguish at all sharply between living and inanimate objects, and that they are especially fond of treating their dolls like live people ... the idea of a 'living doll' excites no fear at all; children have no fear of their dolls coming to life, they may even desire it" (232). While I agree with Freud that children have a deep wish to connect with their toys on levels beyond what is possible in reality, I contend that he misses a vital piece of truth: children above the age of four know on a very conscious level what is real and not real, what is actually alive and what is not. The difference between adults and children in this realm is that the mind of a child allows for the possibility that what they think they know *might not be true*. This is the essential work of childhood: manipulating, experimenting, rearranging, disregarding, fearing and conquering the rules of space, time, identity, and reality through the use of play materials. Many adults misunderstand this process as the inability of a child to know the boundaries of the universe, but in actuality, the child is playing with those boundaries in order to know them from all angles. It is not at all true that children do not fear their toys coming alive; they wish for it and play at it precisely *because* they fear it.

Above and beyond Wright's use of Edith as a proxy for secret fears and anxieties of the young reader, Edith is also the embodiment of an ultimate fantasy for any highly imaginative child. The reader does not know just what circumstance has made Edith a lonely doll. Just as it is possible that a person discarded her, it is also possible that Edith has chosen to abandon the person who loves her. The child who gifts her dolls with life and invests real emotions in their care and play narratives takes many risks: what would happen if my doll abandoned *me*? If my doll could do this, who *else* could? Simultaneous to this is the converse fantasy: what if I suddenly had no family? What would I be in the world and who would take care of me? What if I were *lonely*? Outwardly expressing these essential questions

"Goodbye, our duck. See you in the spring, dear duck. Oh, Mr. Bear, why is spring so far away?"—*Edith and the Duckling*

from a child's developmental experience in a nonthreatening and fantastical is the core of the art and poetics of Dare Wright, but this is also the absolute power of Edith The Lonely Doll.

The last book of the series, *Edith and the Duckling*, is Wright's most frank expression of the themes Edith embodies for her readers. In this story, Edith and Little Bear find an egg, which hatches a helpless little duckling. Edith very seriously cares for the duckling and even tells Mr. Bear that she is the duckling's mother. When Edith is faced with the inevitable abandonment by the growing duck because of its desire to fly south with a flock of other ducks, Edith is immensely upset. Edith knows that she has to let this duck be a duck. She knows she must allow the duck to go because that is how it will be happiest, but this means she may never see it again. How similar this is to the dilemma of the beloved toy as a child grows up or of parents as their child ages. It also explicitly simulates a central struggle of childhood; the constant push from the adult world for increased emotional and physical separation from one's parents. Wright leaves us with a poignant last moment with Edith: a close-up of her face with tearful eyes. Edith hopes she will see the duck in the spring but laments how far away it seems. In this moment Edith is once again lonely, but not just because of the duck. Edith will not see the reader again after this page.

NOTE

1. The books in *The Lonely Doll* series are not paginated and will be cited by title.

WORKS CITED

Ashley, Brook. Personal Interview. 30 Nov. 2015.
Driscoll, Catherine. "The Doll-Machine: Dolls, Modernism, Experience." *Doll Studies: The Many Meanings of Girls' Toys and Play.* Eds. Miriam Forman-Brunell and Jennifer Dawn Whitney. New York: Peter Lang, 2015. 185–204. Print.
Forman-Brunell, Miriam. "Dolls." *Girlhood in America: An Encyclopedia.* Ed. Miriam Forman-Brunell. Vol. 1. Santa Barbara: ABC-CLIO, 2001. 224–232. Print.
Freud, Sigmond, "The Uncanny." *The Complete Psychological Works of Sigmund Freud.* Trans. James Strachey. Vol. XVII (1917–1919). London: The Hogarth Press, 1955. 217–252. Print.
Hayes, Patricia. "Examples of 1925 Lenci 109 Series dolls." Message to Mary Bronstein. 28 October 2015. Email
Jentsch, Ernst. "On the Psychology of the Uncanny" (1906). Trans. Roy Sellars, *Angelaki* 2.1 (1995): 7–16. Print.
Kuznets, Lois Rostow. *When Toys Come Alive: Narratives of Animation, Metamorphosis, and Development.* New Haven: Yale University Press, 1994. Print.
Nodelman, Perry. *The Hidden Adult: Defining Children's Literature.* Baltimore: Johns Hopkins University Press, 2008.
Sexton, Anne. "The Falling Dolls." *45 Mercy Street.* Ed. Linda Gray Sexton. New York: Houghton Mifflin, 1976. Print.
Winnicott, D. W. "The Theory of the Parent-Infant Relationship." *International Journal of Psycho-Analysis* 41, 585–595. Print.
Wright, Dare. *The Doll and the Kitten.* 1960. Remastered ed. Santa Barbara: Dare Wright Media, 2013. Print.

———. *Edith and Little Bear Lend a Hand*. 1972. Remastered ed. Santa Barbara: Dare Wright Media, 2013. Print.
———. *Edith and Midnight*. 1978. Remastered ed. Santa Barbara: Dare Wright Media, LLC., 2013. Print.
———. *Edith and Mr. Bear*. 1964. Remastered ed. Santa Barbara: Dare Wright Media, 2013. Print.
———. *Edith and the Duckling*. 1981. Remastered ed. Santa Barbara: Dare Wright Media, LLC., 2013. Print.
———. *Edith Learns a Lesson*. 1961. Remastered ed. Santa Barbara: Dare Wright Media, 2013. Print.
———. *A Gift from The Lonely Doll*. 1966. Remastered ed. Santa Barbara: Dare Wright Media, 2013. Print.
———. *Holiday for Edith and the Bears*. 1958. Remastered ed. Santa Barbara: Dare Wright Media, 2013. Print.
———. *The Lonely Doll*. Boston: Houghton Mifflin, 1957. Print.

"Real isn't how you are made"
Heroism and the Power of a Child's Love

KRISTINE LARSEN

"Real" Love and "Real" Toys

In his classic lecture "On Fairy-stories," J.R.R. Tolkien notes that true fairy-stories take place in the "perilous land" he dubs Faërie, which "may perhaps most nearly be translated by magic—but it is magic of a peculiar mood and power, at the furthest pole from the vulgar devices of the laborious, scientific magician" (Flieger and Anderson 27; 32–3). Further explaining his philosophy of Faërie in an essay concerning his late story, *Smith of Wotton Major*, Tolkien muses that it

> represents love: that is, love and respect for all things, "Inanimate" and "animate," an unpossessive love of them as "other." This "love" will produce both *ruth* and *delight*. Things seen in its light will be respected, and they will also appear delightful, beautiful, wonderful even glorious [Flieger 247].

This connection between inanimate objects and love brings to mind Margery William's iconic children's tale *The Velveteen Rabbit*, in which the love of a child is pivotal in fulfilling the toy's desire to become a real rabbit. In the words of the wise Skin Horse, despite the fact that one's outward appearance might become shabby and worn through the intense process, "once you are Real you can't be ugly, except to people who don't understand" (Williams 8). Although the audience of William's tale understands that the story of the Rabbit is not true in the real world sense, while the reader or listener is immersed within the universe of the Rabbit he or she not only willingly suspends disbelief, but as Tolkien offers, actively "believes it, while you are, as it were, inside" (Flieger and Anderson 52). It is the rare reader who has not wiped away a tear at the end of the book. This powerful enchanting of the audience designates Williams as a "successful 'subcreator'" of a wondrous "Secondary World," in Tolkien's words (Flieger and Anderson 52).

While Tolkien's most well-known Secondary World is Middle-earth, he also penned other more whimsical works, such as the children's tale *Roverandom*. The title character is first transformed from a rather foul-mooded canine into a toy dog after a run-in with the wizard Artaxerxes, and then a toy-sized flesh and blood dog thanks to the intervention of sand-sorcerer Psamathos Psamathides. The dog's transition back to real size is fraught with danger and adventure, as he journeys to the moon and the bottom of the sea, and finds that the voyage home involves equal parts love and magic. Kris Swank (31) observes that *Roverandom* is a vastly underappreciated work of Tolkien's, especially given its references to not only Tolkien's larger Middle-earth mythology, but its nods to classical literature and mythologies from across Europe. For example, she methodically lays out how *Roverandom* can be read as an *immrama*, a type of medieval Irish "Otherworld sea-voyage tale" (32). Published posthumously in 1998, the short tale was originally concocted by Tolkien to comfort his second son, Michael, after the nearly five-year-old's much-beloved black and white metal toy dog was accidentally lost on a beach while the family was on vacation at the Yorkshire coast in 1925 (Tolkien ix). The initial tale was fleshed out over the next few years, and although it was submitted to Tolkien's publisher after the submission of *The Hobbit* (1936), it was rejected and apparently forgotten until after the author's death (Tolkien xv).

While the Velveteen Rabbit is a toy who longs to be Real, and Roverandom is a real dog who temporarily becomes a toy, a different permutation of the "toys becoming real" trope is illustrated by the 2007 film *The Last Mimzy*. Loosely based on the 1943 science fiction short story "Mimsy Were the Borogoves" written by Henry Kuttner and C. L. Moore (under the pseudonym Lewis Padgett), the story centers on a young girl, Emma Wilder, and her love for what appears to be a stuffed rabbit (an obvious nod to William's work) but is actually a sophisticated artificial intelligence sent back in time from a dystopian future. Here the goal is not to make the rabbit itself real, but instead to aid Mimzy in completing her mission of returning a pure DNA sample back to the future in order to save the human species. This ultimately involves the entire Wilder family, science teacher Larry White, and his Buddhist fiancée Naomi Schwartz conquering their previously isolated and self-involved worldviews, initial disbelief in Mimzy's true identity, and fears of the wonders they observe, in order to outwit Homeland Security and save Mimzy. Although the central themes of these three works obviously include what it means to be (and become) Real, there are other important refrains that resonate between these works. Among these are definitions of heroes and heroism, the liminal space in which heroes function, the roles of love and magic in the process of becoming Real, and the toy's journey through Faërie. This essay will explore these issues through the complex relationships between children and toys in *Roverandom* and *The Last Mimzy*, and situate these works both in relationship with each other as well as Williams' classic tale.

What Makes a Toy a Hero?

The two rabbits and dog who are central to these three tales are the protagonists of their respective stories, as it is their adventures that drive the action. However, they represent three very different types of heroes. Nilsen and Nilsen discuss various heroic archetypes that can be found in children's literature, with, for example, the titular character of *The Velveteen Rabbit* used as an example of "The Caregiver" archetype (13), a reference to the rabbit standing by the child while he is sick with scarlet fever. Using their definitions, Mimzy fits most clearly into "The Lover or Friend," as Emma is "incomplete without the other" (17). Mimzy can also be seen as a teacher or guide for the children, leading them into increased knowledge and understanding. As Emma explains to Naomi, Mimzy is her "teacher. She teaches me everything" (Shaye, *Last Mimzy*). Roverandom is an example of "The Warrior," one who "moves from fighting and cheating simply for the sake of fighting to fighting within the rules for others and for what really matters on an unselfish level" (12). Roverandom can also be thought of as a trickster character, not the least reasons being his characteristics of "mischief-making, cleverness, and shape-shifting" (Mikkelsen 25).

But what defines a protagonist as a hero in a fairy tale? Joseph Campbell distinguishes between the average hero of a fairy-story as achieving "a domestic, microcosmic triumph, and the hero of myth a world-historical, macrocosmic triumph" (30). On the surface, this is true in the cases of the Velveteen Rabbit and Roverandom, but certainly not for Mimzy. But the dangers of the perilous realm of Faërie should not be made light of. It takes courage, strength, and compassion for the Rabbit to help the Boy recover from scarlet fever. Roverandom flies to the moon, battles dragons, and most importantly, faces his own inner demons. It is through this perilous journey (as much one of self-discovery as physical deeds) that the hero can be defined as such. Faërie takes on a decidedly different form in each of these three tales. The Velveteen Rabbit enters into this Other World when he is forcibly removed from the safety of the nursery and carried outside to be burned with the other scarlet fever infected toys. It is only by happenstance that he is able to escape from the sack and finds himself alone in the perilous world. His tear falling to the ground releases the magic of the nursery Fairy, who is able, through her spells, to grant his wish to become an actual biological rabbit. Emma's tear falling upon Mimzy marks the beginning of the end of the rabbit's and Wilder siblings' journey through Faërie (an adventure begun when the AI was sent back in time on her seemingly hopeless mission and discovered by the children on the beach of their vacation home) as the rabbit is afterwards safely sent home to the future. Roverandom crosses the threshold into Faërie proper not when he is turned into a toy dog, but when he is found on the beach—the realm of "mermen and mermaids, not to speak of the smaller sea-goblins that rode their small sea-horses" (Tolkien 10–11)—by Psamathos and turned into what the sorcerer describes as a "fairy-dog" (Tolkien 12). It is in this form that he visits the fantastical realms of the moon and ocean floor and embarks on his real adventures. Through his adventures Roverandom comes to realize the folly of his selfish ways, and by the end is not only transformed back to his original size, but into a loving and loved pet. Through his adventures in Faërie Roverandom also "grew to be very wise, and had an immense local reputation" (Tolkien 88). The road to becoming Real is not easy, and may lead to permanent separation from those one loves (in the case of the Boy and the Rabbit, and Mimzy and Emma Wilder). No one returns from Faërie the same as they had originally embarked. For example, in the case of Tolkien's most famous tale of Faërie, *The Lord of the Rings*, one need only look at Frodo Baggins, and all that he endured on the quest to save Middle-earth from the One Ring.

The three heroic toys discussed in this essay transgress many boundaries during their trials and tribulations, and at times cannot be easily categorized. Are they toys or animals? They are certainly "real" (i.e., not virtual) yet at times they are not "Real" (i.e., a normal biological entity). It can be argued that Mimzy is never "Real," if we use the narrow definition of a biological entity. Dean Miller (297) describes the hero as a "third thing," outside of the typical binary way of viewing the world as this or that. He suggests that many heroes occupy a liminal position, between "genders and generations, or between the realms of life and death" (296). Such is certainly the case of the characters in these tales as they straddle boundaries between toy and animal. There are other usages of the term *liminal* to describe the hero. Christopher Poulos (487) defines the liminal hero as "the outsider, the loner who rides in from somewhere else, or who shows up out of the blue, or who lives out beyond the edge of town. He is the antihero.... He is often a rogue, a rascal, a rebel." Mimzy is certainly an outsider, an artificial intelligence originating from another time, featuring a technology recognized as alien by Homeland Security. "It's almost as if this thing could be alive," one scientist notes. "It's mimicking a nervous system" (Shaye, *Last Mimzy*). Earlier in the film Emma's parents become alarmed when she and her brother begin manifesting preternatural abilities, such as miraculously improved eyesight, genius level intelligence, and telekinesis. Realizing that somehow Mimzy is not the simple toy she appears to be, Emma's parents relegate the toy to the trash. Like the Velveteen Rabbit after the Boy's scarlet fever, Mimzy is considered diseased and dangerous. It is only after Mimzy speaks through Emma's voice that the parents come to accept that the toy is precisely who Emma claims her to be, and that she wishes their family no harm.

For his part, Roverandom is painted as a "rogue, a rascal, and a rebel" throughout his adventures, daring to defy both social norms and direct orders. For example, his initial metamorphosis into a toy dog is precipitated by biting a wizard and refusing to apologize. When he is treated with compassion by shrimp sharing a shopping basket after he is purchased from a toy store, he rebukes their outreach to him with contempt. He is later exiled to the moon to hide from the wizard after a sorcerer transforms him from a toy dog into a toy-sized real dog. He meddles with the great moon dragon and awakens a sea serpent. Not only is he an outsider because he is on the run from the wizard, and due to his size, but because he has refused to return to his home (a home that he was never fond of). Mew the seagull remarks,

> You can't be called exactly a dog, though you are no longer quite a toy. In fact Psamathos was rather puzzled, I believe, to know what to do with you when you said you didn't want to go home [Tolkien 20].

The Velveteen Rabbit is also viewed as an outsider throughout his story. He is naturally shy and has few friends in the nursery besides the Skin Horse. He is self-conscious of the fact that he is filled with old fashioned sawdust, something that "should never be mentioned in modern circles," and that the more expensive and modern toys regard him with disdain (Williams 3). He is initially unaware that real rabbits even exist, further adding to his isolation. When he finally encounters real rabbits in the garden, he is initially thrilled, until the biological creatures declare that he "isn't a rabbit at all. He isn't real," in direct opposition to the Boy's assertions to the contrary (Williams 19). Even after becoming Real at the end of the tale, the Velveteen Rabbit is markedly different, retaining "strange markings under his fur," palimpsests from his original spotted pattern (Williams 33).

Another liminal state is key to these tales, the dream state between waking and sleeping that is "intermediate between consciousness and unconsciousness" (Stevens 17). Indeed, Tolkien explains that in "dreams strange powers of the mind may be unlocked" (35). Mimzy speaks to the Wilder children in their sleep, teaching them what they need to know in order to send her back to her own time. Emma reports dreaming about a bridge built across the universe while Noah dreams about building an actual bridge modeled after the geometric web he has trained spiders to construct. Once they have been trained by Mimzy, the children can speak telepathically to each other, and others, especially in the dream state. On the dark side of the moon Roverandom meets the boy who had briefly owned him while he was in his toy form. In the boy's dream state, they can communicate clearly as well as engage in real play (such as fetching a ball and running). But the boy suddenly disappears when he awakens in his bed (in the "real world" of the story) and Roverandom is left to wonder what might have been as he takes a peek through a telescope at the boy walking along the shoreline, "Looking for shells or for me?" (Tolkien 47). Roverandom asks the Man-in-the-Moon if dreams come true and is told, "Some, but not all; and seldom any of them straight away, or quite like they were in dreaming them" (Tolkien 46). The possibility that this dream might, indeed, become reality becomes a sustaining hope to the dog during the rest of the book, as he eventually becomes single-minded in his desire to not only regain his physical stature and status as a "real" dog, but specifically to be the boy's real dog.

While dreams as such do not play a role in the transformation of the Velveteen Rabbit, the most important plot points in the story take place at night. Firstly, the Rabbit becomes Real to the Boy through sleeping with the child each night. One very special night the child is unable to sleep because the Rabbit has been accidentally left outside, and he proclaims to his Nana that the Rabbit "isn't a toy. He's Real!" (Williams 13). This is the first stage in the Rabbit's road to becoming Real. The final transition also takes place at night, after the Rabbit and other germ-infected toys have been thrown outside at the end of the garden, abandoned for the moment but under the imminent death threat of being burned with the coming dawn. The dreamlike nature of the Rabbit's subsequent encounter with the nursery magic Fairy also highlights the importance of the liminal nocturnal state in Williams' novel. It is under the cover of darkness that magic comes to life.

Magic, Love and the Metamorphosis

Flieger and Anderson (85) explain Tolkien's Faërie as a "parallel reality tangential in time and space to the ordinary world ... [including] the practice of enchantment or magic, especially through the use of words, for example spells or charms." As previously noted the characters in these works are liminal by definition of their transitional states between toys and real animals. Kuznets (5) offers that when "toys become self-consciously alive, they blur the lines between self and other, subject and object, and require the reader to note those blurred dividing lines, imaginatively if not analytically." In undergoing a multistage process of becoming Real the toy protagonists of these tales can be thought of as shape-shifters. Indeed, Wisker (715) argues that "all forms of metamorphosis" can be said to involve shape-shifting. Not only is the metamorphosis accomplished in well-defined stages, but involves both the love of a child and magic to bring it about.

Williams explains that "nursery magic is very strange and wonderful, and only those playthings that are old and wise and experienced like the Skin Horse understand all about it" (4). The Velveteen Rabbit is initially very much loved on Christmas morning, when he is fresh from the stocking, but is subsequently forgotten until the boy's nursemaid hands the rabbit to him in exasperation when he cannot find the toy he wants. The boy rediscovers the rabbit, who becomes his favorite plaything, and, as a result quite shabby. He no longer resembles a rabbit to anyone other than the child, who alone thinks of him as beautiful. Williams notes that the "nursery magic had made him Real" which meant that his outward appearance to others was of no importance (20). But as Kuznets explains, the metamorphosis of a toy into "an independent subject or self rather than an object or other" involves "submitting to the gaze of more powerfully real and potentially rejecting live beings" (2). As previously noted, the Rabbit experiences this rejection firsthand, discovering that he is only Real in the boy's eyes when he is rebuked by biological rabbits. It is not until the nursery Fairy intercedes that the Rabbit truly becomes "Real" in the sense that he is accepted as a biological rabbit by both humans and other rabbits. Kuznets disagrees with critics of the tale who claim that the Fairy's "intervention exalts self-pity and helplessness," instead reminding us that the Fairy is only able to complete the Rabbit's journey to becoming Real because the Boy had loved Rabbit so deeply. In the end we are reminded that it is as the Skin Horse had warned—the process of becoming Real not only involves magic and love, but considerable pain.

It can be argued that *The Last Mimzy* is a tale of technology, not magic, but as Arthur C. Clarke argues, "any sufficiently advanced technology is indistinguishable from magic" (Inglis-Arkell). The futuristic technology of the "toys" Mimzy brings with her into the present certainly appears to be magic to all who witness it. For example, the babysitter runs out of the house when Emma innocently displays her ability to set stones into motion with her mind, the woman later claiming that the family members are aliens when interviewed by government officials. Just as the Rabbit cannot be ugly once he is Real to the boy "except to people who don't understand" (Williams 8), Mimzy is very much Real to Emma, but merely a stuffed animal to her parents. The parents cannot see the magic in the toys; for example, the luminescent green rectangle that allows Noah to create a small wormhole appears as a dull, lifeless black paperweight to his mother. Just as the Boy of Williams' tale argues to his Nana that the Velveteen Rabbit is not merely a toy, the unnamed boy of Tolkien's story exclaims when he is reunited with Roverandom during their dream adventures "I always thought he was real" (Tolkien 44). In each of these cases we see the magic of the nursery at work, a magic that adults cannot (or will not) accept or comprehend.

It is also important to acknowledge that the nursery magic of *The Last Mimzy* has an urgency that is absent in the other two works. Her journey is not one of becoming real, but rather decaying and being rejuvenated. This transformation is also achieved for the human species as a whole, through the "magic" of time travel. After Emma proclaims her love for Mimzy and her desire to help Mimzy save the future, the toy's smile is visibly widened. This parallels a scene in *The Velveteen Rabbit* in which the rabbit has a "knowing expression" the next morning after the boy declares him to be Real (Williams 13). But in the film, the following day Mimzy's smile has visibly shrunken, and continues to fade after she is seized by Homeland Security, as the toy's technology begins to disintegrate—the magic is failing. It is only Emma's heart wrenching grief and the resulting tears falling on Mimzy that stop the death of the rabbit—and humankind—as the collection of this pure genetic material fulfills the rabbit's mission and saves the future. Mimzy's liminal position between present and future, biological and mechanical, uniquely situates her as the hero of this film, as it is this liminal state that allows her to complete a mission that a Real (biological) organism could not (due to the dangers of time travel). In having Mimzy save the world we subvert one of the tropes that Kuznets identifies in stories where toys become "real": "our fear that technologically sophisticated human creations may take on a life that will outlast human life" (5). Mimzy's life will end once she returns her precious biological cargo to the future, but humanity will live on, as will Emma's love for her.

Both magic and the love of a child are also central to the metamorphosis of Roverandom. When he is turned into a toy dog, Roverandom isn't exactly a normal toy, because, like the Velveteen Rabbit, he can communicate with other toys (and, interestingly, the shrimp stuck into the shopping bag with him), and finds that he can move (unlike the other toys owned by the young boy). After Roverandom is transmuted into a toy-sized biological dog by Psamathos, the tiny fairy-dog is not allowed to enter the "Isle of Lost Dogs, where all the lost dogs go that are deserving or lucky" and is instead banished to the moon (Tolkien 20). Once in this alien environment, magic continues to transmute the dog, as he finds he can imagine himself up white wings with black spots to match his fur so that he can fly with the moon-dog. When he is later sent to the ocean realm Artaxerxes changes Rover's feet and fur and gives him a tail to adapt him to swimming. The final act of magical metamorphosis occurs when Artaxerxes finally changes him back into a full-sized ordinary dog, but Roverandom's journey to becoming real does not solely depend on the changes in his outward appearance. As previously noted, it is the realization of the deep love between him and the child that affects a deep change in the dog's attitude and outlook on life, and the final fulfillment of his wish to be reunited with the boy, completes his transformation. It is what finally makes him "Real." But as in the case of the other two works, that realization does not come without pain. While Roverandom is driven by the seemingly vain hope that his dream on the dark side of the moon might become reality, his hopes are momentarily dashed when he is warned that he must return to his original owner. His joy is palpable when he realizes that his original owner is none other than the grandmother of his beloved boy—the magic does not fail, and neither it seems, does the ultimate power of love.

What Does It Mean to Be "Real"?

A key step in Roverandom's transformation occurs in the midpoint of the story, between his adventures on the moon and on the ocean floor. He notes, "I left my wings behind; they didn't really belong to me. And I should rather like to be an ordinary dog again" (56). As Kuznets (2) describes, stories of toys becoming "live beings, embody human anxiety about what it means to be 'real.'" But what does this entail? What common lesson do these three works provide as to what it truly means to be "real" beyond a simplistic desire to be made of flesh and blood? Tolkien (Flieger and Anderson 34–5) explains that the "magic of Faërie is not an end in itself," but rather related to its ability to satisfy "certain primordial human desires" including traveling in "space and time" and to "hold communion with other living things." It is this final point that defines what it truly means to be "Real" in these tales. But like all aspects of Faërie, this one is fraught danger. Kuznets (75) warns that "magic metamorphosis into flesh and blood for toy or toy-like characters obviously takes more than a wave of a wand," noting that "it can hurt." Thus, she explains, "these narratives resonate with the suffering, confusion, and release of psychic energy that dominate the process of coming to feel independently real, a subject rather than an object." Being "Real" in these stories centers largely not on biology but compassion—interacting with humans and loving them (and being loved in return), and accepting the pain what comes with such relationships (including the pain of letting go). It is as the Skin Horse explains to the Rabbit—being "Real" does not depend on the situation of one's birth, but rather depends on a process of *becoming*—a metamorphosis that can only occur through the process of love. It involves pain and decay, where one is no longer shiny and new but old and shabby—well-loved—and involves more than a modicum of strength. As the Horse warns, "it doesn't often happen to people who break easily, or have sharp edges, or who have to be carefully kept" (Williams 5), as Roverandom discovers.

At the beginning of his journey, Roverandom—back when he was plain Rover—was decidedly not ready to become "Real" despite the fact that he was, in fact, a full-sized biological dog. What Rover lacked was a connection with others. Rover was a loner at beginning of story, a decidedly unpleasant, ill-tempered being. Only the love and patience of the boy allow Roverandom to face and defeat his selfish, self-centered attitude, as it is when he realizes how much he loves the boy in return that he has a clear mission and raison d'être. Rover "felt he could bear it no longer. 'I've got a pain in my inside,' he said. 'I want to go back to the little boy, so that his dream can come true'" (49). This is the birthing pain of Roverandom beginning the process of becoming "Real." When he is reunited with the boy Roverandom finally grows up, putting aside his selfish childhood to become "a large and dignified dog" (Tolkien 88).

Mimzy has a similar effect on the entire Wilder family. Emma is considered an introverted freak by the other kids in her school (including her brother) due to her love for science and music. Her brother is also largely disconnected from the world through his love for technology (his phone and video games). The kids are, in turn, disconnected from their parents; a workaholic father who doesn't recognize changes in his own children, and a mother who does not know how to effectively communicate with her family. Mimzy is the catalyst who brings the family together. First the children establish a telepathic link to Mimzy and each other, and develop a greater connection with nature. Noah listens to Mimzy's conch shell and is able to communicate with insects and spiders. Through this (and his computer skills) he is able to train spiders to weave a bridge-like web that mimics the wormhole needed to send Mimzy back to the future. He develops the ability to conjure up small wormholes using Mimzy's technology, and finds he can visualize the fabric of space-time itself. Emma develops precognition—she knows when her father is about to call—and her mind seems able to travel through the universe, at least in dreams. After their encounter with the federal agents and the realization that Mimzy is, indeed, who Emma claims she is, the family is reunited, but on a far higher plane of emotional connectedness. Mimzy has left an indelible mark on their lives. She has made them "Real." But Mimzy has, with the children's help, done far more than this. As a teacher in the distant future reveals to her students, Emma's DNA in a sense made all of humanity "Real" again. "Our precious quality of humanity had been turned off," she explains. "But in Emma's tears was the instruction for an awakening" (Shaye, *Last Mimzy*). Thus Emma's love for Mimzy allows the AI to act as the intermediary between technology and biology, present and future, and helps make future people "Real" by allowing them to reclaim their humanity.

Emma's tear falling onto Mimzy just as all hope seems lost brings about the happy ending that Tolkien (Flieger and Anderson 75) believes that "all complete fairy-stories" must contain, what he calls a eucatastrophe. More specifically, it is not the happy ending that was expected all along, but a "sudden and miraculous grace" that occurs at the darkest hour (Flieger and Anderson 75). Tolkien also notes that "when the sudden 'turn' comes we get a piercing glimpse of joy, a heart's desire" (Flieger and Anderson 76). The Velveteen Rabbit becomes "Real" just as he is abandoned by the Boy and about to be burned. Roverandom is unexpectedly reunited with the boy who taught him how to love, and Mimzy—the last of her kind—successfully returns to the future and saves humanity. It is certainly appropriate that all three moments bring a tear to the eye. As Tolkien explains, when such moments of eucatastrophe occur in a high quality fairy-story, it causes "a catch of the breath, a beat and lifting of the heart, near to (or indeed accompanied by) tears, as keen as that given by any form of literary art" (Flieger and Anderson 75–6).

Conclusion: Recovering What Is Essential

Singh and Lu (2) note that one of the signatures of "good literature" is complex heroes. In rising above "their own negative traits or weaknesses" they can become strong positive role models for children. Jones and Watkins (11) argue that "moments when the hero is depicted as vulnerable and displays what might traditionally be regarded as feminine characteristics" may especially resonate with girls. All three of the toy heroes discussed here certainly demonstrate weakness and are saved through the intervention of the stereotypically feminized characteristics of love and compassion. For example, the Velveteen Rabbit's ultimate transformation into a biological rabbit comes at a moment of self-pity that is transformed through the love and compassion of both the Boy and the Fairy. The same can be said for Roverandom—forever altered by his love for the boy, he reluctantly obeys the order to return to his original owner. Only Mimzy, the completely immobile—most toy-like of all— the one who never becomes "Real" in the biological sense, acts out of what appears on the surface to be pure compassion, but is actually merely her programming. To be "real" means to be imperfect, to have flaws, to act selfishly on occasion. But while Mimzy undoubtedly manipulates the children into helping her complete her mission, she never actively takes a DNA sample from Emma, a gift that is offered freely and completely out of love. Love, as we have seen, has a magic all its own, and can seemingly work miracles, granting us that eucatastrophe that Tolkien argued was essential to a good fairy-story.

Tolkien also considers an important purpose of the fairy-story to be Recovery, what he describes as "a regaining of a clear view" (Flieger and

Anderson 67). Fairy-stories allow us to "clean our windows; so that the things seen clearly may be freed from the drab blur of triteness or familiarity" (Flieger and Anderson 67). In each of these tales we discover through the eyes of a toy what it means to love unconditionally, without conceit, and to recognize and honor what is beautiful in ourselves and others. Without love and fellowship, life has no meaning. It is our connection to others that makes us truly alive—it is what makes us Real. Finally, Tolkien reminds us that the Faërie has "beauty that is an enchantment, and an ever-present peril; both joy and sorrow as sharp as sword" (27). This essay began with Tolkien's warning that the love born of Faërie "will produce both *ruth* and *delight*" (Flieger 247). These tales remind us that in life, as in Faërie, we cannot have one without risking the other. It was Michael Tolkien's love for, and pain at losing, a toy dog that brought the story of Roverandom to life. What could possibly be more "Real" than that?

WORKS CITED

Campbell, Joseph. *The Hero with a Thousand Faces*, 3rd ed. Novato, CA: New World Library, 2008. Print.
Flieger, Verlyn. *A Question of Time: J.R.R. Tolkien's Road to Faërie*. Kent, OH: Kent State University Press, 1997. Print.
_____, and Douglas A. Anderson, eds. *Tolkien on Fairy-stories*. London: HarperCollins, 2008. Print.
Inglis-Arkell, Ester. "Technology Isn't Magic: Why Clarke's Third Law Always Bugged Me." io9.com. 28 April 2013. Web. 14 Oct. 2015.
Jones, Dudley, and Tony Watkins, eds. *A Necessary Fantasy? The Heroic Figure in Children's Popular Culture*. New York: Garland, 2000. Print.
Kuznets, Lois Rostow. *When Toys Come Alive: Narratives of Animation, Metamorphosis, and Development*. New Haven: Yale University Press, 1994. Print.
The Last Mimzy. Dir. Bob Shaye. Perf. Joely Richardson, Rainn Wilson, and Timothy Hutton. New Line Home Cinema, 2007. DVD.
Mikkelsen, Nina. "Strange Pilgrimages: Cinderella was a Trickster and Other Unorthodoxies of American and African-American Heroic Folk Figures." *A Necessary Fantasy? The Heroic Figure in Children's Popular Culture*. Eds. Dudley Jones and Tony Watkins. New York: Garland, 2000. 21–50. Print.
Miller, Dean A. *The Epic Hero*. Baltimore: Johns Hopkins University Press, 2000. Print.
Poulos, Christopher N. "The Liminal Hero." *Cultural Studies: Critical Methodologies* 12.6 (2012): 485–90. Web.
Singhe, Manjari, and Mei-Yu Lu. "Exploring the Function of Heroes and Heroines in Children's Literature from Around the World." *ERIC Digest*, ED477609. 2003. Web. 1 Oct. 2015.
Stevens, Anthony. *Private Myths: Dreams and Dreaming*. Cambridge: Harvard University Press, 1995. Print.
Swank, Kris. "The Irish Other World Voyage of Roverandom." *Tolkien Studies* 12 (2015): 31–57. Print.
Tolkien, J.R.R. *Roverandom*. Ed. Christina Scull and Wayne G. Hammond. Boston: Houghton Mifflin, 1998. Print.
Williams, Margery. *The Velveteen Rabbit or How Toys Become Real*. New York: Delacorte Press, 1997 [1922]. Print.
Wisker, Gina. "Shapeshifters." *The Greenwood Encyclopedia of Science Fiction and Fantasy*, Vol 2. Ed. Gary Westphal. Westport, CT: Greenwood Press, 2005. 715–7. Print.

Goodbye, Get Lost, Come Back!
Parting Ways with Special Toys

VALERIE H. PENNANEN

Life is transient, childhood is brief, and most children look forward to growing up. Yet growing up is a painful process to endure and (for compassionate adults) to watch. In literature as in life, saying goodbye to childhood often involves parting ways with a special toy, a "hero" whose faithful companionship is no longer at the center of the child's world, but who typically lives on in a corner of that world and may never quite "die." This essay explores memorable goodbyes between fictional children and their best-loved toys and aims to compare them, in their full variety, ambivalence and messiness, to real-life goodbyes.

Midway through Margery Williams Bianco's classic *The Velveteen Rabbit* (1922)[1] the Boy, recovering from a near-fatal bout with scarlet fever, allows his faithful Bunny to be taken from him with (so far as we know) neither a word of protest nor a word of farewell. The Boy's lack of concern for the companion (and sickbed guardian) he once called Real may be explained in part by physical weakness—he still cannot walk from bedroom to balcony—and being out of earshot when the doctor orders nursemaid Nana to burn all the infected toys. Moreover, it seems the Boy's dangerous illness has changed him psychologically, making him care less about toys and more about real-life adventures. Forgetful of his lost Bunny and never so much as dreaming of Nursery Magic, the Boy now sleeps beside a "splendid [new] bunny, all white plush with real glass eyes" but is "too excited to care very much about *it*" (emphasis mine). "For tomorrow he was going to the seaside, and that in itself was such a wonderful thing that he could think of nothing else" (Bianco 25). There is actually one person in the household who tries to save the

Velveteen Rabbit: this is Nana, who has come to respect the Boy's feelings about his old Bunny even if she cannot share them.

Nana perhaps understands that in days if not years to come, the Boy will look back on the time before his illness and miss his velveteen companion. And there is indeed a hint of wistfulness on the story's last page, where the Boy pauses in his outdoor play to observe a rabbit with "strange markings under his fur, as though long ago he had been spotted, and the spots still showed through" and whose "little soft nose" and "round black eyes" evoke strong memories (33). The convalescent Boy's indifference to the Rabbit's fate is here softened by the well Boy's touch of nostalgia for his toy and the peaceful, secure early childhood to which it belonged. Sensing the dreadful fact that he could have died—and that the toy was powerless to save him— the Boy no longer views his lost Bunny as a hero or literally thinks of him as Real, yet he vividly recalls the closeness and happy times he shared with the toy. These memories may help the Boy grow into an adult who understands, as do the narrator, the Skin Horse, and the little Rabbit himself, that magic is both real and permanent when we care enough to make it so.

Whereas the Velveteen Rabbit survives neglect, escapes being burned, and receives a happy new life through Nursery Magic, the doll Annabella who appears in Louisa May Alcott's novel *Little Men* (1871) is far less fortunate. Annabella is the favorite toy of three-year-old Teddy Bhaer, who perhaps needs her more than ever since his flesh-and-blood hero Dan left Plumfield. One day Teddy, with doll in hand, trails behind his older brother and cousins en route to a "sackerryfice" of their best-loved toys; ten-year-old Demi is in charge of this odd event, inspired by ancient Greek practice and held in honor of an "invisible sprite called 'The Naughty Kitty-mouse'" who has long haunted the children's imaginations (Alcott 126). Lead soldiers and paper dolls are among the toys consumed in this blaze, but Teddy above all lives to regret his share in the game:

> The superb success of [the] last offering excited Teddy to such a degree, that he first threw his lamb into the conflagration, and before it had time even to roast, he planted poor dear Annabella on the funeral pyre.... First one leg curled up, then the other, in a very awful and lifelike manner; next she flung her arms over her head as if in great agony; her head itself turned on her shoulders, her glass eyes fell out, and with one final writhe of her whole body, she sank down a blackened mass on the ruins of the [toy] town.... [Teddy] looked, then screamed and fled toward the house [Alcott 130].

When "Marmar" arrives on the scene, she finds "the blind worshippers of Kitty-mouse mourning over the charred remains of the lost darling" (130) and though her initial response is sympathetic, empathy is beyond her; she is soon laughing uproariously at the children's "game," afterwards trying to exploit it to teach them a lesson. Yet it is striking to note that Demi, unlike his aunt, *gains* empathy from watching his playmates' distress and proposes a funeral for the doll.

Granted Annabella will never come back, her hero-toy status is reaffirmed through Teddy's grief (he'd never really *meant* to send her to a fiery death!) and Demi's remorse.[2] A mere inanimate object from "Marmar's" (and Alcott's) point of view, Annabella nonetheless has helped both boys—Demi in particular—to do some important growing up.

Saying goodbye to early childhood via farewell to a special toy is sad. Sadder by far is a break with everything the child has ever believed in or hoped for, expressed through violent rejection of a favorite toy. In the opening chapter of Frances Hodgson Burnett's *A Little Princess* (1904) Sara Crewe is placed in a London boarding school by her rich, indulgent, clueless father, who fails to see headmistress Miss Minchin for what she really is: a cold-hearted tyrant who values her pupils solely for the income they bring. Before he goes back to India, Captain Crewe takes his daughter shopping for a very special doll who is to be her "friend when papa is gone" (Burnett 5), i.e., to substitute for his company. After a while Sara "recognizes" Emily in a shop window, looking out at them with "intelligent" gray-blue eyes; a moment later, the doll is "cradled in her arms" (7). In the months following her father's departure Sara carefully cultivates a relationship with her new "friend." Though her seven-year-old mind knows perfectly well that the doll cannot really read, listen, or care about what is happening: she "pretends to believe" Emily can do all these things and more, and this pretending "makes it seem as if it were true" (19). This is clearly an immense comfort, since the doll (in marked contrast to Captain Crewe) is *always there*, patiently "listening" to Sara's fanciful stories and "allowing" Sara be the center of *her* world, just as the child was previously the center of her father's world. Years go by and still, as Sara writes in what turns out to be her last letter to her father, "No one could ever take Emily's place" (44). Of course, no one could, except for Captain Crewe himself; but both relationships are about to be shattered. When Sara's eleventh birthday party is interrupted by news that Captain Crewe is dead—and that he died penniless—Sara flees to her room, locks the door, and implores the doll to listen; her anguished plea "Do you hear? Do you hear…?" evokes the terror of a child being pushed all of a sudden into the adult world. In this world people die and never come back, no matter how much they are needed, and dolls lose their power to love, listen, and understand. Fortunately for Sara, she still feels some connection with her doll. After dressing herself in black, she wraps a piece of black cloth around Emily and carries her still-cherished toy downstairs to help her face the headmistress:

"Put down your doll," said Miss Minchin. "What do you mean by bringing her here?"

"No," Sara answered. "I will not put her down. She is all I have. My papa gave her to me"[Burnett 60].

But as months of cruel treatment by Miss Minchin and Cook turn her into a hungry, dispirited maid-of-all-work, Sara has more and more trouble drawing comfort from Emily. She still talks to her doll, but the doll's response feels less and less like quiet sympathy and more and more like silence. Efforts to pretend that Emily is "a kind of good witch who could protect her" fall apart as the doll "merely sat upright and stared" (89).[3] The void left by Emily's silence is to some extent filled by Sara's friendship with scullery maid Becky; occasional visits from junior pupil Lottie and dim-witted but loyal former classmate, Ermengarde; and, last but not least, companionship with an attic rat whom Sara names Melchisedec. The contrast between these warm, real-life, comparatively "grown-up" connections and her dying friendship with Emily (and dimming sense of herself as a "little princess") at last overwhelms Sara:

> "I shall die presently," she said [to Emily].... "I can't bear this...." "I know I shall die. I'm cold; I'm wet; I'm starving to death.... Do you hear?"
>
> She looked at the staring glass eyes and complacent face, [till suddenly] ... heart-broken rage seized her. She lifted her little savage hand and knocked Emily off the chair, bursting into a passion of sobbing....
>
> "You are nothing but a DOLL!" she cried. "Nothing but a doll—doll—doll! You care for nothing. You are stuffed with sawdust. You never had a heart. Nothing could ever make you feel. You are a DOLL!" [Burnett 89–90].

Even as she cries and rages over Emily's heartlessness, Sara still cannot quite shake the feeling that her doll is a real presence and, as such, ought not to be trashed. Her emotional storm over, she looks up to discern "a kind of glassy-eyed sympathy" in Emily's face, and a twinge of old love brings her back to the doll's side:

> "You can't help being a doll," she said with a resigned sigh, "any more than Lavinia and Jessie can help not having any sense. We are not all made alike. Perhaps you do your sawdust best." And she kissed her and shook her clothes straight, and put her back upon her chair [Burnett 89–90].

Sara's apology to her doll, in effect following up "Get lost!" with "Oh, all right, come back," does not truly renew their friendship. Like Captain Crewe, who failed his daughter first by leaving her at Miss Minchin's and secondly by dying, Emily has failed in the hero's role. Her inability to hear and care about Sara's troubles mattered little when those troubles were light, but now that they are heavy, Sara feels betrayed. Her sense of abandonment is heightened by the doll's refusal (so to speak) to ward off harm; Emily can no more protect her than Captain Crewe can return from the dead.

When Captain Crewe's business partner rescues Sara and adopts her as his "princess," helped by newfound wealth from the diamond mines, there is no mention of Emily's share in the happily-ever-after. Has Emily accompanied

Sara to her new home? Will the doll, or memories of the doll, keep at least some hold on Sara's heart along with memories of Captain Crewe? Or is Emily too closely linked to that desolate attic and time of abandonment for Sara ever to want her back? With the doll getting the silent treatment from heroine and author alike, perhaps the most likely answers to these questions are No, Maybe, and Yes. To put it another way, Sara has moved from angry rejection of her hero-toy ("Get lost!") to sadness over the loss ("Come back") to near-indifference (a careless sort of "Goodbye").

A slow, ambivalent farewell between child and hero-toy is common in real life, and fiction provides memorable examples of this type. Midway through A.A. Milne's *The House at Pooh Corner* (1928), Christopher Robin begins withdrawing each morning from Pooh and the other animated toys. Eeyore somehow uncovers the mystery and reveals to Rabbit and Piglet that Christopher Robin is becoming "Educated" (Milne 89).

Christopher Robin himself has mixed feelings about this new venture: part of him would rather spend the rest of his life playing, or as he puts it, doing Nothing—yet he also takes pride in knowing the "Twy-stymes," which he unsuccessfully tries to teach Pooh (111). Toward the end of the book—just before his parents send him off to boarding school—the child proudly recites a hodgepodge of other things he's learned:

> People called Kings and Queens and something called Factors, and a place called Europe, and an island in the middle of the sea where no ships came, and how you make a Suction Pump (if you want to), and when Knights were Knighted, and what comes from Brazil [Milne 173–174].

Once he runs out of things to recite, though, Christopher Robin's ambivalence returns, and he sits there "looking out over the world [i.e., *his* special world and Pooh's], and wishing it wouldn't stop" (176). Then in response to a wistful query from Pooh, he picks up a long stick and knights him "Sir Pooh de Bear, most faithful of all my Knights" (177). Pooh slides into a daydream where he, along with noble knights Pomp, Brazil, and Factors, serves King Christopher Robin, but he soon worries, "I'm not getting it right" and wonders "if being a Faithful Knight meant that you just went on being faithful without being told things" (177–178). Here Christopher Robin breaks in, asking Pooh to keep watch over their favorite spot much as a Faithful Knight would; and the book ends with a touching affirmation of childhood magic and love of a hero-toy. By now it's clear the little boy simply cannot—and, in Milne's view, should not—cut ties with his animal friends, above all not with Pooh, lest in the process he lose an important part of *himself* and forget how to enjoy sunlit days, happy songs, little adventures, and exchanges of simple kindness. Preparing to enter a world that will order him to work hard and turn himself into "somebody" (as if he weren't somebody already!), Christopher Robin draws comfort from Bear's promise to wait for him in the enchanted wood and hold a place for him there, no matter how many years or even decades pass and whether or not he comes back changed. Forever true to himself and to the child who loves him, Pooh thus transcends his role as toy-protagonist and becomes the hero of the book.

Whereas Christopher Robin hopes to keep Pooh in his life forever, Prince Freedling, protagonist of Laurence Housman's 1890s tale "Rocking-Horse Land," outgrows one of childhood's ugliest traits—self-centeredness—through learning first to love and then to let go of a hero-toy. When we first meet Freedling, he is a brat whose fairy godmother assumes he will be destructive and encourages him to be so, sending him a toy in honor of his fifth birthday which she marks with the message, "Break me and I shall turn into something else" (Housman 97). After wrecking the toy repeatedly, then losing it for good, Freedling spies a new and far better source of magic in the shape of a beautiful, black rocking horse:

> The Prince scampered across the room, and threw his arms around the beautiful creature's neck. All its bells jingled as the head swayed gracefully down; and the prince kissed it between the eyes [Housman 99].

After a full day's play on the horse's back, Freedling goes to bed and dreams of still more riding adventures. Waking up suddenly with a heart "full of love for his black rocking-horse," he decides to check "to make sure it was all safe and not afraid of being by itself in the dark night." To his astonishment, he finds the toy has come alive and is standing by a window, shedding tears because it—or rather, he—misses home and family in Rocking-Horse Land. "Sweet Master," the horse beseeches him, "let me go this night, and I will return to you when it is day!" He reveals his name, Rollonde, and he instructs the Prince, "Search my mane till you find in it a white hair; draw it out and wind it upon one of your fingers; and so long as you have it so wound you are my master; and wherever I am I must return at your bidding" (100–102). Thus begins both a nightly ritual and a close friendship. Every day, Rollonde remains cooperatively stiff and (except for his bells) silent as Freedling rides him; every night, he grants Freedling the joy of watching him come alive and fly out the window and early each morning, he thanks the prince with loving words and a kiss. Learning to value another being's happiness as much as his own and finding that he thereby *gains* happiness points Freedling on the way to maturity, even though he briefly regresses (like many a real-life child) on his *next* birthday:

> As six is to five, so were the presents he received on his sixth birthday for magnificence and multitude to the presents he had received the year before. His fairy godmother had sent him a bird, a real live bird; but when he pulled its tail it became a lizard, and when he pulled the lizard's tail it became a mouse, and when he pulled the

mouse's tail it became a cat. [Further tail-pullings and transformations follow.] ... Now a guinea-pig has no tail to pull, so it remained a guinea-pig, while Prince Freedling sat down and howled... [Housman 104–105].

Freedling's new burst of bratty behavior (thankfully, Housman does not depict the animals as normal flesh-and-blood creatures *hurt* by the tail-pulling) is cut short by the appearance of the King his father, who announces the prince is now old enough to learn to ride a *real* horse. Soon Freedling is so preoccupied with his new mount—that he forgets about Rollonde till three nights later when he hears sobs and a well-known voice, asking once more for the old favor. Overcome with shame, Freedling springs out of bed, embraces his hero-toy, and opens the window to send him on his way, but this time the kindness is permanent as the prince slowly lets go of the white strand, forever.

"Good-bye, Rollonde," he murmured softly, "brave Rollonde, my own good Rollonde! Go and be happy in your own land, since I, your Master, was forgetting to be kind to you." And far away he heard the neighing of horses in Rocking-Horse Land [Housman 106].

While Rollonde's final homecoming is certainly Freedling's loss, the Prince is left in possession of a generous heart—a gift surpassing ownership of even the most wonderful toy. The story affirms that even a child can make wise and good choices, inasmuch as the Prince freely chooses to let go of his toy and the Eden-like world it represents, rather than being pressured (like Teddy Bhaer and Christopher Robin) or forced (like the sick Boy or the impoverished Sara Crewe) to make the decision. And though Rollonde himself is gone forever, his son, "a beautiful foal rocking-horse, black, with deep-burning eyes" one day mysteriously appears in the room of King Freedling's son (107).

Between Housman's lyrical tale and Sylvia Cassedy's half-real, half-surreal novel *Lucie Babbidge's House* (1989) lie many cultural differences; yet both involve children who ultimately let go of their cherished toys for someone else's sake, and both depict powerful, life-changing magic worked jointly by the children and their toys. Unlike pampered Prince Freedling, Lucie Babbidge endures the life of a social outcast in a dreary boarding school. Emotionally withdrawn—yet far more attentive than her teacher realizes, and more imaginative than anyone else dreams—Lucie, a twentieth-century American girl, finds solace in playing with a nineteenth-century dollhouse and its china-faced family of four, to whom she adds three new figures of her own making. Through the persona of the little-girl doll, Lucie becomes once again the child of two loving parents, "Mumma" and "Dada," whose lives revolve around "china Lucie" even as they care for baby "Maud" and endure the silliness of middle child "Emmett." The game blends the doings of a fictional family with memories of Lucie's parents, whose penchant for finding beauty in ordinary things is part of their legacy to her. In time she discovers that her ability to control the dolls (including the heroic Mumma-Dada-Lucie trio) is linked to power over a real-life family in England, whose daughter Delia is the great-great-grandchild of the dollhouse's original owner. When a gang of mean girls invades Lucie's play space and confiscates the dolls, thus usurping her powers, Lucie falls ill from shock; but on recovering, she manages to find the dolls and restores the toy household to normal. She also decides the time has come to leave the toys behind and reach out for new friendships: a friendship with Delia, whose well-being she has already learned to care about through reading her letters, and (as the final chapter reveals) friendship with herself. Yet the tenderness with which Lucie handles the little figures for the last time, her repeated farewells to them, and her draping of her old green sweater over the dollhouse suggest that they will always mean a lot to her—in effect, they have healed her—and she hopes whoever finds them next will treat them well. She cannot even bear to ignore the "tiny crash" which tells her, as she is about to leave the storeroom, that the clothespin maid "Olive" has fallen:

> The sweater had to be removed then, so she could reach inside and stand the maid doll up once again, very carefully this time. She even held her open hand above the maid doll's head for a while, as though to steady the air around it. "Good-bye," she said aloud once more, and she draped the sweater over the roof, letting the sleeves trail along the floor like two broad paths [Cassedy 232–233].

That even the most special hero-toy-and-child friendship cannot last forever, at least not with the same intensity, is sensed by any child who has ever watched an older sibling pack toys away or wondered why adults seem little interested in toys. The child may therefore perform dress rehearsals, so to speak, for saying goodbye to a favorite toy. He or she may offer it to someone else as a gift or loan, or else simply place it out of reach for a time. In *Little Bear's Friend* (1960), author Else Minarik and illustrator Maurice Sendak offer a gently humorous portrayal of a girl who is almost but not quite ready to say goodbye to her doll—in whose company she, Little Bear, and their talking-animal friends have spent a happy summer. Little Bear respects Emily's friendship with Lucy; he holds the doll by one hand to help make her walk, agrees "Emily knows what Lucy wants" (Minarik 38) and fixes the doll's arm with tape after she falls from a tree. But he personally does not love the doll so he is not at all offended when Emily offers to let him keep Lucy and then rescinds that offer:

> Emily made Little Bear hold Lucy.
> Then she said to him, "Little Bear, you can have Lucy for keeps. I will give her to you."

"Oh—" began Little Bear.
But before he could say anything, Emily took Lucy back again.
"Oops!" she said. "I forgot. Lucy has to come to school with me" [Minarik 53–55].

Emily gives Little Bear a pen, a present he clearly prefers, and he reciprocates with a toy boat. The boat however is absent from the book's closing illustration, where Emily sits beside Lucy while reading a letter from her *other* best friend, Little Bear. Lucy, not ready to give up both of her best friends in a single day, must mature and try again.

Finally, in literature as in life, there are times when a child has no choice but to leave a hero-toy behind without farewell. Eugene Field's well-remembered poem "Little Boy Blue" (1888) depicts a child called away to heaven in his sleep, leaving his two new but already beloved toy friends (he's just kissed them good-night) to wonder where he's gone. The toys stand, literally and figuratively, for faithfulness, inasmuch as one is a dog, that most loyal of creatures, while the other is a soldier and thus embodies loyalty in the face of death itself. For a young, fanciful reader, "Little Boy Blue" is a poem about sentient toys who heroically wait out their companion's return, whereas to an adult, the toys' continued presence on the little boy's chair evoke heartbroken parents who treasure them for the child's sake. Generations of readers old and young[4] have wept over this poem, especially its final lines:

> And they wonder, as waiting the long years through
> In the dust of that little chair,
> What has become of our Little Boy Blue,
> Since he kissed them and put them there.

The motif of a young person's transformation as he or she parts ways with a special toy is handled uniquely by Carlo Collodi at the end of *Pinocchio* (1881–1883). Here the title character, now a "bright, intelligent boy with chestnut hair and blue eyes," takes a literal last look at his old self: "a big puppet leaning against a chair with its head on one side, its arms dangling, and its legs so crossed and bent that it was really a miracle that it remained standing" (Collodi 167). Remarking to himself how "ridiculous" ("*com'ero buffo*") he used to be, Pinocchio rejoices that he's become "a well-behaved little boy" ("*ragazzino perbene*")—an odd choice of words, since he is in fact a young man. He has not only rescued Geppetto from the belly of the Dogfish (Monstro the Whale in Disney's 1940 film version) but also (in a sequence omitted by Disney) spent five months laboring at a water-pump and weaving and selling baskets to provide for his old, sick "father." Whereas at the close of Disney's film the drowned wooden boy changes magically into a live, real boy ready to resume his childhood, in Collodi's original we are shown two distinctive Pinocchios. For readers of the book, Pinocchio's boyhood self lies dead in the wooden body that can no longer run, dance, play, get into mischief, and entertain them as it has done for some 200 pages. Pinocchio the young man is admirable, and he represents a dream come true; but when he chuckles at his old wooden self, in effect telling it to "Get lost," he is bound to disappoint "young readers "who have joyfully followed the adventures of this Good Bad Boy and who view the boy—*not* his mature counterpart—as their hero. The story ends as it must, but children often like to re-read it ("Come back!").

Given that in real life dolls, puppets and other miniature figures have kept company with the world's children for millennia,[5] we can only wonder how many real-life goodbyes have occurred between youngsters and hero-toys. It is true that *solitary* play, through which a child can grow exceptionally close to one, two, or at most a small handful of toys, was rarer in pre-modern times than it is today. Moreover, in centuries past as in some cultures today,[6] the number and variety of fantasies a child could attach to his or her toy(s) was limited—somewhat, anyhow—by adult expectations. In seventeenth-century Europe for instance, parents who could afford to buy "babies" for their little girls did so to encourage them to practice mothering skills, while giving "elaborate sets of toy soldiers" to boys so they could rehearse battle strategies (Kuznets 15). Yet we should not overlook the possibility that in the eyes of an imaginative child, anytime and anyplace on earth, a miniature figure of a living being holds potential to be a friend—and so, perhaps, a hero.

Adults of past ages typically assumed that children would "put away childish things" by a certain deadline, and the change would be permanent. In classical antiquity the process was ritualized: girls about to be married would dedicate dolls and other playthings at a goddess's shrine, while adolescent boys offered up toys to Apollo or to Hermes / Mercury (Elderkin 455; "Coming of Age in Ancient Greece").[7] Both the medieval Church and medieval lawmakers defined girls twelve and up and boys fourteen and up as adults, and puberty also was when many youth left home to work as apprentices or servants—presumably leaving behind their dolls, their leaden knights, their riding-sticks and so forth, as they went! (Orme 1–2; "Childhood Objects: Medieval Toys"). Belief in childhood as a lovely time that should be safeguarded and prolonged did not emerge till the Romantic era, side-by-side with newfound respect for individuality (Stearns 156–157). In a culture where childhood is idealized, where imagination and creativity are encouraged, and where the line between childhood and adulthood seems hazier than ever before, it makes sense that each child lucky enough to own a hero-toy will find a unique way to say "Goodbye," if necessary adding "Get lost," and sooner or later (be it two minutes later or well into adult life) calling, "Come back!" We have sampled the rich variety of such goodbyes in children's fiction from the nineteenth century on, and real-life parallels are not far to seek.

The refugee child who hastily gives her doll to a fellow refugee but finds herself missing the doll years later (Westheimer) is perhaps not so different from the Boy in *The Velveteen Rabbit*.[8] The preschooler who flings his cherished toy animal out the car window, weeps for it, gets it back, then throws it away again (Junod 132–134, 135) is reminiscent of little Teddy Bhaer. Rainer Maria Rilke's bitter recollections of the inert, uncaring dolls of his childhood, which he felt deserved to be "flung into a corner…[and] scorned, spurned, done with" (43) provide a striking parallel to Sara Crewe's rage at Emily. Johnny Gruelle's determination to keep his lost Marcella alive through "Raggedy Ann" stories and mass-produced "Raggedy Ann" dolls (Hall 92) recalls the lonely toys (and implied parental sorrow) in "Little Boy Blue." The real-life girl who re-enacts "Sleeping Beauty" with her dolls by charming them to sleep[9] is rehearsing her eventual, long-term goodbyes to these miniature heroes and heroines, à la *Little Bear's Friend*. The real-life boy who grieves for his pet dog while play-acting death and resurrection of a *stuffed* dog (Rogers 145) is undergoing spiritual growth, just as surely as Prince Freedling, Lucie Babbidge, and even Pinocchio do, thanks to the real or perceived magic of hero-toys.

Finally, when we recall how adults (more so than children) wept openly in theaters at the end of *Toy Story 3* (Teodorczuk); when we observe how often dolls and stuffed animals accompany young adults to college (Klass, Wood) and persons of all ages to their graves[10]; when we consider how many women and men love to collect vintage toys and visit toy museums; and when we reflect on the powerful nostalgia for toy-hero relationships behind writings as diverse as *The House at Pooh Corner* and *Calvin and Hobbes* (Kuznets 34–58)—we must conclude saying goodbye to a hero-toy is a sad and unforgettable experience for many people. Inevitably the bond between child and hero-toy loses power, "grows thin," and snaps; yet as Naomi Lewis points out, it does not truly disintegrate but instead "moves into other paths; another name for it is imagination" (12). Psychologist D.W. Winnicott goes even further in his celebrated work on "transitional objects" (admittedly a rather chilly term for the likes of Raggedy Ann, Winnie-the-Pooh, and other close hero-companions of early childhood). According to Winnicott, the child's ability to bond with a material object and turn it into something beloved and wondrous is an important first step toward "the magic of imaginative and creative living" (Winnicott xvi). I would add that in particular, a child who retains warm feelings for a hero-toy *beyond* the main goodbye is—like Freedling—apt to be all the more open to real-life happiness, wonder, and adventure in years to come.

NOTES

1. Publication dates mentioned in the body of this essay refer to first editions. Page references refer to editions actually used in preparation of this essay (see Works Cited).

2. A remarkably similar scene occurs in D.H. Lawrence's 1913 novel *Sons and Lovers*, with young Paul accidentally breaking his sister Annie's doll (*Arabella*) and then convincing Annie to "sacrifice" the doll by burning her. For analysis of the latter scene, see Kuznets 100.

3. It would be interesting to know if the Russian folktale "Vasilisa the Beautiful," in which a dying mother bequeaths a magic doll to her daughter, was known to Burnett.

4. For early public response to "Little Boy Blue" and Field's ongoing legacy as "The Poet of Childhood," as well as for the complete text, see "Eugene Field, 1850–1895" at the Poetry Foundation web site.

5. For a sampling of toys from Roman Egypt see Gazda 29, fig. 52 and the British Museum's online photograph of a rag-and-papyrus stuffed doll, GR 1905.10–21.13. Jointed dolls from antiquity are the subject of a classic study by Elderkin. A charming scene of Chinese children putting on a puppet show was painted ca. 1200 by Liu Songnian (Song Dynasty period).

6. Consider, e.g., the use of kachina dolls as teaching toys by the Hopi Indians and of Mossi dolls among the people of Burkina Faso, West Africa (Roy).

7. The poignant presence of dolls and doll accessories in the graves of young Roman girls has also been noted by archaeologists (Galinier 103, with references in fn 124).

8. Like the fictional Boy, Ruth Westheimer was menaced by a danger which could easily have taken her life; in her case it was the Nazi regime in her native Germany, from which she fled on a Kindertransport. Her story shows how a toy can temporarily lose its meaning to a frightened or exhausted child, yet be fondly remembered and missed after the crisis fades.

9. I did this myself as a child, each year "charming" my dolls to sleep from Thanksgiving afternoon through Christmas morning—quite a sacrifice, as I otherwise played with them daily!

10. Per her request, a member of my extended family was interred with the two stuffed animals she had cherished for more than eight decades. Journalist McKenzie Romero writes of the 2014 burial of a teenage girl with souvenirs of the girl's brief life, including "favorite toys."

Works Cited

Alcott, Louisa May. *Little Men: Life at Plumfield with Jo's Boys*. New York: Little, Brown, 1901.
Bianco, Margery Williams. *The Velveteen Rabbit, or, How Toys Become Real*. New York: Doubleday, 1991.
Burnett, Frances Hodgson. *A Little Princess*. Middlestown, DE: Maestro Reprints, 2015.
Cassedy, Sylvia. *Lucie Babbidge's House*. New York: Avon Books, 1989.
"Childhood Objects: Medieval Toys." *The Apricity*. Bulletin Solutions, Inc., 2016. (Previously published on the University of Michigan website.) http://theapricity.com/forum/archive/index.php/t=188336.html, 17 May 2016.
Collodi, Carlo. *Pinocchio*. Trans. Arthur Pober. New York: Sterling Children's Books, 2014.
Elderkin, K.M.K. "Jointed Dolls in Antiquity." *American Journal of Archaeology* 34 (1930): 455–479.
"Eugene Field, 1850–1895." *Poetry Foundation*. http://www.poetryfoundation.org/poems-and-poets/poets/detail/eugene-field, 17 May 2016.
Galinier, Martin. "À vendre. Les sarcophages romains dans les ateliers, suggestions méthodologiques." *Iconographie funéraire romaine et société: Corpus antique, approches nouvelles?* Ed. Martin Galinier and François Baratte. Perpignan: Presses Universitaires, 2013, 81–115.
Gazda, E.K., ed. *Karanis, an Egyptian Town in Roman Times: Discoveries of the University of Michigan Expedition to Egypt (1924–1935)*. Ann Arbor: Kelsey Museum of Archaeology, 1983.
Hall, Patricia. *Johnny Gruelle: Creator of Raggedy Ann and Andy*. Gretna: Pelican, 1993.
Housman, Laurence. "Rocking-Horse Land." Reprinted in *The Silent Playmate: A Collection of Doll Stories*. Ed. Naomi Lewis. London: Victor Gollancz, 1979. 97–107.
Junod, Tom. "Can You Say … 'Hero'?" *Esquire* 130, no. 5 (November 1998): 132–179.

Klass, Perri. "A Firm Grasp on Comfort." *New York Times* 11 March 2013. http://well.blogs. nytimes.com/2013/03/11/a-firm-grasp-on-comfort/?_r=0, 17 May 2016.
Kuznets, Lois Rostow. *When Toys Come Alive: Narratives of Animation, Metamorphosis, and Development*. New Haven: Yale University Press, 1994.
Lewis, Naomi. *The Silent Playmate: A Collection of Doll Stories*. London: Victor Gollancz 1979.
Milne, A.A. *The House at Pooh Corner*. New York: Puffin Books, 1992.
Minarik, Else. *Little Bear's Friend*. New York: Harper and Brothers, 1960.
Orme, Nicholas. "Childhood in Medieval England, ca. 500–1500." *Representing Childhood*. University of Pittsburgh, 2005. http://www.representingchildhood.pitt.edu/medieval_child.htm, 17 May 2016.
Poetry Foundation. "Eugene Field, 1850–1895." http://www.poetryfoundation.org/bio/eugene-field.
Rilke, Rainer Maria. "Some Reflections on Dolls," in *Where Silence Reigns: Selected Prose*. Trans. G. Craig Houston. New York: New Directions, 1978: 43–50.
Rogers, Fred, and Barry Head. *Mister Rogers Talks with Parents*. New York: Berkley Books, 1983.
Romero, McKenzie. "Family Honors Fremont High Cheerleader's Last Wish at Funeral." KSL Radio 14 June 2014. http://www.ksl.com/?nid=148&sid=30193901, 17 May 2016.
Roy, Christopher D. "Mossi Dolls." *African Arts* 14, 4 (August 1981): 47–88.
Stearns, Peter N. *Childhood in World History*. 2nd ed. Abingdon: Routledge, 2011.
Teodorczuk, Tom. "Why 'Toy Story 3' Plays with Men's Emotions." *The Telegraph* 27 June 2010. http://www.telegraph.co.uk/culture/film/7856218/Why-Toy-Story-3-plays-with-mens-emotions, 17 May 2016.
"Vasilisa the Beautiful." Ed. and Trans. Irina Zheleznova. *Russian Fairy Tales*. Moscow: Progress Publishers, 1966. Unpaged; accessed online at www.arvindguptatoys.com/arvindgupta/65r.pdf, 24 May 2016.
Westheimer, Ruth, as told to Christina Ianzito. "Toy Story: In Dr. Ruth's Apartment, the Past Is Present Every Day." *AARP The Magazine* June / July 2015: 64.
Winnicott, D.W. *Playing and Reality*. London: Tavistock, 1971; reissued in 2005 by Routledge Classics, Abingdon.
Wood, Alaina Ellis Archbishop. "Saying Goodbye to a Favorite Toy Not as Easy as It Sounds." *Bucks County Courier Times* 15 November 2013. http://www.buckscountycouriertimes.com/life-style/reality/saying-goodbye-to-a-favorite-toy, 17 May 2016.

About the Contributors

Thaddeus **Andracki** is a middle school librarian at the University of Chicago Laboratory Schools. His research focuses on theoretical and practical aspects of race, gender, sexuality and indigeneity in children's and young adult literatures.

Michael **Brodski** is an associate lecturer at the Institute of Film, Theatre and Empirical Cultural Studies at the Johannes Gutenberg University of Mainz, where he is also a Ph.D. student studying the representation of child protagonists in Soviet and Russian cinema.

Mary **Bronstein** is a rogue scholar, radical feminist, educator and artist in Brooklyn, New York. Her work includes feminist analysis of *The Baby-Sitters Club* book series (2016), original theory on the metaphysics of mother/daughter relationships (2017) and critical analysis of boys' action hero toys (2017).

Rachel L. **Carazo** is earning a graduate degree (M.A., English) at Northwestern State University. She has undergraduate degrees in English, history, and French from Southeastern Louisiana University.

Tanya **Jones** is a former high school English teacher and department chairperson turned academic author in Charlotte, North Carolina. Her last collection, coedited with Joseph Abbruscato, *The Gothic Fairy Tale in Young Adult Literature*, was published with McFarland in 2014.

Kristine **Larsen** is a professor of astronomy in the Geological Sciences Department of Central Connecticut State University. Her teaching and scholarship focus on the intersections between science and society, including science and popular culture.

Craig Ian **Mann** is an associate lecturer in film studies at Sheffield Hallam University, where he was awarded his doctorate in 2016. He has contributed to *Science Fiction Film and Television* as well as several edited collectons and is co-organizer of the Fear 2000 conference series on contemporary horror cinema.

Dina Schiff **Massachi** teaches *The Wizard of Oz* for UNC–Charlotte's

American Studies department. Outside of the classroom, she divides her time between academic and creative writing.

Kirsten **Møllegaard** is an associate professor of English at the University of Hawai'i at Hilo. She teaches courses in literature, film, gender and women's studies and folklore. Her publications reflect the broad scope of her teaching activities.

Rebecca Gorman **O'Neill** is a professor of English at Metropolitan State University of Denver, where she teaches playwriting, screenwriting, cinema studies and the graphic novel. Her original plays have been produced across the United States and in Canada.

Valerie H. **Pennanen** is an assistant professor of history and the coordinator of the History Support Area at Calumet College of St. Joseph. Her research interests include sacred and spiritual themes as reflected in literature, art, and popular culture through the ages and the use of first-person accounts in autobiography and memoir.

Nathan **TeBokkel** is a Ph.D. student at the University of British Columbia, where he studies poet-farmers from Robert Burns to Wendell Berry. He has published articles in *PostScriptum, The Apollonian, Word Hoard* and *The Goose.*

Index

abandonment 9, 76, 145, 150, 172–173
Abrams, M.H.A. 27, 43
agency 11, 94, 109, 132, 135, 150, 152
Alcott, Louisa May 170, 180
Alice's Adventures in Wonderland 15
alterity 10, 95, 98
alters 95–96, 99–101, 103–104, 110
Alves, Pedro Ferreira 104, 111
Andersen, Hans Christian 17, 27–44
anxiety 2–3, 16, 23–24, 165
archetype(s) 159
Ashley, Brook 146–147, 155
Ashliman, D.L. 69, 77
the authentic 115, 128
autonomy 55, 85, 149

Bader, Barbara 115, 128
Bæksted, Anders 34, 43
Bamber, Martyn 138, 141
Banks, Lynne Reid 14, 17, 45–60
Barker, Joane 126, 128
Baum, L. Frank 10, 78–93
Bell, Jason 89, 93
Bell, Jessica 89, 93
belong(ing) 7–8, 11, 20–21, 48, 90, 126, 136, 140, 150, 152–153, 165
Bennett, Jane 47–48, 53–54, 121, 126, 128
Bernstein, Robin 116–117, 121, 128
Biedermeier 9, 28–30, 35–36, 41–43
binaries 94–95, 105, 109
the Boogeyman 4, 5–7, 13, 17–25
Booth, Allyson 14, 25
Bradford, Clare 122, 129
Brew, Simon 130, 141
Brown, Bill 45, 53–55, 57–60
Buckingham, David 64–66, 67
Burnett, Frances Hodgson 171–172, 180

Buzz Lightyear 10, 16, 19, 23, 94–105, 108, 138
Byrd, Jodi A. 122, 128–129

Calvin and Hobbes 12, 16, 18–20, 23, 26
Campbell, Joseph 38, 159, 168
cannibalism 80, 93
Caputo, John D. 103, 108–111
Carpenter, Carole Henderson 117, 129
Carroll, Lewis 15, 25
Chen, Mel Y. 126, 129
Child's Play 63–64, 66–68, 70
Child's Play 2 64, 67
Cinderella 81, 93
Collier, J.P. 74, 77
Collington, Peter 15, 25
Collodi, Carlo 14, 25, 177, 180
colonialism 10, 115–117, 121, 125–128
comfort object 5, 6, 147; *see also* transitional object
commercialization 71–72, 77
conjunction 95
consumerism 16, 45–46, 48, 60, 63–69, 71–73, 76–77, 132, 137–138, 140
contingency 98–101, 108, 110, 112
Corduroy 15, 23, 25
Corsaro, William A. 132, 136, 141
Coulombe, Joseph 52, 60
Cross, Gary 65–66, 77
Curry, Agnes B. 81, 93

Daverio, John 42–43
death 24, 30, 35, 39, 40–41, 72, 118, 139, 149, 160, 179
de Duve, Christian 110–112
Deloria, Philip J. 126, 129
Derrida, Jacques 104–106, 110–111
Despret, Vinciane 109, 111

185

186 Index

disability 33–34, 41–44
the Disney effect 138
The Doll and the Kitten 155
Dolls (film) 10, 62–77
Doyle, Margaret 29, 43
Driscoll, Catherine 148, 155
duality 32, 151
dynamism 46–47, 51, 53, 56, 59

Edith and Little Bear Lend a Hand 152, 156
Edith and Midnight 156
Edith and Mr. Bear 144, 149, 156
Edith and the Duckling 154–156
Edith Learns a Lesson 151, 156

Faërie 157, 159–160, 162, 165, 168
fairy tale(s) 9, 28–29, 31–32, 37, 40–43, 116, 159
falterity 94–113
favorite toy 1, 4, 6–7, 15, 17, 19, 22, 24, 99, 100, 103, 163, 170–171, 176, 180–181; *see also* primary plaything
favoritism 2, 99–100
fear 4–5, 17, 21–22, 25, 33, 50, 62, 66–67, 76–77, 98, 133, 153–154, 158, 164; of being abandoned/lost 3, 24, 145, 149–150; of parting 24; *see also* replacement anxiety
feminist 81, 84
Ferguson, Frances 81, 84
Field, Eugene 177, 180
Field, Rachel 13, 126
Forman-Brunell, Miriam 146, 155
Freud, Sigmund 37, 132–133, 135, 141, 152, 154–155

Garroutte, Eva 126, 129
gender roles 39
Giddings, Martha 54, 59–60
Giroux, Henry A. 138, 141
Godden, Rumer 15, 18, 25, 144
Gordon, Stuart 62, 67–68, 72, 77
Gruelle, Johnny 13, 25, 179–180

Haahr, John 33, 43
Hade, Daniel D. 45, 60
Halverson, Charles F. 54, 59–60
Hansel and Gretel 69, 72–73, 76
Haugaard, Erik 29, 43
Hayes Patricia 147–148, 155
hero: liminal 160, 168; romantic 9, 27–28, 31, 38
Hersholt, Jean 31–32, 34, 43

hierarchal issues 31, 78–79, 81, 86, 90, 92, 120, 146
Hitty: Her First Hundred Years 13–14, 22, 126–127
Hoffmann, E.T.A. 15, 31
Holland, Patricia 134, 141
Holling, Clancy 114–129
home 3–5, 8, 18, 20, 22, 25, 29–30, 32, 36–37, 40, 42–43, 65, 71, 103, 117, 150–152, 158, 161, 173–174, 178
The House at Pooh Corner 14, 16, 23, 173, 179
Housman, Laurence 174–175, 180
Howarth, Michael 3, 12, 131, 141
Humphries, Reynold 70, 72–73, 76–77

identity 10, 16, 52, 55–56, 65, 70, 106, 119, 132, 145, 148, 154, 158
Igartua, José E. 119, 128–129
inanimateness 19–20
inclusion 117, 121–123, 127
The Indian in the Cupboard 14–15, 45–61
Inglis-Arkell, Ester 163, 168
innocence 18, 22, 63, 65–66, 68–71, 73, 76, 149

Jenks, Chris 131, 141
Jentsch, Ernst 152–153, 155
Johansen, Ib 35, 43
Jones, Dudley 167, 168
Joyce, William 1, 7–9, 12
Junod, Tom 179–180

Karp, Andrew 79, 85–86, 88, 92–93
Kierkegaard, Søren 30, 95, 97–98, 104
killer toy 62–64, 66, 68, 76
Kincaid, James R. 132–133, 141
King, Geoff 66, 77
Kitzinger, Jenny 133, 141
Klass, Perry 179, 181
Kline, Stephen 64–66, 77
Kofoed, Niels 31, 43
Kuznets, Lois R. 4, 9, 12, 14, 17–18, 25, 42, 44, 115, 118, 129, 141, 144, 155, 162–165, 168, 178–181

The Last Mimzy 158–168
Lennard, Dominic 68, 70, 77
Levinas, Emmanuel 95, 98, 103–104, 109, 112
Lewis, Naomi 179–180
Lingis, Alphonso 95, 110, 112
"Little Ida's Flowers" 31, 42
A Little Princess 171, 180

Loncraine, Rebecca 84, 93
loneliness 11, 17, 32, 88, 148–151
The Lonely Doll series 11, 143–156
Lury, Karen 135–136, 141

MacLean, Robert 35, 42, 44
Mancini, Don 64, 67
materialism 10, 45–46, 48–49, 65–69
Mattingly, Emily A. 82, 93
maturation 10, 45, 51–53, 55–57, 59–60
Meek, Barbara A. 48, 51, 60
Meillassoux, Quentin 98–99, 109, 112
metamorphosis 161–165; *see also* transformation
Mikkelsen, Nina 159, 168
Miller, Dean A. 160, 168
Milne, A.A. 3–4, 12, 14, 16, 25, 151, 173, 181
Minarik, Else 176–177, 181
Mr. Punch 74; *see also* Punch and Judy
Mitchell, David T. 33, 44
Moreton-Robinson, Aileen 120, 129
Muir, John Kenneth 68, 77
Muñoz, José Esteban 119, 129
Murray, David 51, 60

Nancy, Jean-Luc 102, 104, 110, 113
Nava, Mica 45–46, 48, 60
Ngai, Sianne 119, 129
Nikolajeva, Maria 14–17, 26, 149
Nodelman, Perry 149, 155
nonsublimation 101–102, 108
nursery magic 14, 162–164, 169–170
The Nutcracker and the Mouse King 14–15, 31

objectification 45–46, 51
O'Brien, Jean M. 124, 126, 129
Ollie's Odyssey 7–9, 12
op de Beeck, Nathalie 116, 119, 128–129
Ordbog 30, 44
other(ed) 133–134, 142

Paddle-to-the-Sea 114–129
Parten, Mildred B. 104, 106, 113
pataphysics 105–107, 111–112
the Patchwork Girl 78–93; *see also* Scraps
patriarch 36, 74
Pinocchio 14–15, 20, 63, 126–127, 177–179
Porter, Joy 51–52, 60
possession: of object 2, 6, 11, 29, 45–46, 51, 53, 58, 69, 72, 74, 90, 144; of person 52, 90; problematic 10, 45–61; of self 45, 47–48; white-possession 10, 120, 126
posthumanism 10, 155

Poulos, Christopher N. 160, 168
Powder of Life 78, 84–86, 88
primary plaything 5; *see also* favorite toy
Pugh, Tison 80, 91–93
Punch and Judy 74, 77; *see also* Mr. Punch
punctum 121

Raggedy Ann 13–14, 179
Raicht, Mike 5–7, 11–12, 26
Realness 14, 20–21, 115, 125–128
Reese, Debbie 114, 127–129
replacement anxiety 16, 23–24; *see also* fear
Rilke, Rainer Maria 179, 181
Roemer, Kenneth M. 51, 60
Rogers, Fred 179, 181
Romantic era 28, 178
Rosenbaum, Jonathan 130, 138, 142
Roverandom 11, 158–168
Russell, David 13–14, 25–26
Rustin, Margaret 54–56, 59, 61
Rustin, Michael 54–56, 59, 61

Sackett, S.J. 80, 82, 91, 93
Salvi, Carolyn 135, 142
Schaller, Michael 66, 77
Schmiesing, Ann 41, 43–44
Schrödinger, Erwin 95, 97–98, 100, 103, 105, 109, 113
Scott, A.O. 106, 110, 113
Scott, Sharon 68, 77
Scraps 78, 80, 92; *see also* Patchwork Girl
scriptive thing 116, 120–121, 127
Secondary World(s) 15–16, 18–20, 158
self 2, 10, 50, 52, 60, 94, 96, 99, 101–103, 121, 126, 162–163, 177; self-possession 45, 47–48; self-reflection 48–49; self-worth 45, 47–48
sentience 13–14, 69, 76, 78, 80, 88, 177
"The Shepherdess and the Chimney-Sweep" 28, 37–43
Sinnbild 41
Small Soldiers 10–11, 63, 130–142
Smirnova, E.O. 2, 12
Smith, Brian 5, 12–13, 26
social norms 11, 36, 48, 57, 59, 161
The Steadfast Tin Soldier 9, 17, 27–44, 115
Stevens, Anthony 161, 168
Stewart, Michelle Pagni 49–50, 56, 61
Strong, Pauline Turner 55, 61
The Stuff of Legend 5–9, 12–26
Sullivan, Laura 3, 12
Swank, Kris 158, 168

188 Index

"The Sweethearts, or The Ball and the Top" 28, 39, 43

Tatar, Maria 29, 32–33, 35–36, 38–39, 42, 44
Tolkien, J.R.R. 11, 157–168
toy literature 13, 18
Toy Story 3, 15–21, 23, 26, 94, 98, 101, 110, 113, 137–139
Toy Story 2 16, 20, 26, 66
Toy Story 3 16, 18, 20, 23, 26, 179
tragic lover 9, 27–28, 38
transcendence 97
transformation 50, 65, 72, 90, 162, 164–165, 167, 125; *see also* metamorphosis
trope(s): coming-of-age 131; fairy tale 81; toy 9–10, 13, 15–18, 22–25, 80, 132, 135, 141, 158, 164
Turcotte, Edmond 120, 129
Turnbull, J. 104, 113
Ulrich, Laurel Thatcher 50, 58, 61

the Uncanny 133, 152–153
unheimlich 37
utopia 78–80, 84, 87–89, 91–92

Vanellope 94, 100–104, 107–108
The Velveteen Rabbit 11, 14, 16, 20, 126–127, 157–159, 161–164, 167, 169–170, 179
Victorian 64

Williams, Margery 14, 157, 159, 161–165, 168–169
Wilson, Charles, Paul, III 5, 12, 19, 26
Winnicott, D.W. 2, 8, 11–12, 150, 155, 179
Winnie-the-Pooh 3, 14–16, 179
Wisker, Gina 162, 168
Wojcik-Andrews, Ian 140, 142
Woody (the Cowboy) 15–16, 18–20, 23, 94, 96–106, 108, 110, 138
Wreck-It Ralph 94, 100, 102–103, 106, 110–111
Wright, Dare 143–156
Wullschlager, Jackie 28, 40, 42–44

Zelizer, Viviana A. 65, 77
Zipes, Jack 43, 93, 138, 142
Zwicky, Jan 108, 110, 113